PRAISE FOR BU BRAND EXPERIENCES

'The key for effective brand management is creating a positive and memorable 360-degree brand experience for customers. In this book, you can find out how you can implement it in a clear and practical way. Absolutely the best guide to successfully managing brand experience.'
Barbara Meneghini, Head of Corporate Customer Relationship Management, TOD'S Group

'Creating meaningful, distinctive brand experiences is the key to business success for virtually all organizations. With *Building Branding Experiences*, Coleman offers a comprehensive and highly practical roadmap that illuminates and inspires. Following his principles and guidance will help firms design and deliver powerful brand experiences to ensure long-term relevance and profitability.'
Kevin Lane Keller, Tuck School of Business, Dartmouth College

'This book is an excellent all-in-one primer for today's digital entrepreneur. It contains a delightful guide full of case studies from different industries for those of us who want to widen the brand experience of our best companies.'
Mert Dorman, Senior Vice President, Corporate Marketing and Distribution Channels, Turkish Airlines

'Building a successful brand doesn't happen overnight. If you want insight on how to do this from conception to launch, strong performance in the market and reputation building, this is the book for you. Coleman provides case studies that make the messages clear and easily translate to real-life experience. The approaches suggested are systematic and offer a great perspective.'
Steve Profit, Global Sales and Marketing Director, Novo Nordisk Pharmatech A/S

'An informative book packed with real-life and practical examples that clearly outline how adopting a holistic approach to building brand experiences improves business performance. Coleman demystifies the process of building brand experiences through digestible, bitesize chapters, and he writes in an accessible

and engaging style that even the most experienced marketing executives will appreciate.'
Colette Murad, Vice President, Senior Communications Manager, Barclays

'Building compelling and cohesive brand experiences is key to retaining brand relevance. Coleman's book gives practitioners a powerful, insight-informed tool that will help build and leverage brand experiences. This is a must-read for senior marketing executives who want to realize the full potential brand experiences can deliver to their organization.'
Professor George Christodoulides, Assistant Dean (Research),
Head of Marketing Group and Professor of Marketing at Birkbeck,
University of London

Building Brand Experiences

A practical guide to retaining brand relevance

Darren Coleman

KoganPage

First published in Great Britain and the United States in 2018 by Kogan Page Limited

2nd Floor, 45 Gee Street	c/o Martin P Hill Consulting	4737/23 Ansari Road
London	122 W 27th St, 10th Floor	Daryaganj
EC1V 3RS	New York, NY 10001	New Delhi 110002
United Kingdom	USA	India

www.koganpage.com

ISBN   978 0 7494 8156 8
E-ISBN   978 0 7494 8157 5

British Library Cataloguing-in-Publication Data

A CIP record for this book is available from the British Library.

Library of Congress Cataloging-in-Publication Data

Names: Coleman, Darren (Marketing researcher), author.
Title: Building brand experiences : a practical guide to retaining brand
   relevance / Darren Coleman.
Description: 1st Edition. | New York, NY : Kogan Page Ltd, [2018] | Includes
   index.
Identifiers: LCCN 2018012301 (print) | LCCN 2018013595 (ebook) | ISBN
   9780749481575 (ebook) | ISBN 9780749481568 (pbk.)
Subjects: LCSH: Branding (Marketing) | Consumers' preferences. | Consumer
   satisfaction.
Classification: LCC HF5415.1255 (ebook) | LCC HF5415.1255 .C646 2018 (print)
   | DDC 658.8/27–dc23
LC record available at https://lccn.loc.gov/2018012301

Typeset by Integra Software Services, Pondicherry
Print production managed by Jellyfish
Printed and bound by CPI Group (UK) Ltd, Croydon, CR0 4YY

I hear and I forget.
I see and I remember.
I do and I understand.

Confucius

CONTENTS

About the author xii
Foreword by Claire Cronin xiii
Acknowledgements xv

01 **Introduction to retaining relevance through brand experiences** 1

Who this book will help 2
What are brand experiences? 3
Why build brand experiences? 4
How this book is structured 9
Endnotes 11

02 **The Brand Experience Blueprint: A practical management tool** 14

How will the Brand Experience Blueprint help you? 14
The three stages of the Brand Experience Blueprint 16
Getting the most out of the Brand Experience Blueprint 20
Conclusion 21

PART ONE Brand Experience Environment 23

03 **Understanding your stakeholders** 25

Profiling stakeholders 25
Helping stakeholders get 'jobs done' 36
Encouraging stakeholder engagement 41
Managing stakeholder expectations 48
Conclusion 48
Endnotes 49

04   Fine-tuning your perspective 51

Embracing transparency 51
Adopting a holistic mindset 54
Competing primarily through value not price 59
Having patience 61
Accepting a loss of control 65
Conclusion 67
Endnotes 68

05   Considering the mechanics of delivery 70

Creating an emotional connection 70
Facilitating co-creation 75
Delivering omnichannel experiences 80
Conclusion 84
Endnotes 85

06   Adopting a data-driven approach 87

Obtaining robust insights 87
Measuring holistically 101
Conclusion 102
Endnotes 102

07   Summary: Brand Experience Environment 104

PART TWO Brand Experience Essentials 107

08   Brand values 115

What are brand values? 115
Why give a brand values? 117
How to create great brand values 123
Conclusion 127
Endnotes 128

09   Brand essence 129

What is brand essence? 130
Why is brand essence important? 131

How to define your brand essence   134
Is a brand essence a tagline?   135
Conclusion   136
Endnotes   136

10   Brand promise   137
What is a brand promise?   137
How to distinguish benefits from features   140
Types of benefits   140
Conclusion   143
Endnotes   143

11   Brand positioning   144
What is brand positioning?   146
Defining your competitors   149
How to write a positioning statement   151
Conclusion   152
Endnotes   153

12   Brand personality   154
What is brand personality?   154
Why give brands a personality?   157
Conclusion   162
Endnotes   164

13   Summary: Brand Experience Environment and Essentials   165
Endnote   167

PART THREE Brand Experience Enablers   169

14   Behaviour   175
Employee behaviour and brand experiences   176
Recruitment   178
Induction   183
Training   184
Appraisal   186

Reward   188
Exit interviews   189
Conclusion   190
Endnotes   190

15   Communications   192

Communications and brand experiences   193
Internal brand communications   193
Don't be seduced by social media   194
Understand content and the conversation   196
The power of communities   199
Mind your brand language   204
Making the most of mobile   205
Crafting brand stories   208
Explore gamification   212
Conclusions   213
Endnotes   214

16   Design   216

Design and brand experiences   217
Multisensory design   218
Service design   226
Conclusion   238
Endnotes   238

17   Summary: Brand Experience Environment, Essentials and Enablers   240

PART FOUR Measuring Brand Experiences   243

18   Getting started with measuring brand experiences   245

Obtaining Big Picture and Touchpoint metrics   245
Conclusion   249
Endnote   249

19   Adopting a holistic approach to measuring brand experiences 250

The dangers of focusing on purely financial metrics   250
Obtaining employee, brand and financial metrics   252
Conclusion   254
Endnotes   254

20   How to measure brand experiences scientifically 256

Understanding constructs, dimensions, measures and indices   256
The practicalities of measuring scientifically   260
Conclusion   261
Endnotes   261

21   Closing thoughts: Building brand experiences as a route to retaining brand relevance 262

'Brand purpose': A cautionary note   265
Further reading   268
Index   272

This book is supported by a series of Toolkits: tried-and-tested techniques, tools and templates that will help you think about building brand experiences in the context of your organization. These can be found online at **koganpage.com/building-brand-experiences**.
Use password: B83APGT4BR.

ABOUT THE AUTHOR

Dr Darren Coleman has over 20 years of global branding experience spanning Europe, the Middle East, Southeast Asia and Japan. He has helped brands such as Johnson & Johnson, Orange (UK and Group), Maybank and Standard Life. Darren is the Founder and Managing Consultant of Wavelength Marketing. Wavelength specializes in helping services brands retain relevance through the experiences they build.

Darren is frequently invited to speak at international conferences, run executive-level workshops, comment on brand-related issues in the media, and has published articles in leading journals. He has a penchant for travel, tennis, scuba diving, mountain biking, yoga and Birmingham City Football Club. Granted, some are more enjoyable than others.

FOREWORD

The Virgin Atlantic brand experience was built on the master brand promise of making it deliciously irresistible and truly addictive. When Sir Richard Branson first conceived of creating an airline, it was driven by the same underlying thought that has inspired all his business ventures: to create a truly unique brand experience that was predicated on making the banal feel brilliant – and it fixed a genuine customer problem. Back in the 1980s, airline travel was a joyless experience that was stressful, uncomfortable and required everyone to conform. Richard's response was to create Virgin Atlantic, to restore the joy and romance of flying by helping people enjoy the journey as much as the destination.

At Virgin Atlantic we are forensic in our examination of the brand experience but we're playful in our interpretation of the opportunity and the translation into the brand experiences we build. No business case in the world could have been built to support the introduction of Wilbur and Orville (our on-board salt and pepper shakers that are shaped like planes). We introduced them because they made us smile – and we thought they would make our customers smile too; they were a brilliant example of translating the Virgin master brand value of 'Delightfully Surprising' into a tangible brand experience touchpoint. In fact, our customers loved them so much they stole them in droves. We saw this as a brilliant opportunity for our brand to be more enduring and to continue to live on in our customers' homes, rather than viewing it as a breakage in the brand experience which required fixing.

Richard's ambition is just as relevant today as it was in 1984. As a company, we continue to obsess over every aspect of the brand experience we build and to challenge ourselves to think, what would Richard do?

That entrepreneurial zeal is embedded in our brand ambition – to be Everyday Pioneers – and that innovative spirit is something we seek in every recruit, whether they work in Cabin Crew, Catering or Cargo. We don't differentiate between front-office employees and back-office staff. Everyone is encouraged and empowered to re-imagine processes, products, services and communications for the benefit of our customers – and also other colleagues. We hire for attitude and train for skill; irrespective of which function they report into, we expect our people to embody our three core personality traits: to be Inclusive, Optimistic and Adventurous. That approach has created a culture in which our brand promise can be expertly executed and brought to life via our brand experiences. Our brand personality also plays a central role in guiding our brand communications and overall tone of voice. For example, on our website we refer to destinations in the context of 'Your adventure starts here'.

Over 30 years later, as we partner with more suppliers globally and expand our network reach, the customer journey has become more diffused. It is vital that everyone in our supply chain understands our core brand proposition and can accurately translate that into the target brand experience through their own behaviours. Many CEOs have responded to this challenge by adding a new role to the board – the Chief Customer Officer – accountable for defining the brand promise and galvanizing everyone across the business to deliver brand experiences that bring that promise to life.

As I read through this book I found myself saying to myself, 'My team should try to do this', or 'I should talk to my colleagues in HR, Operations or Revenue Management about that', with the goal being to enhance the brand experiences we collectively build.

This book will help you to understand the challenges of delivering a cohesive and compelling brand experience. It will equip you with practical solutions that will help your brand to retain relevance through the experiences it builds and ultimately to drive brand performance.

In closing, and as you think about your own brand experience, I will leave you with a final thought from our fearless founder: 'Don't think what's the cheapest way to do it or what's the fastest way to do it. Think what's the most amazing way to do it.' I would encourage you to hold this thought as you read this book.

Claire Cronin
Chief Marketing Officer, Virgin Atlantic

ACKNOWLEDGEMENTS

A number of people have helped with this book and I would like to express my thanks.

Experts who reviewed drafts of the manuscript: Sandra Horlings, Dr Cristián Saracco, Stephen Wunker, Professor George Christodoulides, Hilton Barbour and Benjamin Erwood. Your direction and dedication are much appreciated.

Claire Cronin for writing the foreword and more importantly being refreshingly straightforward to work with.

The leaders, executives and senior managers who have shared their expert insights. I realize you are busy so I am grateful for your time and am delighted you are involved.

Additional advice, support and sense checking I have received from other specialists in their field: Dr Erich Joachimsthaler, Rishita Jones, Mark Brill, Jonathan Gabay, Dr Nebojša Davčik, Dr Roland H Bartholmé, Dr Achilleas Boukis, Tarek Khojah, Sophie Le Rae, Claudio Naccari, Karen Ng, Ahmed Al-Aamri, Dr Jiyao Xun, Susanna Enrico Gansin and – last but by no means least – Lisa Gee.

Wavelength Marketing clients who have placed their faith in us to advise them on a spectrum of projects over the years. The experiences we have built have provided insight and anecdotes that are central to this book.

The team at Kogan Page: Jennifer Volich, Commissioning Editor, for believing in my ideas; Charlotte Owen, Development Editor, for being dedicated to developing my manuscript and patient when I was a pain; and other members of the Kogan Page team, in particular Chris Cudmore, who made my ideas happen.

Derrick Daye for facilitating my introduction to Kogan Page; but for this I would not be sharing these words with you now.

Finally, my family, friends and loved ones. Your encouragement and empathy, at just the right times, have been invaluable.

Keep right on.

Introduction to retaining relevance through brand experiences

Kodak, Blockbuster, Sears and Woolworths Group (UK). Iconic brands that have faded or even fallen from grace. During their peak these brands appeared invincible. Almost indestructible. They were admired, respected and even loved in their home markets and beyond.

How did things go so wrong? Simple. They failed to retain relevance, so their customers moved on. Their fortunes contrast sharply with the likes of Amazon, Apple and Google who currently represent the world's most valuable brands.[1] These brands thrive and flourish, with their success being primarily driven by the brand experiences they build.

Apple, Amazon and Google aren't alone when it comes to understanding the importance of brand experiences. 'Share a Coke' let consumers customize bottles with their name to deliver a more personalized experience. Porsche holds driving days at the iconic Silverstone racetrack, giving new owners the chance to experience the exhilaration of their new car. Smirnoff hosts pumping house music nights in the world's coolest clubs, so people can enjoy the brand as part of an immersive experience. Red Bull organizes races in weird and wonderful vehicles around the globe to deliver experiences that are all about 'adrenaline-fuelled extreme fun'. The Guinness 'Storehouse' in Dublin lets people savour the heritage and history of the brand whilst guzzling a pint or two.

These brands don't bow to fashions or fads that change with the direction of the wind. They know it's not *what* they do, but *how* they do it that keeps them relevant. In other words, they build brand experiences. But building experiences is difficult and is a challenge I see many senior executives facing. It's hard to know where to start and how to structure brand experience-building initiatives. Reading this book will help you solve that problem.

Companies have considered customer experience (CX) a strategic priority for quite a while, but executing with excellence has proven to be quite a challenge.[2]

Only 32 per cent of executives (versus 40 per cent polled in the same research in 2014) working at B2B brands feel they are well equipped with the skills, tools and resources necessary to deliver the desired experience.[3]

Who this book will help

This book can help:

- **People that work in brand, marketing, experience or service design, or a related profession (eg communications or creative).** If you're a chief marketing officer, senior manager or executive, it will help you:

  - lead brand experience-building initiatives with greater confidence;
  - develop a robust brand experience business case for the boardroom;
  - apply a broad range of advanced yet practical insights, tools, templates and techniques you will be able to use straight away;
  - defend your brand experience proposals with more self-assurance;
  - demonstrate in a scientific way the value delivered to your business by the brand experiences you build.

- **Executive managers who work closely with brand teams.** This could include the CEO, head of HR, finance, customer services, information technology, sales, strategy or operations. The knowledge, tools, techniques and Expert Insights provided by this book will help you:

  - work more productively with those who are primarily responsible for building brand experiences;
  - appreciate the role you and your team play in building brand experiences;
  - feel more confident about contributing to the 'brand experience' conversation that may be happening at your organization.

This may seem like a broad list. It is. That's because delivering brand experiences is everyone's job. It doesn't matter if you're the CEO or the concierge. You have a role to play in building brand experiences. It's that simple.

What are brand experiences?

I find it useful to define brand experiences as *carefully sequenced, synchronized and selected touchpoints that combine to emotionally engage stakeholders as they progress through their entire journey with your brand.*

Delivering an experience requires touchpoints to be *carefully sequenced.* Customers and other stakeholders[4] need to progress through each part of your experience so that, step by step, you help them solve a problem, achieve a goal or get a relevant 'job done'. This should be your ultimate goal when building brand experiences.

Customers or other stakeholders need to move or 'transition' from one touchpoint to the next with minimal effort or 'friction'. Disrupting the flow of the experience between touchpoints within or across channels could give stakeholders good reason to go elsewhere. Their experience should be 'seamless'. This requires synchronization between touchpoints.[5]

Building brand experiences is an organization-wide effort that can involve customer services, human resources, sales, finance, operations and more. It involves everyone in your organization, not just brand or marketing. This requires synchronization across your organization.

You need to identify, then focus on delivering *carefully selected* touchpoints. The sheer number of brand experience touchpoints can be overwhelming. Where choice is concerned, less is often more.[6] If part of an experience does not deliver relevant value it should be removed. It will add noise, cost and dilute the clarity of the experiences you deliver. It's the way your touchpoints *combine* to create the whole experience that delivers the magic. This makes your experiences unique and hard to emulate.

You need to *emotionally* engage stakeholders with your brand because it's primarily our emotions that drive choice.[7] That doesn't mean you should ignore rational and cognitive processes. However, I find it useful to stress the importance of emotion because it plays such an important yet often overlooked role in a surprising number of boardrooms.

Focusing on how stakeholders *engage* with your brand is important because people are decreasingly passive. They seek out immersive experiences they can take part in, actively contribute to and share with their friends and networks. They also look for opportunities to assess the authenticity of a brand's claims. Engagement provides this.

You need to be mindful of the *entire journey* because the overall brand experience you deliver will only be as good as the weakest touchpoint. When building brand experiences, stakeholders need to engage *with your brand*. It's the substance of your brand – its values, essence, promise, positioning and personality – that your stakeholders should connect with as part of the brand experiences you build. Not its trappings in the form of brand logo or other visual cues that bring your brand to life.

I have used the word 'stakeholder' intentionally to help distinguish brand experiences from customer experiences. This is a subtle but important point, and should frame your perspective whilst reading this book. Brand experiences and customer experiences are related, but brand experiences cast a wider net, as they are built with a spectrum of stakeholders in mind. This includes customers, but also local communities, employees, suppliers and others. People tend to use the words 'brand experience' and 'customer experience' interchangeably. Doing this narrows your perspective and will prevent you from thinking about the important stakeholder groups your brand should engage with via the experiences you build.

As you progress through this book you will find that some research and statistics refer to 'customer experience'. Don't let this deter you. Customer experience is a subset of brand experience. The purpose of this book is to share tried and tested principles via the Brand Experience Blueprint that will help you deliver brand experiences to a broad range of stakeholders, including customers. To support this goal, I have included a range of case studies and 'Expert Insights' from a spectrum of organizations to show how the brand experience-building principles apply.

Why build brand experiences?

Brand experiences drive brand performance

Brand performance in this context includes revenue,[8] brand awareness and associations,[9] advocacy,[10] perceived quality,[11] reputation,[12] satisfaction,[13] and loyalty.[14] To help you bolster your brand experience business case, additional sources and statistics have been included in Toolkit 1.1 – available to download from koganpage.com/building-brand-experiences (password found at the end of the contents). Well worth a look.

In his Expert Insight, Peter Walshe outlines how, based on over a decade of global data collection, brand experience drives brand valuation.

EXPERT INSIGHT 1.1 Brand experience drives brand valuation
– Kantar Millward Brown

Peter Walshe, Global BrandZ™ Strategy Director, Kantar Millward Brown

A positive brand experience is crucial in driving financial success. Analysis of WPP's BrandZ™ Top 100 Most Valuable Global Brands study shows that a poor brand experience actually retards growth.

Table 1.1 BrandZ™ Top 100 Most Valuable Global Brands 2006–16

	Brand experience		
	Bottom third	**Middle third**	**Top third**
11-year value change (USD)	−0.4%	+62%	+166%

SOURCE Methodology and valuation by Kantar Millward Brown, 95 brands valued in both 2006 and 2016

Aspects such as the experience with the brand 'meeting the consumer's needs', being 'unique', and, increasingly important these days, being 'better online', are ingredients of the brand experience measure.

The five factors in brand wellness

Brand experience does not work in isolation. Just as there are many contributors to human well-being, there are multiple factors that contribute towards a healthy brand. BrandZ™ analysis has identified five key attributes shared by healthy, strong and valuable brands:

1 Brands must be **innovative**, which means they're seen as leading the way in their sector and shaking things up.

2 They must also be **creative**, with powerful, memorable advertising.

3 They provide a great **brand experience** that meets consumers' needs and is available when and where consumers need it.

4 There's a strong sense of **brand purpose**, so the brand makes people's lives better.

5 Over time, consumers develop a strong sense of **love** towards the brand.

When a brand has all five of these attributes, they have healthy 'lifeblood'; if they are lacking in any one area, they are at risk of damaging their brand health and underperforming in the market. If they fail on all five measures, they are classed as being out of shape. Some of the best-known and most valuable brands in the world score highly on all five of these measures, including Google, Disney and Starbucks.

Over the last 11 years, brands with healthy lifeblood grew by 225 per cent, whilst the out of sorts declined by 10 per cent. Brand health, including a great brand experience, gives a return more than 100 times larger.

Kantar Millward Brown is a leading global agency specializing in advertising effectiveness, strategic communication, media and brand equity research.

Brand experiences bring people more enduring happiness than possessions[15]

> 'Respondents from various demographic groups indicated that experiential purchases – those made with the primary intention of acquiring a life experience – made them happier than material purchases.'
>
> Van Boven and Gilovich[16]

Waiting for an experience is also more pleasurable than waiting to receive a possession[17] because dopamine (the primary neurotransmitter that signals reward and pleasure in our brains) is released when we anticipate a positive emotion.[18] For example, to capitalize on their sense of anticipation, The Wizarding World of Harry Potter sends early ticket holders a park map in advance of them visiting Hogwarts.

> 'Consumers derive value from anticipation, and that value tends to be greater for experiential than for material purchases.'
> Kumar, Killingsworth and Gilovich[19]

At a more detailed level, research[20] suggests material and experiential purchases both provide momentary happiness during consumption, but in different ways. Possessions delivered more frequent momentary happiness whilst experiences delivered more intense momentary happiness. The practical implication being 'do you want to go for quantity or quality of happiness when building brand experiences?'

Brand experiences provide almost unlimited sources of differentiation

Years ago brands tried to differentiate through physical product features. Cars focused on electric windows, sunroofs, leather seats, alloy wheels and sound systems. Banks focused on interest rates, number of ATMs and credit card design. This strategy is problematic because a physical product has a finite number of features. Once you've used all those features you commoditize your offer and the only competitive route is price. As margins evaporate, something has to give, so the quality of experience delivered suffers. In the long run, no one wins.

This contrasts sharply with brand experiences that provide many sources of differentiation. Take a bank as an example. You walk into a branch and what do you experience as your first impression? A welcoming member of staff, customers looking at home on a comfortable sofa, a vibrant feature wall, ambient music and open retail format? Just one touchpoint that provides many opportunities to differentiate your brand. Now extend this to other parts of the retail experience. The customer waits in a queue, deals with a cashier then leaves the branch. Even more opportunities to differentiate the brand. Then add digital, social, telephone and other channels into the experiential mix, and opportunities to differentiate grow exponentially. TD Bank delivers a wonderfully engaging touchpoint through its Penny Arcades. These allow customers to deposit coins at branches and win prizes for doing so. The otherwise dull activity of depositing coins at a bank is transformed into a fun, interactive experience.

Brand experiences help co-ordinate the management of the ever-growing number of touchpoints organizations need to wrestle with

Cast your mind back five years and think about how many traditional and digital media channels existed. Now add social media and mobile into the mix. The number of potential brand touchpoints is increasing rapidly and shows no signs of relenting. Brands that understand how to build brand experiences embrace such change and thrive. They have clearly defined

Brand Experience Essentials that inform, guide and focus their decisions when it comes to identifying relevant channels then delivering experiences within or across them.

Brand experiences facilitate interaction between people

Chief marketing officers are increasingly focused on 'digital transformation' and in some cases see it as a cure for all their brand experience ills. Whilst digital's appeal is understandable, I would encourage you not to overlook the importance of people in your brand experience-building efforts. One study[21] found that whilst 78 per cent of financial services consumers said they would welcome computer-generated support, nearly two-thirds still value interaction with other people, especially to deal with complaints (68 per cent) and advice about complex products (61 per cent).

> Lasting brand differentiation is realized through your employees. This simple idea has never been more important, as companies rush to deploy new digital ways for customers to engage and transact with them.[22]

> 'You must embrace tech and digital but you can't let it lead you, you have to take the lead. Humans still want human exchanges and I still feel that's the best way to connect on a deeper level. Human interactions are still the primary and core driver of loyalty, and that's where we're putting a lot of our energy.'
> Becky Brock, Marketing Director, John Lewis[23]

Brands are increasingly investing in technology to automate brand experiences. BP is testing an artificial intelligence (AI) gas pump called Miles. SoftBank and IBM are collaborating on a robot called Pepper, and Burberry used 'bots' in the run-up to the 2017 London Fashion Week. But research shows chatbots are failing to meet customer expectations because they cannot deal with the idiosyncrasies and nuances of human behaviour.[24] Such technologies also struggle to identify then respond appropriately to our emotional states in an empathic or relevant way. This could include sensing increased customer frustration on the phone, dealing with impatient investors at a shareholder meeting or allaying noise pollution concerns with members of the local community. Whilst new developments in facial recognition and AI's ability to sense our emotional state through tone of voice could go some way to addressing this challenge, they are not there, just yet.

The interpersonal nature of B2B markets means personal contact holds particular value when building brand experiences. This is even more evident in B2B services markets such as consulting and professional services, where the light shines particularly brightly on the adage, 'people business with people'.

How this book is structured

This book is structured around the *Brand Experience Blueprint* (Chapter 2). The Blueprint is a practical management tool that will help guide and structure your approach to building brand experiences. It's based on over 20 years of global branding experience, robust commercial and academic research, and has been validated through extensive application in client organizations around the globe.

The Brand Experience Blueprint comprises three stages:

1 Brand Experience Environment.

2 Brand Experience Essentials.

3 Brand Experience Enablers.

The *Brand Experience Environment* (Part One) encompasses the context you need to be mindful of whilst developing and defining your Brand Experience Essentials. It includes four elements: understanding stakeholders; fine-tuning your perspective; considering the mechanics of delivery; and adopting a data-driven approach to building brand experiences.

Brand Experience Essentials (Part Two) are intangible brand assets: values, essence, promise, positioning and personality. They inform and guide the brand experiences you build through Brand Experience Enablers.

Brand Experience Enablers (Part Three) are three tools you can use to bring your Brand Experience Essentials to life: employee behaviour, communications and design.

These stages are explained fully in the next chapter.

By the end of Part Three, you will understand the sequential, iterative and practical relationship that exists between the Brand Experience Environment, Brand Experience Essentials and Brand Experience Enablers. As a result, you will be well placed to build brand experiences that help your brand retain relevance.

Part Four of this book provides actionable advice on how you can measure brand experiences in a scientific, rigorous and robust way. Although measurement is not a direct brand experience-building activity, you need to couch your efforts within a measurement mentality. This will give your brand experience business case credibility and clout in the boardroom.

Alongside the book are a series of downloadable brand experience-building Toolkits. These are a treasure trove of tried-and-tested tools, techniques and templates I have used with clients around the globe. The Toolkits, which can be found online at koganpage.com/building-brand-experiences (please use the password found at the end of the contents), will help you think about building brand experiences in the context of your organization in structured, applied and so highly relevant ways. You can use them both individually and with your team(s). By sharing these Toolkits with you, my ultimate goal is to help you build brand experiences with greater confidence and conviction.

This book also contains a number of 'Expert Insights'. These are mini-case studies written by experienced senior executives and managers from blue-chip brands, thought leaders with extensive experience, inspiring entrepreneurs, and leading academics located around the globe. I'm absolutely delighted they are a part of the book as they help bring to life the ideas I'm trying to convey in unique, informative and engaging ways.

When it comes to building brand experiences it's important to realize that one size doesn't fit all. Every organization and brand is unique, so the process of building brand experiences cannot be expressed through a universal law. That would confuse simplicity with simplification. This book will guide you through the Brand Experience Blueprint. But how you apply the Blueprint in the context of your organization will depend on your organization's individual characteristics, culture, markets, competitive environment and the specific challenges you face. For this reason, the Brand Experience Blueprint will provide you with freedom to think within a framework instead of being overly prescriptive.

I have had the pleasure and privilege of working with many wonderful people in organizations located around the globe. To ensure they're on the right track, they invite me to speak, run workshops, advise, mentor or coach them through the ideas I will share with you in this book. At Wavelength we also use the Brand Experience Blueprint to audit clients' brand experiences before offering them advice, and use the associated measurement techniques as a baseline to assess progress – if subsequent measurements are taken. Clients' questions, conundrums and contributions inspired and informed this book. I thank them for that.

I hope you enjoy reading this book and that it shares insights you can use to build experiences that will help your brand retain relevance. If you would like to contact me for additional advice, direction, support, or simply to share some thoughts and reflections on how the Blueprint works in practice, you can reach me via the following channels:

Twitter: @onthewavelength
Email: info@wavelengthmarketing.co.uk
Website: www.wavelengthmarketing.co.uk

Do let me know how you get on. I would be delighted to hear from you.

This chapter is accompanied by Toolkit 1.1.

Endnotes

1 Kantar Millward Brown (2017) 2017 BrandZ Top 100 Global Brands [online] http://bit.ly/wavelength-KMB

2 IBM (2016a) The experience revolution: mobilizing to win – are you ready? September [online] http://bit.ly/wavelength-IBM-win

3 Accenture (2015) Majority of B2B companies missing out on revenue growth due to poor customer experience performance, Accenture study finds, 01 December [online] http://bit.ly/wavelength-accenture-2015

4 Stakeholders are individuals who are influenced by, or come into contact with a brand. These could include employees, shareholders, creditors, local communities, suppliers, distributors, vendors or trade unions, to name a few.

5 Some authors feel that friction or 'pain' for the customer is a good thing, eg Sampson Lee (http://bit.ly/wavelength-PIG) whilst others such as Brian Solis don't (*X: The Experience when Business Meets Design*, Wiley). I would encourage you to explore both sides of the argument to balance your perspective and inform your approach.

6 Schwartz, B (2004) *Paradox of Choice*, Harper Perennial

7 Du Plessis, E (2011) *The Branded Mind: What neuroscience really tells us about the puzzle of the brain and the brand*, Kogan Page

8 Schmidt-Subramanian, M et al (2017) Drive revenue with great customer experience, 18 January [online] http://bit.ly/wavelength-forrester-CX2017

9 Biedenbach, G and Marell, A (2010) The impact of customer experience on brand equity in a business-to-business service setting, *Journal of Brand Management*, **17** (6), pp 446–58

10 Maechler, N, Neher, K and Park, R (2016) From touchpoints to journeys: seeing the world as customers do, *McKinsey Quarterly* (March) [online] http://bit.ly/wavelength-mckinsey-cx

11 Biedenbach, G and Marell, A (2010) The impact of customer experience on brand equity in a business-to-business service setting, *Journal of Brand Management*, **17** (6), pp 446–58

12 Özyer, Y (2016) Understanding the impact of the brand experience on brand reputation by the moderating role of technology turbulence, *International Journal of Marketing Studies*, **8** (1), pp 161–69

13 Brakus, J J, Schmitt, B H and Zarantonello, L (2009) Brand experience: what is it? How is it measured? Does it affect loyalty? *Journal of Marketing*, **73** (3), pp 52–68

14 Nysveen, H, Pedersen, P E and Skard, S (2013) Brand experiences in service organizations: exploring the individual effects of brand experience dimensions, *Journal of Brand Management*, **20**, pp 404–23

15 Carter, T J and Gilovich, T (2010) The relative relativity of material and experiential purchases, *Journal of Personality and Social Psychology*, **98** (1), pp 146–59

16 Van Boven L and Gilovich, T (2003) To do or to have? That is the question, *Journal of Personality and Social Psychology*, **85** (6), pp 1193–1202

17 Kumar, A, Killingsworth, M A and Gilovich, G (2014) Waiting for merlot: anticipatory consumption of experiential and material purchases, *Psychological Science*, **25** (10), pp 1924–31

18 Dubol, M et al (2017) Dopamine transporter and reward anticipation in a dimensional perspective: a multimodal brain imaging study, *Neuropsychopharmacology*, 22 August

19 Kumar, A, Killingsworth, M A and Gilovich, G (2014) Waiting for merlot: anticipatory consumption of experiential and material purchases, *Psychological Science*, **25** (10), pp 1924–31

20 Weidman, A C and Dunn, E W (2016) The unsung benefits of material things: material purchases provide more frequent momentary happiness than experiential purchases, *Social Psychological and Personality Science*, **7** (4), pp 390–99

21 IBM (2016b) The experience revolution: new teams, new rules, November [online] http://bit.ly/wavelength-ibm-gameon

22 Accenture (2017) Seven out of 10 consumers globally welcome robo-advice for banking, insurance and retirement services [online] http://bit.ly/wavelength-accenture2017

23 Hobbs, T (2017) John Lewis: human interactions are still the primary driver of loyalty, *Marketing Week*, 6 October [online] http://bit.ly/wavelength-johnlewis

24 Ask, J A et al (2016) The state of chatbots: pilot chatbots as part of your app+ mobile strategy, *Forrester*, 20 October [online] http://bit.ly/wavelength-forrester-chatbots

The Brand Experience Blueprint: A practical management tool

During the introduction, I provided context for this book: senior executives know that brand experiences provide a route to retaining relevance but find it difficult to build them. This book solves that problem. I also defined brand experiences, outlined why you should build them, and detailed how this book will help you build brand experiences. In this chapter, I will introduce the Brand Experience Blueprint (Figure 2.1), which is a robust and practical management tool designed to guide you, step-by-step, through the brand experience-building process.

How will the Brand Experience Blueprint help you?

The Brand Experience Blueprint forms the backbone of this book:

- It helps you structure and sequence your approach to building brand experiences.
- It provides an overarching framework that enables you to:
  - organize the development of your initial brand experience-building thoughts;
  - think about brand experiences in the context of your organization in applied and so more relevant ways;
  - lead brand experience-building initiatives in ways that suit your organizational structure and leadership style.

Figure 2.1   The Brand Experience Blueprint: a practical management tool

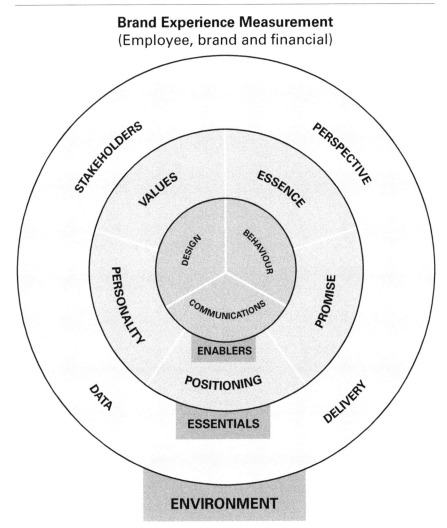

Brand Experience Measurement
(Employee, brand and financial)

- It challenges you to deepen and broaden your thinking through the Brand Experience Essentials and Brand Experience Enablers respectively.

- It includes practical Toolkits – tools and templates you can use straight away to start building brand experiences by yourself or with your team(s). These Toolkits can be found at koganpage.com/building-brand-experiences (please use the password found at the end of the contents).

Before we dive into the detail of the Brand Experience Blueprint it is important to place this practical management tool in the context of brand, marketing and corporate strategy. I want to stress that building brand experiences can't be an independent or standalone brand marketing activity. It should always dovetail with broader brand, marketing and corporate strategy.

At this stage it's also important to acknowledge your brand experience-building efforts should happen within the context of brand experience measurement. As I will cover in Part Four, this entails:

- obtaining employee, brand and financial metrics before you start building your brand experiences so you have a holistic suite of baseline measurements;

- re-administering the same measurements at regular intervals so you can demonstrate the value your work is delivering.

The three stages of the Brand Experience Blueprint

The Brand Experience Blueprint is divided into three stages: Brand Experience Environment (Part One), Brand Experience Essentials (Part Two) and Brand Experience Enablers (Part Three).

The Brand Experience Environment represents the context managers and senior executives should be mindful of when developing and defining Brand Experience Essentials. It comprises four elements:

1 understanding your stakeholders;

2 fine-tuning your perspective;

3 considering the mechanics of delivery;

4 adopting a data-driven approach.

Table 2.1 highlights how each element is made up of various topics including 'profiling stakeholders', 'embracing transparency', 'creating an emotional connection' and 'obtaining robust insights'.

The second stage of building brand experience entails defining your Brand Experience Essentials. These are the intangible elements of your brand experience and need to be developed and defined in the context of the Brand Experience Environment. The Brand Experience Essentials are powerful brand assets and comprise:

- brand values;

- brand essence;

Table 2.1 The Brand Experience Environment: overview and rationale

Familiarizing yourself with the Brand Experience Environment entails	This is important because you need to
Understanding your stakeholders	
1 Profiling stakeholders	Identify then empathize with key stakeholders so you can build relevant brand experiences.
2 Helping stakeholders get 'jobs done'	Understand how your brand will help key stakeholders solve problems or accomplish specific tasks that are relevant to them.
3 Encouraging stakeholder engagement	Appreciate that stakeholders expect brands to interact with them in relevant ways and not just talk at them.
4 Managing stakeholder expectations	Deliver on what you say to a spectrum of stakeholders.
Fine-tuning your perspective	
1 Embracing transparency	Accept there is nowhere for brands to hide in today's digital world.
2 Adopting a holistic mindset	Realize that delivering relevant brand experiences is everyone's responsibility at your organization.
3 Competing primarily through value not price	Appreciate that the majority of stakeholders make decisions based on value, not just price.
4 Having patience	Remember that it can take time to build a brand and the associated experiences.
5 Accepting a loss of control	Acknowledge brands can no longer completely control how they are perceived.
Considering the mechanics of delivery	
1 Creating an emotional connection	Associate your brand with a relevant emotion because the decisions we make are primarily influenced by our emotions.
2 Facilitating co-creation	Facilitate opportunities for stakeholders to create relevant value for themselves.
3 Delivering omnichannel experiences	Realize that stakeholders expect brands to deliver relevant experiences when, where and how they want.

(*continued*)

Table 2.1 *(Continued)*

Familiarizing yourself with the Brand Experience Environment entails	This is important because you need to
Adopting a data-driven approach	
1 Obtaining robust insights	Make brand experience decisions based on robust quantitative and qualitative insight, not anecdote.
2 Measuring holistically	Appreciate the need to obtain employee, brand and financial metrics when measuring brand performance.

- brand promise;
- brand positioning;
- brand personality.

These are important concepts that you need to understand so you can build brand experiences at scale with consistency. Some of your colleagues might consider them 'brand jargon' and this can be dangerous. Jargon can cloud clarity which can alienate people or, worse still, provide a political tool that antagonists can use to derail your project. I recommend explaining Brand Experience Essentials more practically (Table 2.2).

Table 2.2 The Brand Experience Essentials explained in practical terms with supporting examples

Brand Experience Essentials	Explained in practical terms by answering these questions	Example for an outdoor recreation/brand
Values	How would you describe your brand in four or five words?	Inspiring, dependable, driven and down-to-earth.
Essence	If you were asked to sum up your brand in two or three words, what would you say it's all about?	Active outdoor excellence.
Promise	What benefits – NOT features – does your brand deliver?	All of our clothes are made from natural fabric *which means* that they are extremely lightweight and warm.

(continued)

Table 2.2 *(Continued)*

Brand Experience Essentials	Explained in practical terms by answering these questions	Example for an outdoor recreation/brand
Positioning	How are you different from your main competitors?	Believe competitive/outdoor activities can be enjoyed by everyone: 'Everyone can compete'.
Personality	If you were to describe your brand as a person who would they be?	Jessica Ennis-Hill

It's important to define your Brand Experience Essentials in the context of the Brand Experience Environment so they help your brand resonate with stakeholders and form foundations for how you enable your brand experiences.

Brand Experience Enablers are the tools that help you bring your Brand Experience Essentials to life. They include employee behaviour, communications and design. They are important because they help your stakeholders get a 'handle' on your Brand Experience Essentials in tangible and palpable ways. The Brand Experience Enablers are summarized below (Table 2.3).

Table 2.3 Brand Experience Enablers: overview and scope

Enabler	Scope
Behaviour	Human resource processes including recruitment, induction, training, appraisal, reward and exit interviews.
Communications	Traditional media and public relations, eg TV, radio and print; internal communications; social media content, conversations and communities; mobile; stories and gamification.
Design	Multisensory design: using all the senses to build brand experiences, ie sight, taste, touch, sound and smell. Service design: eg customer personas, customer empathy maps, customer journey maps, use case scenarios, service/experience prototyping, mood boards, storyboards and stories.

Getting the most out of the Brand Experience Blueprint

Working through this three-stage Environment–Essentials–Enablers process will help you develop, define and deliver brand experiences that are relevant to your stakeholders. For example, your brand's positioning (Brand Experience Essentials) should be mindful of key stakeholders, create an emotional connection, enable co-creation and be based on data-driven insight (Brand Experience Environment). You can then bring this positioning to life through your employees' behaviour, your communications and/or design (Brand Experience Enablers).

The Brand Experience Environment isn't a rigid checklist, where every item influences every Brand Experience Essential in equal measure. I have watched some clients and workshop participants tying themselves in knots, trying to establish rigid and prescriptive rules to guide their decision making. It's not possible for the Brand Experience Blueprint, or any framework, to work in that way, because every organization and its context is unique.

I would encourage you to adopt a fluid and flexible approach. Use the Blueprint as a helping hand to guide you on your brand experience-building journey. Think of the Brand Experience Environment as the context within which you define your Brand Experience Essentials. Once the Essentials have been defined, behaviour, communications and design – the Brand Experience Enablers – can be used to breathe life into your brand experiences.

The true value of the Brand Experience Blueprint lies in its whole – not just its parts. It's important that you work through all three stages rather than scanning and skipping to the Brand Experience Enablers to save time. Following the sequential approach will help you to:

- Think about how relevant your brand (Brand Experience Essentials) is in today's market (Brand Experience Environment). This will help you build experiences that resonate with your stakeholders.

- Develop clear principles that focus, guide and shape the expression of your brand through the Brand Experience Enablers. This will help you accelerate and scale the delivery of the brand experiences you build.

- Build experiences with substance that are informed by well-thought-through Brand Experience Essentials.

At a glance, *some* of the ideas contained within the Blueprint may feel familiar, but it's likely the way these ideas combine to create the Blueprint won't be. For that reason, I recommend reading all of the following chapters. Words like *values*, *essence* and *personality* are used in everyday brand experience language but when you dig deeper the associated understanding can be quite diverse and even superficial. If we're going to build brand experiences, we need a common understanding of these key terms – and so does your team – so the brand experiences you build have depth, meaning and substance.

A lot of branding terms such as *values*, *essence* and *positioning* are intangible. This makes them slippery and elusive beasts that can be difficult to apply in straightforward and practical ways. This book solves that problem by connecting Brand Experience Essentials and Brand Experience Enablers.

There is a tendency to equate brand experiences with customer experiences or, more specifically, user experience design. But the brand experience-building process encompasses much more than that. Thinking about brand experiences in terms of behaviour, communications and design will broaden your horizons and elevate your level of sophistication when it comes to building brand experiences.

Although the stages of the Brand Experience Blueprint are sequential, the practicalities of building brand experiences mean it's likely you'll need to adopt a more iterative approach. Guided by the Brand Experience Environment you may, for example, define your brand as outlined in Table 2.2 but when it comes to enabling your Brand Experience Essentials through employee behaviour, communications and design, realize this doesn't accurately reflect your brand. If this happens, you would be wise to revisit your Brand Experience Essentials in the context of the Brand Experience Environment. That way, they can be brought to life in a more realistic way through your various Brand Experience Enablers. Don't worry if you need to do this: it's a perfectly normal part of the process and is time well spent. Embracing this thorough and iterative approach will help you to develop greater confidence in the brand experience decisions you make because you'll be building experiences on solid foundations.

Conclusion

In summary, I have introduced the Brand Experience Blueprint, which consists of three stages:

1 *Brand Experience Environment*. This provides the context within which your Brand Experiences Essentials development definition needs to be couched.

2 *Brand Experience Essentials*. The blocks upon which your brand experiences are built.

3 *Brand Experience Enablers*. The tools you can use to bring your Brand Experience Essentials to life.

We will be using this practical, three-stage management tool to structure your approach to building brand experiences, with actionable advice on how you can best use the Brand Experience Blueprint to help you develop, define and deliver relevant brand experiences. Adopting a fluid, flexible and holistic approach to using the Blueprint is also advocated.

PART ONE
Brand Experience Environment

Figure P1.1   The Brand Experience Blueprint: time to focus on the Brand
Experience Environment

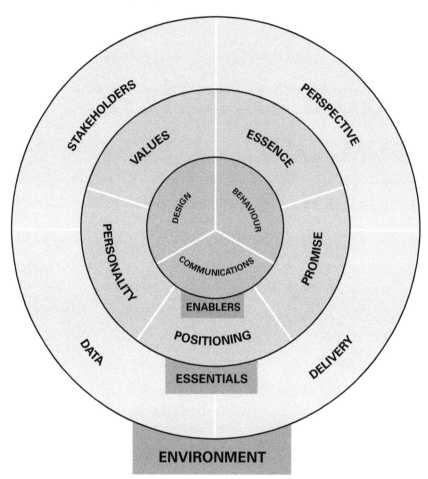

Brand Experience Measurement
(Employee, brand and financial)

The Brand Experience Environment provides the context within which you
should develop and define your Brand Experience Essentials (Part Two).
Understanding the Brand Experience Environment is the first stage of the
Brand Experience Blueprint (Figure P1.1).

Part One consists of four chapters and covers the four elements of the
Brand Experience Environment:

- understanding your stakeholders;
- fine-tuning your perspective;
- considering the mechanics of delivery;
- adopting a data-driven approach.

Understanding your stakeholders 03

There are four elements of the Brand Experience Environment: under-standing your stakeholders; fine-tuning your perspective; considering the mechanics of delivery; and adopting a data-driven approach.

This chapter focuses on understanding your stakeholders and covers:

- profiling stakeholders;
- helping stakeholders get 'jobs done';
- encouraging stakeholder engagement;
- managing stakeholder expectations.

Understanding your stakeholders will help you consider points such as: who you are building brand experiences for; how the experiences should be delivered; where the experiences should be delivered; and how your experi-ences will help various stakeholders. Armed with these insights you will be well placed to deliver relevant experiences that resonate with your key stakeholders.

Profiling stakeholders

Organizations are influenced by an increasing number of stakeholders. Table 3.1 identifies a range of stakeholders that brands may come into contact with, and provides examples of experiences different groups may expect brands to deliver.

Table 3.1   Examples of stakeholder-based experiences

Stakeholder	Type of experience you may build for this stakeholder group
Customers (existing/ prospective; B2B/B2C)	• Online (desktop/mobile). • Retail (shopping centre, pop up etc). • Experiential events to educate buyers, agents, distributors or other intermediaries/partners that sit between your organization and the end customer.
Employees (existing/ prospective)	• Induction and training to educate and engage employees. • Recruitment fairs/employer branding experiences to attract and engage potential employees. • Apprentice schemes which help bring young people into the workplace and equip them with valuable skills. • Company away days to show appreciation/build team spirit and break down team or functional silos.
Suppliers	• Events to share your expectations of suppliers in terms of service levels, costs, ethics etc so you can learn how you can work more closely with them and ultimately deliver a better experience to your customers or other stakeholders. • Joint training sessions where you learn about each other's values (and other Brand Experience Essentials) so you can appreciate what informs each other's approach to doing business.
Competitors	• Industry events so you can collaborate on standards or ethics-based best practice, for the good of the industry and society at large.
Organizations you could collaborate/ partner with	• Events/stands at trade shows that demonstrate how your brand experiences complement each other. • Creating joint thought leadership content, eg webinars to highlight the value your organizations can collaboratively deliver.
Trade unions	• Meetings to listen to union members' concerns and/or share strategic plans in an open and transparent way.
Governments/ politicians	• Invite national/local government to your premises to showcase your brand experiences to encourage inward investment.

(continued)

Table 3.1   *(Continued)*

Stakeholder	Type of experience you may build for this stakeholder group
Potential/existing investors/ shareholders/ analysts	• Quarterly/annual investor updates to outline how funds have been invested, returns delivered and plans for the future. • Organize online debriefings to share market insights/ forecasts that demonstrate thought leadership.
Local, national or international media	• Invite to press days to showcase new experiences you are about to launch. • Provide clearly presented and informative industry data that media can use in articles or reports. • Invite prominent social media influencers to special events so you can start to build relationships with them and ultimately their communities.
Local communities	• Educational experiences to engage the local community with your brand and show how you make a positive contribution to the local area. • Town hall meetings to allay anxieties concerning noise, disruption or pollution associated with your premises, planned factory expansion, etc.
Lobby groups	• Approach or invite lobbyists to share insights, initiate dialogue so you can build relationships based on mutual understanding and benefit.
Volunteers (for charities or religious organizations)	• Public events that recruit volunteers. • Training so volunteers know how to fundraise in ways that align with your Brand Experience Essentials.

Sime Darby is a diversified Malaysian multinational with a US $11.74 billion market capitalization. The company has 123,410 employees across 26 countries and spans sectors including plantations, industrial equipment, the automotive industry and property.[1] The organization's scale means it needs to identify, understand and engage with a broad range of stakeholders, as their 2016 Annual Report outlines (Table 3.2).

This chapter focuses on customers, as they tend to represent the most familiar stakeholder group. However, the tools and templates introduced here can be used just as easily and effectively with other stakeholders. The same principles apply whether you are profiling a customer, employee, channel partner or potential investor.

Table 3.2   Sime Darby stakeholders

Stakeholder	How we engage
Investors	• Roadshows and regional investor conferences • Group and one-on-one meetings • Annual general meeting, quarterly results briefing sessions
Customers	• Tradeshows and exhibitions • Product launches • Direct engagements and surveys • Direct visits to sites and factories operated by the Group
Suppliers/Business Partners	• Relationship building/networking sessions • Vendor development programme
Employees (current and potential)	• Town halls, events and activities • Focus group discussions on targeted issues and engagement surveys
Communities	• Community engagement and outreach • Community development programmes • Strategic partnerships
Governments/Authorities/Regulators	• Regular engagements, communication and dialogue • Consultation on regulatory matters
Civil Society/NGOs	• Industry roundtables • Strategic partnerships • Direct engagements
Others (Media, Academics, Industry, Association)	• Stakeholder engagement surveys • Periodic updates on corporate developments, key events and press release issuance • Group and one-on-one Q&A sessions

SOURCE Sime Darby 2016 Annual Report

Profiling your target customers facilitates empathy. This enables you to see the world through their eyes. Once you have this perspective, you will start to understand their lives and the type of experiences that will be relevant to them. It also helps to 'sense check' whether you *really* are the target customer, or if you have erroneously assumed you are. This is important because it's unlikely a target market of one will be very lucrative. Profiling will help everyone in your organization develop a shared understanding of your customer segments. When everyone has a similar understanding of who your customers are, the challenges they face and how the brand experiences you build will help them address those challenges, you will be able to deliver experiences that are consistently more relevant.

Eighty-one per cent of companies say they have or are close to having a holistic view of their customers but only **37 per cent** of consumers say their favourite retailer understands them.[2]

Twenty-three per cent of 1,300 senior executives 'don't have a consolidated, accurate, 360-degree customer view across all touch points'.[3]

When you profile target customers, it's a good idea to ask yourself the questions outlined in Table 3.3.

Table 3.3   Stakeholder profiling template

Components of stakeholder profiling	Understanding this will help you:
How old are they? What's their gender (does this matter?), their marital status, income, educational level and occupation?	Think about your stakeholder persona from a high level before going into more detail.
Where do they go for dinner?	Appreciate their tastes, attitudes, disposable income, interests, cultural perspectives, eg local or cosmopolitan.
Where do they go grocery shopping?	Know if they are interested in organic, local, international, premium brands etc, and make inferences about disposable income and underlying values which inform purchase behaviour.
What do they drink (alcoholic/non-alcoholic)?	Understand the types of brands they enjoy, eg premium sprits, vintage wine, real ales, organic juices, artisan coffee etc. This will provide a basis for understanding their social context, eg rooftop bars, cosmopolitan coffee shops, juice bars or urban hangouts, and so the basis for where and how to deliver brand experiences.
What music do they like?	Choose the tracks to play at corporate events, in your retail space or whilst a stakeholder is waiting on the phone etc.

(continued)

Table 3.3   *(Continued)*

Components of stakeholder profiling	Understanding this will help you:
Where do they go on holiday?	Realize the type of lifestyle they live, eg active, relaxed, cultural, as the basis for assessing how relevant your brand is to their lifestyle.
What TV programmes do they watch, websites they visit etc?	Plan more effective brand communications on and across relevant channels that are relevant to your target stakeholder.
What type of entertainment do they like?	Identify experiences that may engage them, eg cultural, sporty, relaxed, underground, sophisticated, refined.
What sports do they play or watch?	Understand sports they are passionate about so you can align your brand via sponsorship or relevant experiential events, if appropriate.
What films do they watch?	Appreciate their tastes for entertainment so you can focus communication or other brand activations around relevant films or types of media.
Where do they live?	Identify income levels, where/how to communicate with them and the types of brands they may perceive as relevant, eg rural vs urban.
What is their life mantra, eg YOLO (you only live once), fortune fancies the brave, win some/lose some?	Understand their philosophical approach to life and whether your brand's philosophy aligns with this.
Do they suffer from any disability (physical, mental or otherwise)?	Tailor the experiences you build so they are mindful of this important but often underserved group.
What are their purchase channels?	Determine how your stakeholders buy (online, eg desktop, tablet, mobile, or offline, eg retail, agent) so you can focus your efforts on a relevant channel(s).
Where are their social media hangouts? What technology do they use?	Know where to build communities and engage with your stakeholders digitally; understand where to distribute content, focus online and spend or influence marketing activity. Deliver your experiences through relevant technology.
Who influences their choice, eg parents, celebrities, business leaders, social media influencers?	Understand who you need to engage with as part of your brand experience-building efforts.

(continued)

Table 3.3   *(Continued)*

Components of stakeholder profiling	Understanding this will help you:
What value do they seek? (Try to think of non-monetary points.)	Build experiences that deliver relevant benefits.
What stories have shaped their life?	Craft brand stories which are personally relevant so they can identify with your brand via the narratives you use.
What emotion(s) drive their decision making, eg fear, ego, acceptance, peace of mind, competitiveness, pride?	Build brand experiences that are emotionally relevant to their lives, eg family, social circles, career progression, emotional well-being.
What motivates them in life? eg family care, personal status, well-being.	Deliver experiences which enable them to achieve their motivations in life.
What worries them/keeps them awake at night?	Position your brand experiences as something that will solve a problem and/or alleviate these worries.
What are their values?	Define brand values that are relevant to them.

Addressing the above points will help you understand your key stakeholders in a more sophisticated and nuanced way because you'll see them in the context of their lives and not just as a customer, investor or member of the local community. You'll also start to understand their world view. This will help when it comes to building relevant brand experiences because empathy will inform your ideas.

Whilst it's common for brands to segment based on age, gender and other demographic characteristics, I would encourage you to dig deeper and focus your efforts towards the bottom of Table 3.3. Focusing on age, gender and demographics is quite rudimentary. It could also be argued segmenting your market in this way will become less important as Gen Z mature into adult buyers.[4]

You may be wondering how some of the questions are relevant to your brand. Some examples may help:

Why understand customer interests?

When Dell wanted to reach out to senior business executives who heavily influence technology purchase decisions they created a Dell 'Play Through' golfing app (for iPhone and Android) emulating an interactive golfing experience (they also invited senior executives to attend a golfing tournament in Austin, Texas, where the company is based). Within a few months, the brand enjoyed a 33 per cent increase in perceptions of it being a 'leader in the IT industry'.[5]

Understanding their lifestyle

If you understand the lifestyle a customer has or aspires to have you can locate your brand within this. Premium cooler brand Yeti does not focus brand communications on its products but on outdoor adventures such as fly fishing and kayaking. By focusing on the lifestyle and its associated experiences the brand becomes relevant to the target customer, stimulating demand for their product, and opening the door to new revenue streams courtesy of other goods, services and experiences which sit comfortably within the scope of Yeti's brand essence.

Which social media channels and technology do they use?

LaCroix sparkling water realized that 55 per cent of online 18–29-year-olds are active on Instagram. Based on this insight they encourage and promote user-generated photos amongst their Instagram community, which sits just shy of 115,000 followers (as of January 2018). Whilst social media isn't a numbers game, a quick flick through their Instagram posts highlights a very engaged community. Understanding social media, and technology in general, will become increasingly important with the advent of Gen Z, who are particularly dependent on technology.

What values do they have?

Research[6] shows that people increasingly evaluate brands based on their values. If you understand your stakeholders' values, you can seek out stakeholders whose values align with yours as the basis for connecting with them at a deeper, more emotional level. Bank of Singapore's 'Building on Your Values' campaign depicts financially successful people who have not forgotten their roots. The campaign shows, for instance, someone helping their chauffer change a wheel on their limousine. This sends a clear message. If you have money but are humble, then Bank of Singapore is for you. This is an effective way to facilitate identification with the brand's values via a relevant story that existing and potential customers can relate to.

In the context of stakeholder profiling it's always a good idea to supplement personal anecdote with insight (see Chapter 6). Nielsen research supports this point.[7] Their data showed that Gen X-ers spend more time on social media than the Millennial generation.[8] Given a cursory glance at the tops of heads as you walk down the street, this is a result few would predict. That's why it's good to check and challenge your assumptions; that way your personal views and biases won't colour your judgement.

When profiling your target customers, it's useful to visualize them, then provide details around the drawing to elaborate on your insights. Figure 3.1 provides an example from a workshop held at a large Southeast Asian bank. The target customer was called Ben. He loved gadgets, music, fast cars and spending time with friends. The problem was, he didn't have a lot of money. This is where he needed some help. This exercise provided the inspiration for a segment-based strategy that adopted a digital-first approach to managing finances shaped around customers like Ben.

The profile sketch doesn't need to be a work of art, but visualizing your customers is essential. Not only is it great fun but once you understand a target customer you can develop segment personas that make each type of customer real and tangible. This is important because when your customer is a person and not just a number, employees can develop a common understanding of them, relate to who they are and see the world through their eyes. Adopting this more empathetic approach paves the way for insights

Figure 3.1   Customer profiling: Wavelength Marketing client example
(financial services brand, Southeast Asia)

that can inform, inspire and enhance the brand experiences you build. Figure 3.2 shares some personas we developed for the UK Sepsis Trust.

At Wavelength Marketing we have helped clients use segment personas in a number of ways. These include: locating a life-size mannequin for each persona in clients' offices to keep the customer at the front of everyone's minds – this is especially useful in customer services departments, call centres or in organizations where a more customer-centric approach is required; including them in brand books to provide guidance to external agencies; and using them in employee training where, for example, retail employees were trained to recognize segment personas, encouraging them to tailor the in-store experience around different segments.

Figure 3.2   Customer personas: Wavelength Marketing client example (UK Sepsis Trust)

BRAND PERSONAS

1 HEALTHCARE LEADER (BOARD, NON-CLINICAL) | SOMEONE LIKE ROGER

CHARACTER   Intelligent, 'life-experienced', business-savvy individual. New NEDs overwhelmed by complexity of the NHS. CEOs have disaster and job loss looming like an ever-present rain cloud.

PRESSURES   Very challenged by meeting service demand, balancing need for quality, safe care and financial stability and dealing with persistent change.

EMOTIONS   Threatened and anxious about potential for things to go wrong and the personal liability and damage to reputation that would bring.

2 HEALTHCARE PROFESSIONAL – JUNIOR | SOMEONE LIKE NATALIE

CHARACTER   A HCP of 0–5 years' standing. Sees SEPSIS regularly but probably doesn't realize it. Keen to find out more about the practical aspects of treating these potentially terrifying patients well!

PRESSURES   Can be challenged by pressures on time within and outside work. May feel as if 'fighting fires' and always in a rush, rather than having time to address problems. Conflict can exist between their view of what is right and their seniors' views.

EMOTIONS   Threatened and anxious about potential for things to go wrong and the personal liability and damage to reputation that would bring.

3 PROFESSIONAL BODY LEADER | SOMEONE LIKE SIR LIAM DONALDSON

CHARACTER   An ambitious and politically savvy individual. Strong core values but protective of own interests and those of their body. Will occasionally place these interests ahead of those of patients.

PRESSURES   Burdened by frequent meetings, and fatigued by having to constantly fight their corner. External pressures can necessitate decisions against their better judgement.

EMOTIONS   Will be excited by proposals which benefit them and their body, but which also reflect their core values. May find the opportunity to do genuine good refreshing.

Figure 3.2 *(Continued)*

4 HEALTHCARE LEADER – CLINICAL/SHOP FLOOR | SOMEONE LIKE RON

CHARACTER Dedicated to caring and compassion – maintaining professional values, tries to ensure delivery of safe, reliable care.

PRESSURES Struggles with trying to motivate a de-moralized workforce whilst ensuring high standards of quality and safety. Can be overwhelmed by financial targets and burden of compliance.

EMOTIONS Will be excited by genuine opportunities to improve outcomes, especially if ground-up led. Success will generate professional pride and satisfaction.

5 PARLIAMENTARIAN | SOMEONE LIKE SARAH NEWTON MP

CHARACTER A committed individual who commenced her career intending to make a difference. Will do what is right, as long as it will not bring adverse publicity.

PRESSURES Emburdened by workload and constantly trying to balance constituents' needs with commitments to Groups and Committees and to individual votes.

EMOTIONS Genuinely wants to 'do good', but can be frustrated when the 'right' thing is not in the Party's interests. Controls emotion and will not display willingly in public.

6 AFFECTED BY SEPSIS AND ENGAGED | SOMEONE LIKE RHIAN

CHARACTER Sepsis virgin. Has never heard of sepsis before, probably hearing of it for the first time on a death certificate or at post mortem, or if a survivor mentioned in passing by a HCW. Keen to know more, and to help others.

PRESSURES Conflict can arise between different family members' expectations-blame/litigation vs. do good.

EMOTIONS Driven by a desire to ensure this doesn't happen to anyone else. Complex interactions with grief (if bereaved) or personal manifestations (inclusing PTSD) if survivor. Ability to communicate and participate can therefore wax and wane.

7 AFFECTED BY SEPSIS AND ANGRY | LIKE SOMEONE FROM ANGRY BIRDS

CHARACTER Sepsis virgin. Has never heard of sepsis before, probably hearing of it for the first time on a death certificate or at post mortem, or if a survivor mentioned in passing by a HCW. Suspicious of health care, often politically active locally and prone to aligning to patient action groups.

PRESSURES Often driven by a (often misplaced) sense of guilt. Family may fuel and reinforce desire to seek recompense. May feel compelled to seek litigation, blame, or media exposure.

EMOTIONS Can feel guilty – 'what if I'd called the GP sooner' etc. Seeks information and answers, but often to use to gain apology or adverse publicity. May in time engage but unlikely. Will regard UKST as a friend independent of healthcare but may be a transient relationship.

It could be argued that stakeholder profiling in B2B markets is equally, if not more important, than B2C markets. This is due to the importance of the interpersonal relationships which characterize B2B markets. You can profile key stakeholders such as business customers, suppliers, or other channel partners at B2B brands using the template provided in Table 3.3.

Research conducted by Google[9] provides interesting pointers on what is perceived as relevant in B2B markets. Their findings indicate that business customers prefer, and are willing to pay a price premium for, brands that deliver self-image improvements and professional benefits of personal value. In other words, there's an element of 'What's in it for me?' This could be career advancement, impressing the boss, or demonstrating expertise to colleagues. Thorough stakeholder profiling will help you understand this so, when building brand experiences for B2B markets, you need to be mindful of how you can help people achieve these goals or get those 'jobs done'.

Helping stakeholders get 'jobs done'

The origins and authenticity of Henry Ford's famous quote, 'If I had asked people what they wanted, they would have said faster horses', are contested but the value of the sentiment stands. Fast-forward several decades. Did we know we wanted the iPod? No. Did we know we wanted Facebook or Airbnb? It now seems so obvious they should have been launched a long time ago. Why? The answer lies in asking customers or other stakeholders the wrong question during market research.

> 'A lot of the times people don't know what they want until you show it to them.'
>
> Steve Jobs

Research frequently focuses on identifying and satisfying customers' 'needs' and 'wants'. Asking about either isn't terribly helpful because, with the exception of expert users or industry specialists, a lot of the time customers don't *really* know what they want or need. This is especially the case when it comes to detailed specifications or functional features which tend to be the focal points of most research. The solution is to find out what 'jobs' they are trying to get done. Once you understand this you will be well placed to build relevant experiences.

Pfizer's launch of Xeljanz, a pill for rheumatoid arthritis sufferers, provides an example of a brand that focuses on helping customers get jobs done. After conducting extensive research, they understood that one of the key 'jobs' people were trying to get done was to enjoy moments that people without chronic pain don't even think about. These include walking upstairs, swimming, yoga, helping a loved one fasten a necklace, or even standing on tiptoes to give their partner a hug. Such scenarios were incorporated into the campaign, which increased Xeljanz brand awareness by 24 per cent, brand recall by 25 per cent, the likelihood patients would discuss Xeljanz with their doctor by 24 per cent, consideration by 75 per cent and prescription volumes by 95 per cent.[10]

The 'jobs to be done' approach was pioneered by Professor Clayton Christensen from Harvard Business School and subsequently developed by the likes of Stephen Wunker and his team at New Markets Advisors.[11] The main idea is that goods, services, brands, experiences etc, are 'hired' to help people get 'jobs' done. Put another way, what are they trying to achieve in their life? What tasks are they trying to get done? What problems are they trying to solve? Once you understand this then it's your responsibility to build experiences that help stakeholders get 'jobs' done. Clients tend to think the language of 'jobs to be done' is a little cumbersome and awkward. This is precisely why I like it. It's unusual. This draws you in and gets you thinking at a deeper level about what a certain stakeholder is trying to achieve and how you can help them do this.

The 'job' someone wants to get done could be primarily rational, emotional or a combination of the two. Here are some examples of jobs different stakeholders may want to get done:

- be considered cool by their kids (working parents);
- impress their boss (account manager);
- trusted by the local community (chemical manufacturer);
- show their partner they love them (boyfriend, girlfriend, fiancé(e) etc);
- feed their kids balanced and nutritious meals, quickly (parents or carers);
- prove to themselves that they can be a success (graduate recruit);
- retire early (chief executive officer);
- deliver brand experiences through employees' behaviour that delights customers (chief marketing officer or head of human resources).

Armed with this insight you can build brand experiences that help people get specific jobs done, making those experiences much more relevant for your stakeholders. The Expert Insight 3.1 provided by Stephen Wunker outlines how Mini carved out a niche for a premium small car by understanding the jobs a certain customer segment was trying to get done.

EXPERT INSIGHT 3.1 How Mini used 'Jobs to be Done thinking' to drive brand performance

Stephen Wunker, Managing Director, New Markets Advisors

Small cars are boring and unprofitable – a necessary but unattractive part of doing business as an automaker. So went the industry logic through the 1990s.

Enter the reborn Mini, from BMW. The car was undeniably small, yet also vastly profitable. The Mini was a business wonder: customers paid a price premium, and they got an auto with just two basic chassis variants.

The secret was to delve into what people were trying to accomplish with a car – their 'Jobs to be Done' – not just what auto-specific 'needs' the car met. The lens of 'Jobs to be Done' enabled Mini to focus not just on the *what* that customers were seeking, but the *why*. While rivals were defining their market in terms such as 'small sedans' and competing on an almost endless list of functional features, the Mini team saw that its real competition could be clothing, scooters, or larger vehicles such as the Prius. The 'why' lens – and particularly the focus on self-expression – enabled the brand to stake out unclaimed mental real estate, owning the key territory of individuality in a sea of mass production.

By understanding Jobs to be Done, not just customer needs, Mini redefined its marketplace and created its own vectors for performance that enabled a price premium. Moreover, the company appealed not only to buyers' functional desires, but to emotional cravings that customers would pay good money to fulfil.

New Markets Advisors is a Boston-based consulting firm specializing in creating distinct approaches to competing in and growing a broad range of markets.

Research from Saatchi & Saatchi and Mumsnet found that successful and relevant brands help mums in seven ways (note: the research specified 'mums', but could be considered relevant to all parents and carers).[12] Whilst this wasn't described as helping Mum get jobs done the parallels are clear. Mums are drawn to brands with the following characteristics:

- *Precision*: helps shave a few extra seconds from a task and makes things run seamlessly.

- *Sorcery*: can help Mum pull the rabbit out of the bag at the last minute to entertain their kids.

- *Elasticity*: helps Mum work around their busy schedules and be flexible when required.

- *Showmanship*: gives Mum the confidence that she is doing the right thing when it comes to taking care of her kids so she can showcase this to people she knows.

- *Attentiveness*: has a tacit understanding of what is 'right' for mums. They don't need to ask because they intuitively understand.

- *Integrity*: helps Mum feel comfortable and true to herself when around the kids.

- *Enhancement*: helps Mum by supporting her life and empowering her.

Once you understand the various 'jobs' Mum (or another parent or carer) is trying to get done, the type of experiences and the way they should be delivered becomes apparent. To help with 'precision', a washing machine that washes then dries clothes very quickly, leaving them ready to iron (or, ideally, crease-free so they don't need ironing) will save extra time when it comes to getting kids ready for school. To help Mum with some 'sorcery', a content production brand could email educational and informative videos or reading materials at key times in the day so Mum can keep the kids entertained when other things need to get done, eg preparing the evening meal or during the school run. This way of thinking contrasts sharply with starting from customer wants, needs or product features where 'Mum' (or the parent) may not be familiar with, or even care about the technology. They just want to keep the kids entertained so they can focus on getting the evening meal ready. The detail is not their concern.

Around 2002, I was responsible for location-based services at a big mobile telecom company and was guilty of focusing on customer wants and needs rather than the jobs they wanted to get done. Extensive and very costly qualitative and quantitative European-wide research indicated our 'Buddy Finder' service called 'Locate a Mate' would be well received across the European footprint. Locate a Mate enabled customers to identify the location of 'Mates', who had given them permission, before finding a mutually convenient meeting location which they could send as a map and directions to their relevant Mates. Several hundred thousand pounds of application development investment later (on the back of a multimillion-Euro location platform deal) the service failed miserably in pre-launch tests. This was extremely embarrassing and very confusing. Why did I get it so wrong? Simple. Customers were asked the wrong questions during focus groups. These included:

- 'Is an accuracy of 200 metres good enough for locating your friends?'
- 'Once you have located your friends, would you be interested in finding a mutually convenient meeting point and then sending them a map with directions?'
- 'Would reviews of restaurants, bars, etc located in mutually convenient locations be useful?'

The innovative nature of location-based services meant customers couldn't visualize the service, how it would fit into their lives or if the location accuracy provided was acceptable. So they had no idea what features they needed. To solve this problem, we thought it would be useful to provide an extensive feature list so they could select the most relevant service features. This was a bad move. They said they wanted everything (no surprise). On reflection, this was a masterclass in how not to design brand experiences. We should have understood the jobs the target customers were trying to get done, then built experiences around these. We later discovered they just wanted to find their friends then give them a call to meet up in the local area. Simply sending an SMS to a short code to identify their friend's location would have sufficed. They didn't need maps, directions or restaurant reviews. Based on the focus group insight we aimed to launch a Rolls Royce experience when a mid-range Mercedes would have sufficed.

You can identify the jobs that a customer wants to get done by using a simple framework which consists of three steps:

1 context/situation;

2 anxiety or motivation;

3 job you want to get done.

These can be tied together using the following template: *When* (context/situation) *I want* (anxiety/motivation) *so I can* (job to be done). For example: '*When I don't have any cash* (context/situation) *I want to ensure I can pay to get around town* (anxiety) *so I can live my life without any stress* (jobs to be done).' Once this task has been completed you can start to build targeted experiences that enable customers to pay without cash and so avoid payment-related stress.

Another way to identify the jobs a customer needs to get done is to consider:

1 Who?

2 What?

3 Why?

You can use the following template to bring these together: *As* (who) *I want* (what) *so that* (why, ie job to be done). For example: *'As an ambitious chief marketing officer* (who) *I want to equip my team with advanced brand experience knowledge* (what) *so we can drive the financial performance of our brand and so command the respect of my chief financial officer in the boardroom* (why).' This insight could inform the type of experiences an agency delivers so they, ultimately, help the CMO drive financial performance and earn the respect of the CFO.

When you start to adopt a 'Jobs to be Done' perspective clarity emerges. An iPod helps customers carry their entire CD collection on the move. Airbnb helps customers live like a local whilst travelling away from home. Facebook satisfies our fundamental need to connect with other people. If you think in this more abstract way the type of experiences you need to take to market become apparent. Unfortunately, most brands focus on needs and wants which are 'satisfied' by functional product features. This results in irrelevant innovation and unnecessary product features that cloud the clarity of the experiences you build and inhibit stakeholder engagement.

Encouraging stakeholder engagement

The increasingly connected and complex nature of today's business environment means that brands interact *with* a diverse range of stakeholders. The days of focusing purely on customers and talking *at* them have long gone. Brands need to engage *with* stakeholders via immersive and relevant experiences. This a challenge many, especially corporate brands, face as they aim to retain relevance. In their Expert Insight piece, Hari Nair and Rafiza Ghazali outline how the Sime Darby Young Innovators Challenge addresses this issue by engaging with the Millennial generation through innovation and the sustainability agenda.

EXPERT INSIGHT 3.2 How Sime Darby engages Millennials with sustainability through innovation

Hari Nair, Group Chief Strategy and Innovation Officer, Sime Darby
Rafiza Ghazali, Senior Vice President, Group Innovation and Performance Management, Sime Darby

Sustainability is an integral part of Sime Darby. Balancing economic, social and environmental considerations allows Sime Darby to deliver sustainable value to our stakeholders. This involves engaging and empowering them to be part of this agenda. The Sime Darby Young Innovators Challenge (SDYIC) encourages teenagers to embrace sustainability through an innovation challenge. The winning proposal is then developed with the support of Sime Darby. A total of 168 participants joined the regional workshops in March 2016 across four different regions in Malaysia. The regional champions proceeded to a national workshop held in conjunction with Sime Darby's inaugural Innovation Day. The event was attended by the Prime Minister of Malaysia, Dato' Seri Mohd Najib Tun Abdul Razak.

Robin Food (http://www.myrobinfood.org), a team of four 16-year-olds from East Malaysia, was the inaugural champion of the Sime Darby Young Innovators Challenge 2016, with a platform (app and www) to reduce food wastage. This highly interactive online marketplace connected hypermarkets and hotels with food banks across Malaysia so surplus food could be distributed to those in need via local charities and NGOs.

Sime Darby and the Sime Darby Foundation (which funds the SDYIC project) worked closely with Food Aid Foundation, a leading food bank in Malaysia, and Tesco to develop the app. The Robin Food app was launched in 2016 and is an example of how external and internal ideation, innovation governance, execution and commercialization can combine to engage tomorrow's innovators and entrepreneurs with the sustainability agenda of today. SDYIC also allows Sime Darby to contribute towards the nation's human capital development. Not only can young people develop confidence, creativity and teamwork, they are also exposed to design thinking, innovation, leadership and entrepreneurial capabilities. More importantly, it develops a deeper understanding of sustainability and highlights the important role it plays in today's business world.

Note: This article was based on materials published in Sime Darby Berhad 2016 Annual Report: *Innovating for the Future.*

Sime Darby is a diversified multinational and a key player in the Malaysian economy, with businesses in key growth sectors, namely, plantation, industrial equipment, motors, property and logistics, with operations in 26 countries and four territories.

Not-for-profit, non-governmental and charitable organizations also have to engage with diverse groups of stakeholders to get their voices heard. Brand experiences play an important role in helping them do this. For example, The UK Sepsis Trust manages stakeholder relations with the following groups:

- healthcare leaders (board, non-clinical) eg National Health Service trusts;
- healthcare professionals (junior position) eg nurses or doctors;
- professional body leader, eg Chief Medical Officer for England;
- healthcare leaders (clinical/shop floor) eg surgeons or anaesthetists;
- parliamentarians, eg MPs (Figure 3.3);
- people affected by sepsis who are engaged/supportive;
- people affected by sepsis who are angry/upset.

Figure 3.3   Jeremy Hunt MP, UK Secretary of State for Health and Social Care, discussing Sepsis with stakeholders

Governments also realize the role building brand experiences plays in the countries they run. Dr Wafa Abu Snaineh's Expert Insight provides an interesting example of how the Executive Council, Government of Dubai engaged internal and external stakeholders so it could deliver more customer-centric government initiatives to the people of Dubai.

EXPERT INSIGHT 3.3   How the Government of Dubai builds customer-centric experiences

Dr Wafa Abu Snaineh, Advisor of Dubai the Model Centre, The Executive Council, Government of Dubai

The Dubai Model for Government Services (DMGS) was launched with the primary objectives of increasing customer-centricity and service efficiency, and encouraging the implementation of creative and smarter government initiatives. Its inception, development and ongoing delivery are guided by four principles: customer engagement; connected government; innovation; and reasoned spending.

These principles inform three DMGS framework components that enable government entities to deliver high-quality government services:

1 **Service Delivery**. Consists of seven critical perspectives for the successful design and delivery of model services: customer insights, service charters, service realization, customer experience, service delivery stars, service improvement culture, as well as efficiency and effectiveness results.

2 **Service measurement**. A set of unified tools for the assessment of service efficiency and effectiveness with a focus on customer-centricity. These tools allow organizations to benchmark their performance internally as well as externally and provide senior management with a strong basis for educated decision making across government.

3 **Service improvement process**. Includes a standard tool for continuous improvement and innovation of services.

The DMGS has delivered real impact in Dubai. In fewer than three years, the model has been adopted by more than 30 government entities. This large-scale, but gradual roll-out helped embed a common culture of service improvement within government. Through the DMGS, government entities have implemented more than 300 strategic initiatives for service improvement since its launch, made cost savings of hundreds of millions of dirhams (the basic monetary unit in the United Arab Emirates), and enhanced customer experience in different ways.

The models also demonstrated that:

- the public sector can improve customer experience by placing customers at the heart of the government service delivery processes;

- efficiency and customer experience can simultaneously improve – there is no need to sacrifice one for the other;

- the government machinery is not necessarily outdated and has the chance to implement leading-edge solutions across bureaucracy and red tape.

The Dubai Model for Government Services (DMGS), managed by Dubai, The Model Centre, is one of the strategic public services transformation programmes implemented by the Government of Dubai.

Although the topic of stakeholder engagement is a book in its own right, the rest of this chapter focuses on engaging two particularly important stakeholder groups: customers and employees.

The role of customers

The days of customers accepting brand communications messages without question are long gone. Customers are not passive. They expect brands to interact with them. They have high expectations. They are discerning, connected, sceptical and demanding. To connect with your customers in relevant ways, you need to build personalized and engaging experiences.

Eighty-one per cent of customer experience decision makers believe it is important to involve customers directly in customer experience efforts. Only 57 per cent actually do it.[13]

Nike used to sign off brand communications with 'nike.com'. Not anymore. That's too passive. Nike now uses the #justdoit hashtag or more focused hashtags such as #NIKExNBA at the end of brand communications to encourage social engagement. More recently, to facilitate customer engagement, Nike launched NikeConnect so basketball fans can access real-time, personalized experiences by connecting their NBA jersey and smartphone.

Starbucks has run the Red Cup Art competition for nearly 20 years. This invites customers to pick up a plain red holiday cup in-store and paint their own work of art to be shared via #RedCupArt, with the best designs being shared via Starbucks social channels. Mondelez encourages an Oreo-dunking culture via its #OREODunkSweepstakes, which gives people a platform to showcase their dunking prowess.

T-Mobile and Samsung ran a promotional event in Times Square, inviting visitors into virtual reality booths to try the Samsung Gear VR headset and immersive experiences such as a skiing adventure. Burberry's 'Art of the Trench' allows customers to share photos of themselves wearing their Burberry trench coats. This approach initiated community-based conversations on social media platforms. It also dovetails nicely with Burberry's strategy targeting the Millennial generation who love to engage with communities around a common interest, which in this case is high-end British luxury fashion.

The importance of brand engagement comes into sharper focus when considering the Millennial generation. The first to grow up with pervasive digital technologies, they represent over a quarter of the global population.

Millennials were also raised during one of the worst recessions in living memory, so are sceptical of many global brands who they hold accountable for the economic hardship they endure. Brand experiences that facilitate engagement help address these challenges because they provide brands with an opportunity to express their Brand Experience Essentials (Part Two) in open, authentic and interactive ways. This appeals to the Millennial generation who want to assess the truthfulness of brand claims before buying and being associated with that brand. Toms Shoes is a good example. Each Toms store has a virtual reality headset featuring 360-degree stories showing how their shoes are helping underserved communities. This helps Toms customers engage with the brand's story and altruistic values.

Understanding the importance of employees

Great brand experiences are built from within so it's essential you engage and involve employees in the brand experience-building process. Adopting this approach helps employees feel a part of and 'own' the brand experiences your organization takes to market. Employees are considered the most credible spokespeople for a range of issues including the treatment of customers, business practices, innovation and societal issues.[14] This makes them a valuable brand asset so it's important that they're engaged in your brand experience-building efforts.

> 'Employees come number one, customers come number two. If you have a happy workforce, they'll look after your customers anyway.'
>
> Tony Fernandes, Founder and
> Group Chief Executive Officer, Air Asia

Wavelength worked on a brand values project with an ambitious boutique corporate finance firm. The company realized the behavioural side of their experience required attention so they could deliver more consistent client experiences across their footprint. The first stage of the project involved running a series of facilitated workshops in all their European markets to educate and engage employees in the brand value definition process, whilst eliciting views on existing and ideal values. We then conducted quantitative research with larger groups of employees to validate the views voiced during the workshops. This fed into a series of brand experience-related work streams that focused on how these values could be brought to life through employee behaviour at key touch points during the client experience.

Organizations that take the time to involve employees in this way tend to be the exception, not the norm, but that firm is reaping the rewards, as their company values are understood and owned across the organization.

When Adidas started to lose market share to Nike and Under Armour, it wanted to reposition itself as a 'creator brand'. To achieve this goal, it initiated projects like 'Futurecraft', which allowed customers to tailor its products with 3D printed soles. Before Adidas could take the changes to market, the company educated and engaged its 55,000 employees through an internal programme focused on their repositioning.

As part of the Virgin Active Australia rebrand launch, the Virgin Active team were invited to a special unveiling at warehouses on the outskirts of Melbourne and Sydney. Upon arrival, the head of brand showed a new brand 'sizzle reel' followed by a curated video in which employees unknowingly described the brand values and what they meant to them. The whole group then completed a 30-minute DJ-led yoga experience which aimed to provide a taster for Virgin Active's new yoga proposition and emphasize its group-based exercise focus. After the class, Virgin Active Australia's managing director provided more detail on the new brand and what it would mean for them in terms of uniform, a commercial partnership with Lululemon, employee behaviour and reward.

High street fast-fashion brand Zara engages its employees by encouraging them to keep their finger on the pulse of fashion trends. The company trains store employees and managers to be sensitive to customer trends in the ways they handle product enquiries and behave on shop floors. Zara empowers and encourages its retail employees to harvest customer insight into cuts, fabrics, styles or lines. Employees feed their insights back to staff at Zara HQ, who decide whether to progress and commercialize their suggestions.

Research from IBM[15] found that customer experience aficionados, referred to as 'Elites', engage employees in the brand experience process as they are considered critical drivers of success. Other studies show employee engagement has a positive influence on organizational performance.[16] More specifically, compared with organizations in the bottom quartile, companies with engagement scores in the top quartile:

- have twice the annual net income ('profit attributable to shareholders' in the UK);[17]
- return seven times more to shareholders over a five-year period;[18]
- experience 2.5 times revenue growth,[19] 12 per cent higher customer advocacy and profitability, and 18 per cent higher productivity.[20]

This is consistent with other research[21] which found that highly committed employees try 57 per cent harder, perform 20 per cent better and are 87 per cent less likely to leave than those with low levels of commitment.

Despite overwhelming evidence supporting the case for engaging employees, most brand experiences are still, in the name of speed, built from the outside in. This entails starting with design and communications work before involving employees as something of an afterthought. I would advise against this. If employees aren't engaged and don't understand the role they play in delivering brand experiences, these experiences will be characterized by employee apathy, even anguish, and not genuine commitment.

Managing stakeholder expectations

A lot of brands promise the universe but deliver far less. 'We'll double your revenues', 'We'll halve your OPEX within a year', 'Your product will be with you tomorrow, I guarantee'. Research conducted by YouGov in 2013 shows this is a particular problem for big corporates.[22] Overpromising but failing to deliver is tantamount to brand experience suicide. Why do so many brands make this mistake? Brands don't want to disappoint their customers or other stakeholders.

It's much better to be realistic and manage expectations, even if this causes short-term frustration. That way you can minimize stakeholder irritation, annoyance and the eroded advocacy that follows in the long run.

Some time ago Wavelength was asked to complete an annual report for a big Middle Eastern bank. To do this we needed to obtain their rather hefty brand guidelines by post. Usually this would not pose a problem but the client's country was experiencing serious civil unrest. To our surprise a DHL courier was in our reception a mere three days later. I told him I was delighted to see the parcel arrive at all, not to mention so quickly! His response was 'We under-promise and over-deliver.' For an organization of DHL's size to deliver a brand experience in this way is a testament to their internal communications and employee engagement efforts.

Conclusion

In this chapter we have explored how you can understand the stakeholder element of the Brand Experience Environment. This entails profiling stakeholders, thinking about how your experiences can help stakeholders get 'jobs done', encouraging stakeholder engagement and managing expectations.

Familiarizing yourself with your stakeholders in this way represents an important component of the Brand Experience Environment. Once you know who your stakeholders are, where they go, what 'jobs' they need to get done in their life, how you can engage with them and are realistic about what you can deliver, you'll be well placed to build experiences that are more relevant to them – especially if you fine-tune your perspective.

This chapter is accompanied by Toolkits 3.1, 3.2 and 3.3.

Endnotes

1 Sime Darby (2016) *Innovating for the Future*, Annual Report, 2016

2 IBM (2015) The great customer experience divide, April [online] http://bit.ly/wavelegth-IBM

3 Oracle (2016) Global insights on succeeding in the customer experience era [online] http://bit.ly/wavelength-oracle

4 Adams, P (2017) Why Gen Z might signal the end of demographic targeting as we know it, *Marketing Dive*, 10 October [online] http://bit.ly/wavelength-generationz

5 Warc (2016) Dell: Play Through Mobile App, MMA Smarties, Silver, 2016 [online] Warc.com

6 Lai, A et al (2007) The values-based consumer: a technographics® 360 report using survey, social listening, and qualitative data, *Forrester*, 6 April [online] http://bit.ly/wavelength-values

7 Nielsen (2016) 2016 Nielsen social media report. Social studies: a look at the social landscape [online] http://bit.ly/wavelength-acnielsen2016

8 Millennials are a generation, not a segment of people, born between the early 1980s to 2000. Whilst it's true certain characteristics predominate, such as being predisposed to digital, they are a diverse group so please note they are not to be considered a segment with homogenous characteristics when referenced in this book. If you would like to read more: Lau, R (2015) *Direct to A New Perspective on Millennials: Segmenting a generation for actionable insights*, Interbrand Design Forum, January; The 2016 Deloitte Millennial Survey: Winning over the next generation of leaders.

9 Nathan, S and Schmidt, K (2013) From promotion to emotion: connecting B2B customers to brands, *Think with Google* [online] http://bit.ly/wavelength-google

10 Warc (2015) Pfizer: Xeljanz 'Body Language', ARF Ogilvy Awards, Silver, Pharmaceutical [online] Warc.com

11 Wunker, S, Wattman, J and Farber, D (2016) *Jobs to Be Done: A roadmap for customer-centered innovation*, AMACOM. This book provides a thorough, practical and accessible overview of 'jobs to be done' thinking.

12 Marketing Week (2017d) The seven characters of brands mums love, 26 April [online] http://bit.ly/wavelength-mums

13 Accenture Interactive (2016) Expectations vs experience: the good, the bad, the opportunity, June [online] http://bit.ly/wavelength-accenture

14 Edelaman Trust Barometer (2017) [online] http://bit.ly/wavelength-edelman-2017

15 IBM (2016a) The experience revolution: mobilizing to win – are you ready? September [online] http://bit.ly/wavelength-IBM-win

16 Macleod, D and Clarke, N (2009) *Engaging for Success: Enhancing performance through employee engagement – a report for government* [online] http://bit.ly/wavelength-employee_engagement

17 Wiley, J (2008) *Engaging the Employee*, Kenexa Research Institute

18 Wiley, J (2008) *Engaging the Employee*, Kenexa Research Institute

19 Royal, M and Yoon, J (2009) Engagement and enablement: the key to higher levels of individual and organisational performance, *Journal of Compensation and Benefits*, 25 (Sept/Oct), pp 13–19

20 Harter, J K et al (2012) *Q12® Meta-Analysis: The relationship between engagement at work and organizational outcomes*, Gallup Organization

21 CEB (2004) *Driving Performance and Retention Through Employee Engagement*, Arlington VA [online] http://bit.ly/wavelength-ceb

22 Nugent, G (2013) What price trust? *Campaign*, 29 May [online] http://bit.ly/wavelength-promise

Fine-tuning your perspective

04

In Chapter 3, I outlined the importance of understanding your stakeholders so you can build brand experiences that are relevant to them. This chapter will help you think through how to fine-tune your perspective in connection with key aspects of the Brand Experience Environment. It outlines why the following are important when building brand experiences:

- embracing transparency;
- adopting a holistic mindset;
- competing primarily through value not price;
- having patience;
- accepting a loss of control.

Understanding these issues will help you develop and define more relevant Brand Experience Essentials as your outlook will be in tune with the salient factors that shape the Brand Experience Environment.

Embracing transparency

Stakeholders, especially the Millennial generation, are increasingly drawn to brands based on *who* they are, *what* they stand for and *why* they exist. This trend looks set to continue and even intensify with Gen Z, who insist on and scrutinize integrity. As a result, brands need to conduct business in an open and transparent way so stakeholders can make an informed judgement about these topics and ultimately whether the brand is relevant to them. In parallel, trust in NGOs, media, government and its officials, business and CEOs has been diminishing for some time.[1] Now add into the mix fading consumer trust in social media due to the advent of fake news.[2] When combined, these factors compel brands to be open and honest, bringing transparency into sharper focus.

Social media brings stories to the masses at electrifying speed. Brands are now increasingly being held to a high social standard and have nowhere to hide. Once fuel is added to the social media fire it's hard to put the flames out.

For example, in November 2015, news channels[3] reported VW had noticed 'irregularities' with the fuel emission software installed in their cars. The resulting scandal has had major implications for the brand, with Bloomberg.com reporting that VW stock dropped from €2.50 (10 April 2015) to about €0.95 (October 2015).[4] Japanese car manufacturer, Mitsubishi, was found to be overstating car fuel efficiency,[5] resulting in the brand's first loss in eight years.[6] A documentary called *The Beautiful Bung: Corruption and the World Cup*[7] led to investigations into corruption in world football. This resulted in the US Department of Justice indicting nine FIFA officials and five corporate executives for racketeering, conspiracy and corruption,[8] with a further 16 FIFA officials being charged by US authorities in December 2015.[9] These are just a few examples and the list keeps growing. In his Expert Insight, marketing provocateur Hilton Barbour outlines how other brands have fallen foul when it came to transparency.

EXPERT INSIGHT 4.1 Why transparency is the backbone of brand experiences

Hilton Barbour, Marketing Provocateur

Transparency is an expectation that no part of your business operation is beyond the scrutiny of your customers or other stakeholders. It is no longer enough to deliver a great service or product; how that service or product is delivered is equally critical.

Just ask Nestlé about their ongoing battle with Greenpeace,[10] the sourcing of palm oil from rainforests or their recurring court cases with municipalities over ownership of ground water.[11] The treatment of workers who manufacture your (very expensive) iPhone is equally open to scrutiny.[12] Your organization's position on gender, race or even sexual orientation can earn or eradicate customer trust – US fast-food chain Chick-fil-A found themselves at the centre of a polarizing debate when their CEO announced he was against same-sex marriage.[13]

For those still struggling with the concept of transparency, consider this. We live in a world where the availability of information and the desire for self-expression has never been higher – or more public. Discovering your organization's practices is a Google search away. The takeaway for executives? It may be popular to obsess about your organization's 'why' but it is perhaps more critical to ensure your 'how' is equally open and transparent.

Hilton Barbour is a Toronto-based strategist who loves nothing more than tackling thorny brand challenges.

Transparency holds brands to account and this can be scary, for good reason. Brands feel exposed and vulnerable because their mistakes are magnified in the public eye. But transparency should not necessarily be viewed with caution or disdain. An increasing number of brands embrace transparency. They use it as the cornerstone of the brand experiences they build, and thrive as a result. For example, Patagonia's Footprint Chronicles show the farms, textile mills and factories it works with around the world. The goal is to use supply chain transparency to mitigate the adverse social and environmental impact a brand can have. Every time Toms sells shoes, eyewear, coffee or a bag it sends a pair of shoes or spectacles to a person in need as part of its Toms One for One® initiative. Unilever invited children to one of their Blue Ribbon farms in Canada[14] to learn what goes into Hellmann's mayonnaise and opened the doors of one of its tomato suppliers in Latin America as part of its 'Grow with Us' campaign.

From a B2B perspective, Procter & Gamble's Chief Brand Officer, Marc Pritchard, is an example of an executive who takes transparency seriously. He insisted that all the company's media partners, platforms and agencies demonstrate greater transparency in their media supply. By the end of 2017, P&G expected all its agencies to adopt MRC (Media Rating Council) accredited third-party verification to comply with the MRC Viewability Standard across all platforms, and that all digital media partners become TAG (Trust Accountability Group) certified to address fraud.

The advent of Blockchain technology – giant, open, decentralized and shared databases – should, ultimately, facilitate greater brand transparency. Once encrypted data is put into a Blockchain it can only be modified when all stakeholders who have permission to change the data have reached a consensus. Also, any changes made on a Blockchain are automatically registered, so you can see what changes were made, when they were made and who made them. Again, this facilitates transparency.

Some practical examples of how Blockchain technology could aid the delivery of more transparent brand experiences include:

- customers having the opportunity to verify the authenticity of luxury goods and identify fakes;
- brands being able to see where their ads have been served online to facilitate greater media spend transparency;
- local communities being able to check if toxic waste from factories is being disposed of in a responsible manner, or if a firm is meeting its recycling targets;
- supply chains being able to release goods or services based on payments or certain contract obligations being met, in view of all parties concerned, by using 'smart contracts';
- governments could make access to public contracts and the management of the tender process more transparent by using a Blockchain.

These examples also highlight the variety of stakeholders a brand can have, showing the importance of adopting a holistic mindset when building brand experiences that are conscious of, but go beyond customers.

Adopting a holistic mindset

'Customer experience is absolutely not a department.'
Andrew Pine, VP, Customer Relations, Porsche, North America[15]

'Marketing shouldn't be the only function responsible for customers.'
Andy Briggs, Chief Executive Officer, Aviva UK[16]

World-class organizations realize that building brand experiences is everyone's job. Research shows that most sophisticated brands adopt a cross-functional approach to building brand experiences.[17] This means brand, marketing, human resources, sales, customer services, operations, IT, facilities and other functions at all levels have a part to play. This can be challenging. It's unlikely human resources, operations, facilities management or customer services think building brand experiences is part of their job. Nothing could be further from the truth. Research conducted with executives from the UK, Germany and France shows how the practicalities of adopting a holistic approach can be problematic:[18] 53 per cent of all companies do not have a clearly defined overarching customer experience strategy that goes beyond marketing and involves different business units, whilst 48 per cent of the companies felt the various departments do not collaborate well enough to provide a holistic customer experience.

> CX responsibility and leadership is expanding beyond the traditional siloed domains of the chief marketing officer (CMO) and marketing departments.[19]

In his Expert Insight, Harun Olcay outlines how Amazon adopts a holistic approach to building brand experiences which entails considering fellow employees as part of its 'customer obsession' Leadership Principle. More companies would do well to follow their lead.

EXPERT INSIGHT 4.2 How 'customer obsession' helps Amazon build brand experiences

Harun Olcay, Pathways Operations Manager, Amazon

Amazon's brand experience is guided by 14 'Leadership Principles'. You can see these 14 principles everywhere at Amazon – posters, meeting room walls, booklets and guides – but you can also hear them from employees in the course of day-to-day conversation.

One of, if not the most important Leadership Principle is 'customer obsession'. When you work with a team of 3,000 people, you cannot just be obsessed with the end customer and assume everyone will understand the role they play in delivering the brand experience. This is too simple. Every employee has to understand and buy into what 'customer obsession' means and appreciate the role they play in delivering the overall experience.

To achieve this goal, our understanding of 'customer' is not restricted to the end customer. It is broader due to the number of people that combine to deliver our brand experience. These could include:

- customer service teams that deal with customer enquiries;
- associates that fulfil the end-customer orders;
- logistics partners who deliver parcels;
- vendors;
- suppliers;
- other support functions in the fulfilment centre.

At Amazon we truly believe that if we go the extra mile for our internal customers and remove their barriers we can serve our end customers better. Adopting this mentality is core to the Amazon understanding of a 'customer' and plays a vital role in the brand experiences we deliver.

Amazon is a US electronic commerce and cloud computing company.

> 'The entire customer journey is very much part of my remit, and it's critical to align ourselves with our operational colleagues who deliver the actual guest experience.'
> Michael Hobson, Chief Marketing Officer, Mandarin Oriental[20]

> 'Every employee's goal is to improve the guest experience and their sentiment toward the brand.'
> Ed French, Chief Marketing Officer, The Ritz-Carlton[21]

Linda Hon's Expert Insight outlines how Malaysia's biggest bank, Maybank, adopts a holistic approach to building brand experiences for small- to medium-sized enterprises (SMEs). This involves co-ordinating a variety of activities and functions spanning communications, retail, recruitment, process and product.

EXPERT INSIGHT 4.3 Building holistic brand experiences for small- to medium-sized enterprises at Maybank

Ms Linda Hon Pei Ling, Head Marketing and Strategy, Retail SME Banking, Maybank Singapore

Maybank Singapore's retail banking strategy for SMEs (businesses with turnover of less than SGD $20 million) is shaped around our desire to deliver a 'Fast, Simple, Hassle-Free' customer experience. We take a multi-pronged approach in order to deliver this. The supporting business model is clearly communicated to all staff so they understand the need to embrace and contribute to delivering this type of experience, which meets the innate needs of SMEs.

The overall customer journey is carefully mapped so we can deliver fast, simple and hassle-free customer experiences. This entails developing a thorough understanding of SME customer interactions and encounters with our brand. We look to develop a deep emotional connection with our SME customers through key marketing moments in order to build trust, loyalty and ultimately sales and profitability.

We also take great care to recruit customer-facing staff whose natural DNA supports this kind of experience delivery to facilitate positive engagement and interactions with our customers. For example, our branch network is optimized so our SME customers can walk into any branch to get their basic banking needs served conveniently and quickly. They are no longer confined to visiting designated business centres.

Business processes have been re-engineered with loan origination to approval procedures designed with speed and efficiency in mind to simplify and expedite the product approval process. Documents for submission and execution are also standardized and streamlined, with on-boarding processes being simplified. This helps to make loan application a smooth and hassle-free process for our customers.

The products and services we take to market tend to be pre-customized, pre-packaged and solution-based. The goal is to deliver quick and easy financial solutions to clearly defined SME customer segments. Advertising and marketing communication are carefully placed along the customer journey. The adopted style is visual and light in content, with infographics increasingly being used for easy reading and better comprehension.

These are just a few examples of how Maybank Singapore facilitates the delivery of 'Fast, Simple, Hassle-Free' SME customer experiences.

Figure 4.1   Maybank BizMortgage advertising tailored for the SME market

Maybank is among Asia's leading banking groups and is Southeast Asia's fourth-largest bank by assets, with an international network of 2,400 offices in 20 countries, and 44,000 employees serving 22 million customers worldwide.

CIMB is a leading Malaysian bank with operations spanning Association of Southeast Asian Markets (ASEAN), has 12 million customers and employs 40,000 employees. CIMB Chief Operating Officer, Mohamed Adam Wee Abdullah, outlines how, during a customer journey-mapping workshop involving employees from a range of CIMB functions including IT, operations and HR, it became apparent that some of its commercial property loans took two-and-a-half months to be approved.[22] To reduce that to less than one month, CIMB embarked on a business process re-engineering project to certify employees as Lean Six Sigma Green Belts. This helped CIMB re-engineer loan-approval processes, increase efficiency and reduce waste across functions. Delivering this type of enhanced experience would have been impossible if the company hadn't adopted a cross-functional, holistic mindset.

Developing a cross-functional mentality that sits at the heart of adopting a holistic mindset is easier said than done. Based on my experience, ego, power, empires, politics, stubbornness and sheer silliness can come into play. The result is defensive, introspective and siloed management behaviour, which is always harmful. Brand experiences can't flourish in this type of environment. When you engage other departments, are open, and seek out colleagues' help in constructive ways, the response tends to be positive. People like to feel their work has value beyond the scope of their department. Historically, departments like marketing, customer services and human resources tend to be politically weaker in organizations. So, combining forces may not be a bad thing.

Competing primarily through value not price

'There was a lot we could have done from a brand perspective because I had a £12 million annual budget for traditional advertising. We were also a top three spender on radio. I guess our message got a lot more aggressive to arrest the decline, but it was primarily sales-driven and based around price.'
Bryn Owen, Blockbuster's UK Chief Marketing Officer (2008–2012)[23]

Competing purely on price can be a dangerous strategy. You reduce your price then competitors retaliate and reduce theirs. You do likewise and a self-perpetuating downward spiral gathers pace as you strive to cut costs and retain margins. A price-driven approach limits you to a finite number of competitive options because once you have set sail on this course it's hard to change tack.

This contrasts sharply with a value-driven approach. If you understand your stakeholders, you can identify relevant sources of value that they'll be prepared to pay for (note: this was a customer profiling prompt). Additionally, because there is also an almost infinite number of potential value sources, you will have a broad spectrum of strategic routes to choose from.

Between autumn 2009 and early spring 2014, we experienced the worst recession since the 1930s. During this time, some British supermarkets entered a price war. Price pressures led to them to cut costs rather than add value, and their supply chains were an obvious target. One retailer ended up with horsemeat rather than beef in its spaghetti bolognese.[24] Although horsemeat is better for you due to its lower fat content, that's not the point. Consumers were paying for beef, not horse (which isn't usually eaten in the UK). The secret was out and the brand's trust was in tatters.

Ryanair, the budget airline, continued to compete on price during the depths of the global recession. The cost-cutting exercises lost them customers and led to the company issuing two profit warnings in 2013.[25]

At the other end of the spectrum, between September 2009 and January 2014, Apple's stock value soared from US $25 to $77.

Whilst the industries are different, these examples illustrate how, even during difficult financial times, customers made buying decisions based on factors other than price.

The importance of brand in comparison to price is borne out by some extensive research from Kantar Millward Brown (Figure 4.2). This outlines how 56 per cent of consumers make a decision based purely on brand whilst just 10 per cent make a decision on price.

It's true that price plays a more important role in some markets than others; commodities, for example. But even in these markets, organizations can weave value into the fabric of their brand experience through

Figure 4.2   The importance of brands compared to price

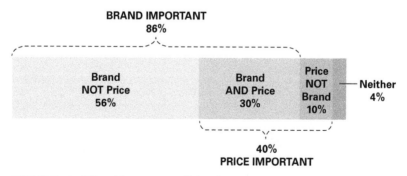

SOURCE Kantar Millward Brown BRANDZ™ (2016)

heritage, reputation, supply chain transparency and after-sales service to facilitate price premiums. British Gas is introducing internet-connected products, smart meters and a reward programme. The goal is to carve out service-based sources of value to distance itself from purely price-driven competitors. Supermarket brands such as Aldi and Lidl have aggressively won market share based on their no-frills price-driven strategy. But even they are diversifying their offer with 'Deluxe' and 'Specially Selected' ranges. It's important to recognize that, even in price-sensitive markets, price represents part of value, but seldom equates to value alone.

Having patience

A cursory glance at the world's most valuable brands (Table 4.1) highlights how most of them have achieved this status due to years, if not decades, of hard work. IBM, Coca Cola, AT&T, Visa and McDonald's illustrate this point. It's true that tech brands like Google, Facebook and Amazon have grown astronomically over a short period of time but they are the exception, not the norm.

> 'Brands must practice patience. Growing a brand simply takes time.'
>
> Byron Sharp[26]

The cold truth is that building a brand and brand experiences takes time. It takes time for your brand values to resonate with stakeholders in a meaningful way. And it takes time for brand positioning to form associations between your brand and the category or categories in which it operates.

It also takes time to build the experiences that enable your brand, due to the structural and cultural changes that can be required. Sometimes, when Wavelength's clients decide to place brand experiences at the heart of what they do, they frequently restructure around stakeholders or customer segments and not channels, product lines or industry verticals. This change also has considerable cultural implications. Shaping an organization around brand experiences requires a different mindset, one which is focused on stakeholders, not products or market verticals.

Table 4.1 The world's most valuable brands

Rank 2017	Category	Brand	Country of origin	Region	Brand value 2017 ($m)	% Brand value change 2017 vs 2016
1	Technology	Google	US	North America	245,581	7%
2	Technology	Apple	US	North America	234,671	3%
3	Technology	Microsoft	US	North America	143,222	18%
4	Retail	Amazon	US	North America	139,286	41%
5	Technology	Facebook	US	North America	129,800	27%
6	Telecom Providers	AT&T	US	North America	115,112	7%
7	Payments	Visa	US	North America	110,999	10%
8	Technology	Tencent	China	Asia	108,292	27%
9	Technology	IBM	US	North America	102,088	18%
10	Fast Food	McDonald's	US	North America	97,723	10%
11	Telecom Providers	Verizon	US	North America	89,279	-4%
12	Tobacco	Marlboro	US	North America	87,519	4%
13	Soft Drinks	Coca-Cola	US	North America	78,142	-3%

14	Retail	Alibaba	China	Asia	59,127	20%
15	Regional Banks	Wells Fargo	US	North America	58,424	0%
16	Logistics	UPS	US	North America	58,275	17%
17	Telecom Providers	China Mobile	China	Asia	56,535	1%
18	Entertainment	Disney	US	North America	52,040	6%
19	Conglomerate	GE	US	North America	50,208	−7%
20	Payments	Mastercard	US	North America	49,928	8%

SOURCE Kantar Millward Brown (2017)

Making such structural and cultural changes requires time to plan, implement and take root. This means you need to be patient when building brand experiences.

I realize that patience requires time and this is something most CEOs don't give chief marketing officers. CMOs are under pressure to deliver returns, yesterday. To address this challenge I would offer the following advice:

- Educate colleagues on what brand experiences are and how they will help your organization (the downloadable practical Toolkit 1.1 may help).

- People frequently don't know what they don't know. Until you explain the scope and intricacies of building brand experiences, a short-term mentality will prevail. Taking this step will help manage expectations.

- Engage colleagues so they take an interest in, and ownership of the brand-building process. It has to be everyone's baby, not just yours.

- Seek out brand experience advocates and supporters across the organization who will breathe life into your work. They can also counter the sceptics who try to suck the life out of your work – often for no good reason beyond their personal agenda or office politics.

- Share relevant case studies, ideally from competitors or the same market, to demonstrate success. These tend to focus executives' minds.

- Outline how you will be taking a scientific approach to building brand experiences (Chapter 20). This will inspire confidence and trust in those who understand numbers but not brand.

- Identify quick wins as part of your brand-building work. Use statistical techniques such as regression or structural equation modelling (Chapter 6) to identify touch points that drive performance. Focus on those to demonstrate the value delivered by brand experiences. People like to be associated with success and demonstrating quick wins will help you do this.

Based on my experience, a lack of patience is one of the main reasons brand experience projects fail. Rushing these projects does more harm than good, as senior management and wider organizational support will seldom exist at the outset. You'll need to devote time to taking your organization's people with you. A failure to do so means confusion reigns, fragmented experiences follow, and disappointing brand performance results.

Accepting a loss of control

Leaders, managers and executives who think they completely control the brand experiences they deliver are mistaken. Take Burberry as an example. Although it is an iconic premium British luxury lifestyle brand, football hooligans like to cover their faces with Burberry scarves when engaging in hooliganism. Burberry can do little about this. When the company started, brand communications could be crafted, and to a large extent controlled, using magazines, newspapers, radio or TV. The advent of social media changed everything. Once in the public domain, brand messages can now be modified or even distorted at frightening speed. This presents brands with a challenge.

They are no longer in complete control of how their brand is perceived. To work with this development, marketers can use social media monitoring software and influencer marketing to help them function in a world where they have to accept less control, but not relinquish it entirely.

Social media monitoring software gives brands a 'fly on the wall' capability. It allows brands to observe, locate (by social platform/physical location) and understand sentiment by 'listening' to online brand-related conversations. Community managers can then try to direct conversations in ways that support their Brand Experience Essentials.

Nestlé created a Data Acceleration Team (DAT) at its headquarters in Vevey, Switzerland in 2011. The DAT is a control room that monitors real-time data feeds from all of Nestlé's brands across its social footprint so they can marshal and guide conversations in a direction that enables their Brand Experience Essentials in the desired way. This may sound covert and clandestine; to a large extent I would agree. But this is what world-class brands are doing to engage customers and guide conversations that are happening around their brand in online communities.

'Influencer marketing' provides another way of asserting some subtle control over how your brand is perceived. This entails brands working with people who have built communities of highly engaged followers through the content they create and curate via their social media channels.

Social influencers have the authenticity, credibility, clout and social currency most brands can only dream of, and it's their perceived objectivity that can really help your brand claw back some control. The value of influencer marketing is especially pronounced amongst the Millennial generation, where 34 per cent of those aged 18–34 (versus 12 per cent of those over 55) say that having an endorsement from a social influencer, blogger or vlogger influences their overall feeling of loyalty toward a brand or company.[27]

Influencer marketing is slowly moving into the mainstream with a number of brands incorporating it into the experiences they deliver.

Google created YouTube Labs, which works with social influencers to shape consumer perceptions around brands owned by the likes of L'Oréal, BMW and Johnson & Johnson. Amazon formed Amazon Affiliates, which pays a sales-based commission. Amazon also has a more exclusive Influencer Programme, which evaluates applications based on number of followers across platforms, levels of engagement, quality of content, and relevance. Again, this provides sales-based commission.

Nike connects with Gen Z by partnering athletes such as Simone Biles and cultural influencers like FKA Twigs. Meanwhile, Adidas has embraced a 'dark social' approach, which entails setting up small groups of hyper-connected brand advocates on messaging apps such as Facebook Messenger, WhatsApp and Line. Adidas's first dark social group was called Tango Squad, named after the iconic football. This group is made up of 100–250 16–19-year-old football fanatics from around the globe, who receive exclusive content before launch which they can share with their communities. They're also invited to meet players so they can take photos to share on social media. This gives community members kudos and makes them feel like valued insiders rather than mainstream consumers.

Chinese telecoms brand Huawei invited 11 key technology influencers to their Huawei Connect conference in Shanghai in September 2016. About 20,000 people attended the event, which gave the brand a reach of 4.6 million people during this time.[28] When cosmetics brand Estée Lauder wanted to tune into a more youthful channel with 'The Estée Edit' they called upon Kendall Jenner (one of the Kardashians), to share make-up tips with her 75 million Instagram followers, using her favourite products from their range.

To encourage a younger demographic to try their new chalupas, Taco Bell invited micro-influencers to 'speakeasies' to try the Central-Southern Mexico speciality, photograph the food and share the pictures with their communities. Iceland, the frozen food retailer, partners with 50 mums on Channel Mum. These 'micro-influencers' are not celebrities but members of the public with an interest in food, the idea being this approach and message will resonate with real mums.

Some may feel that 'influencer marketing' is underhand, insidious and even deceptive. This is understandable, as many people are still oblivious to what it is or how it works. But, in many ways, it's no different to old-school public relations, where agencies would supply journalists with information in the form of press releases for inclusion in the print media. The average reader was unaware this was happening and merely thought the paper was sharing newsworthy content. This ethical debate is one for you to explore in line with your Brand Experience Essentials (Part Two), but influencer marketing is one way brands can try to exercise an element of indirect control over their brand experiences.

In his Expert Insight, Mark Di Somma suggests another approach brands can take to retain an element of control over their brand experiences through a belief system.

EXPERT INSIGHT 4.4 How brands can address a loss of control

Mark Di Somma, Founder, Strategist, The Audacity Group, New Zealand

Who owns a brand today? Many brand managers believe they are in charge. For them, their job gives them the mandate to carefully shape how the brand is experienced. That works well when consumers 'play nice'; when they savour the experiences that are prepared for them at an Apple Store, Whole Foods or Ritz-Carlton. What happens when groups make the brand their own, and those associations clash with the viewpoints the brand wants to extol? Take the case of a popular sports shoe that was reported as having been adopted by far-right groups as their official shoe.[29] Or when the trucks of a global vehicle manufacturer are noticed in videos released by a terror group?[30] The brand is certainly noticed, but this was a profile the brand never asked for, and these associations are not compatible with their brand values.

A solution: every brand should pair its brand with a clear belief system that shapes and informs the delivery of distinctive experiences. That might not stop others hijacking the brand, but it will at least provide evidence that the brand doesn't approve.

Audacity works with senior decision makers and brand agencies to define, articulate and elevate the competitive value of brands at critical moments of change.

Conclusion

To build relevant brand experiences you need to fine-tune your perspective in the context of the Brand Experience Environment. This entails embracing transparency, adopting a holistic mindset, competing primarily through value not price, having patience and accepting a loss of control. If you are mindful of these when developing and defining your Brand Experience Essentials, you will be well placed to build more relevant brand experiences.

This chapter is accompanied by Toolkits 4.1, 4.2 and 4.3.

Endnotes

1 Edelman Trust Barometer (2017) [online] http://bit.ly/wavelength-edelman-2017

2 CMO Council (2017) How brands annoy fans: the impact of digital advertising experiences on consumer perceptions and purchase intent [online] http://bit.ly/wavelength-cmo-council

3 See Hotten, R (2015) Volkswagen: The scandal explained, BBC News, 10 December [online] http://bit.ly/wavelength-vw-fuel-emmissions; Schwartz, J et al (2015) VW engineers admitted rigging CO2 emissions – Bild, *Reuters*, 8 November [online] http://bit.ly/wavelength-VW-emissions

4 See http://bit.ly/wavelength-vw

5 BBC News (2015) Mitsubishi Motors admits falsifying fuel economy tests, 20 April [online] http://bit.ly/wavelength-bbc-mitsubishi

6 Mullen, J (2016) Fuel scandal drives Mitsubishi Motors to first loss in 8 years, *CNN Money*, 22 June [online] http://bit.ly/wavelength-cnn-mitsubishi

7 Jennings, A (2006) The beautiful bung: corruption and the World Cup, BBC News [online] http://bit.ly/wavelength-BBC-FIFA

8 The US Department of Justice (2015) Nine FIFA officials and five corporate executives indicted for racketeering conspiracy and corruption, 15 May [online] http://bit.ly/wavelength-US-DOJ

9 BBC Sport (2015) Fifa crisis: US charges 16 more officials after earlier Zurich arrests, 4 December [online] http://bit.ly/wavelength-fifa-crisis

10 Greenpeace (2010) Ask Nestle to give rainforests a break [online] http://bit.ly/wavelength-greenpeace

11 McClearn, M (2015) Water Fight: Bottles, wells, big business. Who owns water? Nestlé's ambitions in Southern Ontario raise big questions about an essential – and finite – resource, *Globe and Mail* [online] http://bit.ly/wavelength-nestle

12 Blanchard, B (2012) Apple, Foxconn scandal highlights exploitation of Chinese workers by foreign firms, *Huffington Post* [online] http://bit.ly/wavelength-apple-foxconn

13 Shapiro, L (2012) Chick-fil-A anti-gay controversy: gay employees speak out, *Huffington Post* [online] http://bit.ly/wavelength-chick-a-fil

14 See http://bit.ly/wavelength-unilever

15 CXweek.com (2016) Building a model for customer experience at Porsche [online] http://bit.ly/wavelength-porsche

16 Chahal, M (2017), Aviva UK CEO: Marketing shouldn't be the only function responsible for customers, *Marketing Week*, 14 March [online] http://bit.ly/wavelength-aviva

17 IBM (2016) The experience revolution: mobilizing to win – are you ready? September [online] http://bit.ly/wavelength-IBM-win

18 PAC (2015) Holistic customer experience in the digital age: a trend study for Germany, France and the UK [online] http://bit.ly/wavelength-holistic

19 IBM (2016) The experience revolution: mobilizing to win – are you ready? September [online] http://bit.ly/wavelength-IBM-win

20 Deloitte/CMO Council (2016) The CMO shift to gaining business lift, December [online] bit.ly/wavelength-deloitte-cmocouncil

21 Fister Gale, S (2017) NPS: tracking customer loyalty, how global organizations use the net promoter score to elevate the customer experience and improve the bottom line, *Insigniam Quarterly*, Winter [online] http://bit.ly/wavelength-ritzcarlton

22 Alderton, M (2017) Profiles in customer experience, *Insigniam Quarterly*, Winter [online] http://bit.ly/wavelength-CCO

23 Hobbs, T (2017) From iconic to punchline: Blockbuster's CMO reflects on how things imploded, *Marketing Week* [online] http://bit.ly/wavelength_blockbuster

24 BBC (2013) Horsemeat scandal: Tesco reveals 60% content in dish, 11 February [online] http://bit.ly/wavelength-horsemeat

25 Telegraph (2013) Ryanair in second profit warning in two months, 4 November [online] http://bit.ly/wavelength-ryan-air

26 Sharp, B (2010) *How Brands Grow: What marketers don't know*, Oxford University Press

27 Accenture (2016) Seeing beyond the loyalty illusion: it's time you invest more wisely [online] http://bit.ly/wavelength-loyalty

28 Maoz, Y (2016) The story of Huawei and 11 WOWie influencers, *klear* [online] http://bit.ly/wavelength-klear

29 Woolf, J (2016) New Balance sneakers have now been claimed by neo-Nazis, *GQ*, 15 November [online] http://bit.ly/wavelength-new-balance

30 Osborne, S (2015) Why does Isis have so many Toyota trucks? *Independent*, 7 October [online] http://bit.ly/wavelength-toyota

Considering the mechanics of delivery

In the previous chapter I outlined how you can fine-tune your perspective by focusing on a handful of key issues, in the context of the Brand Experience Environment, so you can develop and define more relevant Brand Experience Essentials. This entailed embracing transparency, adopting a holistic mindset, competing primarily through value not price, having patience, and accepting a loss of control.

This chapter is less abstract. It dives into the detail of how you can consider the mechanics of brand experience delivery in the context of the Brand Experience Environment. This entails:

- creating an emotional connection;
- facilitating co-creation;
- delivering omnichannel experiences.

Considering the mechanics of delivery at this stage will be time well spent. It will help you to focus your mind on some of the practicalities associated with building brand experiences.

Creating an emotional connection

'Emotion is the new currency of experience.'

John Mellor, VP Strategy,
Alliances and Marketing, Adobe Systems[1]

We like to think we're rational and logical, that we identify then assess the options, evaluate the consequences then make solid, well-thought-through and reasoned decisions. But the decisions we make are primarily influenced by the emotions we feel. This is why creating an emotional connection is so important when building brand experiences.

The importance of emotion in decision making has been recognized for many years. Ancient Chinese philosophers like Confucius and Mencius acknowledged the importance of the emotion.[2] The influential work of Antonio Damasio[3] and colleagues outlines how human behaviour is primarily driven by the emotions we feel, with rational thought following behind. Professor Dan Ariely[4] and Nobel Prize-winner Daniel Kahneman[5] also highlight the importance of emotion in decision making.

Research shows that creating an emotional connection with stakeholders delivers value. One study[6] found the value of a customer increases as they progress along an 'emotional connection pathway' which gradually deepens their emotional relationship with the brand. Other research[7] highlights the positive influence of creative and emotional rather than factual and rational content on brand favourability. This finding is consistent with another study,[8] which showed the profitability of adverts with purely emotional content was approximately twice (31 per cent vs 16 per cent) that of those with only

Figure 5.1   The effect of emotion on favourability and sales

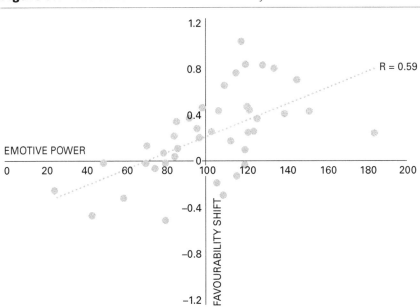

SOURCE Nielsen (2016)

rational content. Another study[9] found a statistically significant and positive correlation (r = 0.59) between emotive brands and perceived favourability (Figure 5.1), whilst adverts with above-average emotional response scores generated a 23 per cent lift in sales volume.

> Businesses that sell to other businesses are made of people – and people have emotions.[10]

The value of emotions in branding is not restricted to B2C markets.[11] A Google study[12] highlighting the personal nature of B2B markets showed how B2B customers feel emotionally connected to B2B brands. This study compared brands with 'no brand connection' and 'high brand connection'. The results demonstrate the value of a 'high brand connection':

- consideration: 15 per cent ('no brand connection') vs 79 per cent ('high brand connection');
- purchase: 5 per cent ('no brand connection') vs 64 per cent ('high brand connection');
- willingness to pay a premium: 2 per cent ('no brand connection') vs 60 per cent ('high brand connection').

Most B2B brands tend to follow a similar brand experience path. They focus on price and functional features, not emotion and experiences. The logic for this approach tends to relate to clients' use of a 'cost, quality and feature' matrix to inform their decision. These tools aim to make people objective and logical. If only life was that simple!

To address this situation you need to understand the emotions that drive your target clients' decision making then build brand experiences that tune into a relevant emotional channel.

The types of emotions that drive B2B choice are qualitatively different to those that drive B2C markets. B2B markets are characterized by complex, high-risk, high-value and long-term investments. This means experiences that mitigate risk, provide security, reassure, give peace of mind and enhance personal or organizational reputation win. IBM's classic 'Nobody ever got fired for buying IBM' was a pioneering example. The emotion IBM played on was fear and they said they could address this problem by being reliable. More recently, other world-class brands have started to adopt a more emotive approach. GE's (General Electric) 'short films' series[13] demonstrates the work GE facilitates, whilst Caterpillar's #BuiltForIt Trials[14] illustrate the durability and strength of their products in a variety of situations.

A few years ago, I spent a week delivering our brand strategy master-class to one of the world's leading laser manufacturers. Beforehand, I was a little nervous due to the technicalities of the market and the scientific profile of the participants. As the first day progressed I started to wonder if the brand was plagued by an irony. They sold exceptionally complex products that had a range of sophisticated applications, but our client focused on technical features such as 'parameters'. Later that night I went back to their competitors to review their websites again. It struck me they were all adopting the same approach, even to the extent that most of the brands' homepages have a picture of a laser. A wonderfully advanced market had focused on function, and so commoditized their offer. The next day we set about exploring how their target customers could be reached in more emotive ways, for instance, outlining how their product could help eminent professors conduct research that would make them candidates for Nobel Prizes.

In his Expert Insight, Joel Harrison outlines how some B2B brands are increasingly leveraging the power of emotion with great effect.

EXPERT INSIGHT 5.1 How B2B brands are winning through emotional experiences

Joel Harrison, Editor-in-Chief, B2B Marketing

Emotion has always been a massive part of B2B marketing, but until recently, most B2B brands have struggled to understand its importance and how to deploy it properly. B2B brands majored on logic and rationality – to list the wealth of important product features in excruciating detail.

Where emotion was used, in the 'broadcast era' of 'one to many' marketing channels, it often focused on the negative. Unless they took action, something really awful was going to happen. They were going to get outmanoeuvred by a competitor, or become uncompetitive due to legislative changes, etc. Fear was the emotional lever.

But today, in the era of social media, the role of emotion in B2B has flipped on its head. Brands rely on positive messages, sharing things that are interesting, exciting, funny, cool… even (whisper it) sexy. The likes of IBM, Lenovo, Hootsuite and Microfocus stand out as particularly good examples. Being robust, solid, dependable… the rational choice, makes you invisible on social media. We're seeing a more informal, friendlier and warmer tone of voice coming to the fore in B2B akin to consumer marketing.

This is refreshing and long overdue. Understanding the subtle but profound differences required in driving an emotional connection for B2B over B2C customers will be one of the key factors in determining which B2B brands succeed in the 21st century.

B2B Marketing is the leading provider of insight and intelligence, helping B2B marketers succeed and develop their careers.

Emotion is the trump card when it comes to building brand experiences but it's important you don't underestimate the role of cognition or 'thinking', especially during the earlier stages of decision making. For example, if you are not aware of a brand it will not come to mind when making a choice. With all the talk about emotion and brands I would encourage you to remember this point.

To appreciate why our decisions are primarily driven by the emotions we feel you need to understand two tightly connected regions of the brain: the prefrontal cortex and the limbic system (Figure 5.2).

The prefrontal cortex sits at the front of our brain and deals with cognitive functions such as decision making, evaluation, logic, working memory, reason, control and problem solving. The limbic system is a complex set of brain structures located in the depths of our brain that supports a variety of functions including our sense of smell, motivation, intuition, impulse,

Figure 5.2   The limbic system and the human brain

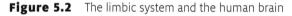
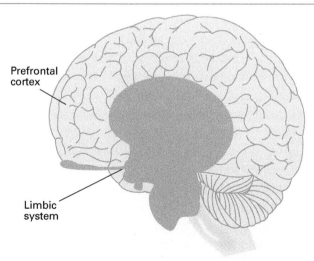

long-term memory and emotions. The fact that the limbic system deals with long-term memories and emotions is particularly important when it comes to building brand experiences. Why? When we make a decision, the front of our brain (prefrontal cortex) accesses our memory, and when we access our memory our brain sends electrical impulses to the limbic system to recall a brand-related emotion. This is important because when we make a decision, it's not the *memory* of the brand that influences our choice but the *emotion we feel* associated with that brand in our memory. This is a subtle yet significant point.

Think about the last time you went out for dinner. Did the rude waiter make you feel uncomfortable? Was the food overpriced so you felt like you had been ripped off? Did the fly sitting proudly on top of your soup make you feel the restaurant was unhygienic? It's not actually the memory of the waiter, food or fly that influences whether you would go back again, recommend the restaurant or send a mail the next day to complain; it's the emotion you feel when you recall the experience. This is why the best brands in the world work hard to generate brand-related emotion.

Coca-Cola associating itself with the emotion of happiness is a classic example. Volvo helps people feel safe. Hallmark helps people feel loved. Ritz-Carlton helps people feel special. Armani helps people feel stylish. The list goes on but these brands understand the importance of creating an emotional connection as part of their brand experience-building efforts.

Facilitating co-creation

'People are best convinced by things they themselves discover.'
Benjamin Franklin

The days of building standardized brand experiences are long gone. It's empowerment and autonomy that give brands appeal.

Stakeholders, especially the Millennial generation and Gen Z, are drawn to brands that enable them to co-create[15] personalized experiences in partnership with the brand so they can make them their own. Fifty-four per cent of 18–34-year-old respondents (compared with 34 per cent of over-55s) say that having the opportunity to personalize the products they buy, to create something unique, influences their overall feeling of loyalty toward a brand or company.[16] The logic is that people increasingly want to have a say in the things they buy. Based on my experience of running a number of focus groups and ethnographic studies for youth-orientated brands, this trend looks set to continue with Gen Z. You will be able to help stakeholders get this 'job' done by equipping them with the relevant:

- *contexts*, eg a welcoming and inviting retail format that encourages exploration or a www homepage that inspires customers to create experiences;
- *tools*, eg self-service kiosks for flight check-ins or an online car configurator;
- *knowledge*, eg online video tutorials, factsheets or reports that share relevant knowledge

as part of the brand experiences you build so they have the ability, and confidence, to build brand experiences for themselves.

Ikea is a co-creation pioneer. The term 'Ikea effect'[17] was coined to highlight how their customers became particularly fond of their products due to the time and effort required to assemble them.

The Ikea experience is brand experience-building brilliance. You drive to a large warehouse, wheel a trolley around, possibly try to escape (but fail miserably), buy flat-pack furniture, then load the furniture into your car. You drive home, possibly bickering with your partner about what you bought, drag the furniture into your house, assemble it, then sit back and admire your domestic masterpiece.

The genius of Ikea relates to a simple insight. They tap into people's deep-seated desire to feel useful; a sense of pride, ownership and achievement. The fact that the process can be tiresome (and, some would argue, unpleasant) doesn't matter. Because when you stand back and admire the piece of furniture you assembled, you feel fantastic because you have played an active role in creating the value you experience. More recently, Ikea have enhanced their ability to co-create experiences with their Virtual Reality Experience, which lets customers co-create their ideal kitchen layout through virtual and augmented reality technologies. This deepens Ikea's bond with customers and entrenches their position in the value chain by co-creating value at the design as well as the assembly stage.

A number of other brands understand the value co-creation delivers. On Nike iD you can create your own shoes. Adidas lets consumers use Snapchat's doodle tool to design their own footwear whilst for their Neo brand they enlisted the help of their Instagram followers to create content around #MyNeoShoot, with the best creators being invited to model in a professional shoot for use on their Instagram channel: this campaign generated 71,000 mentions. You can design your own Audi online or Range Rover in Jaguar Land Rover's London store, whilst Porsche Exclusive provides customers with an opportunity to customize and personalize their car. Burberry Bespoke allows customers to design customized coats, whilst Shinola's #LoveMyCity challenges local influencers and tastemakers to make a city guide they then publish on their social channels, website and blog. Oreo created a #MyOreoCreation contest to encourage cookie-eating enthusiasts to share their ideas with the brand. Pernod Richard launched the world's first Internet of Things (IoT) cocktail library so consumers can collate shopping lists, learn cocktail recipes and order spirits online. Coach Create allows you to personalize your handbag by customizing the strap, rivets and adding your own monogram. Lego Ideas provides an online platform where Lego fans can submit product suggestions for commercial launch. Rolls Royce Aerospace has a CareStore. This is an online portal that gives customers access to a suite of support services such as TotalCare® Life®, TotalCare® Flex®, and SelectCare™ so they can tailor the type of aviation engine support they require as the product progresses through its life cycle.

These world-class brands understand the need to devolve responsibility when building brand experiences. They empower customers with the context, tools and knowledge they require to create experiences for themselves. Facilitating co-creation makes for more personalized, relevant and so more valuable experiences. It also pushes some of the cost of production onto the customer. This can boost profitability because the brand no longer needs to employ people to do the work. It's a major benefit of co-creation that more leaders and managers could leverage.

Managers and executives worry about delegating responsibility for building brand experiences to customers or other stakeholders. It's hard to let go. The concern is that customers may create experiences that breach the brand's values, personality, positioning, along with other Brand Experience Essentials (Part Two) and so dilute or derail the experiences you deliver. These are core brand assets that are not up for discussion, so it's a valid concern.

To achieve a degree of 'delegated control', brands need to provide stakeholders with enough scope to personalize their experience within the parameters of their Brand Experience Essentials. Nike iD, for example, provides a range of trainers and options so customers can tailor their shoes. But the colours are carefully selected, making it hard, if not impossible, to create a fashion disaster.

Some years ago at Wavelength, we developed a portal for an asset management company that enabled their clients to manage their investment portfolio. If a portfolio became too risky or unbalanced, an email was sent to the account manager, suggesting the client required 'a courtesy call' to advise them accordingly. In this way the brand became both a brand experience facilitator and guardian. The onus for creating the experience increasingly lies with the customer, closely supervised by the brand.

In their Expert Insight, members of the Ooredoo Oman marketing team provide an interesting example of how the leading telecoms brand engaged with the youth community to co-create an experience around the relaunch of their 'Shababiah' brand.

EXPERT INSIGHT 5.2 How Ooredoo Oman co-created
experiences with the youth market

The marketing team, Ooredoo Oman

Shababiah is a product brand from Ooredoo Oman, targeted at the youth segment in the telecommunications market. The aim was to create a product that inspires Oman's youth, a generation immune to traditional marketing. The word 'Shababiah' means 'youth' in Arabic and is a widely used term in Oman to refer to youthful behaviour. The brand was initially launched in the early days of Ooredoo Oman. However, it only had moderate popularity, so in 2016, the management decided to tackle the problem by revamping and relaunching Shababiah.

The Shababiah team decided to involve customers and a series of surveys was conducted, asking the youth about their telecommunications goals, behaviour and what matters most to them. The surveys revealed that the youth segment want simple, transparent and affordable services. The concept was to have young Omanis create the product, so that it would be relevant to those young at heart. Ooredoo engaged an Omani calligrapher to create the logotype and a number of diverse Omani artists were selected to create their own version of the logo. The strategy was built around co-creation; the idea was that the best way to make a brand relevant to youth was to have them involved in the development of the product and brand communication.

Ooredoo invited them to create the logo, the visual identity and design all touchpoints of the brand. We wanted youth to show us their world, their Oman, and make Shababiah their product of choice and lifestyle partner.

Some of the artists went beyond the logo space itself, creating entire canvases for the brand which became the campaign's communication assets: SIM card packaging, vehicle livery, press packs and merchandise, as well as online content. This was, in every way, a brand created by the youth, for the youth.

Figure 5.3 Examples of Ooredoo Oman's co-created Shababiah campaign

The effectiveness of Shababiah far exceeded expectations, with all targets smashed since its launch in July 2016. At the end of six months, Shababiah had acquired a big market share of the youth segment, closing the year ahead of customer base target.

Ooredoo Oman was founded and registered in the Sultanate of Oman in December 2004. It launched its service in March 2005 as the challenger mobile

operator in Oman, originally operating under the name Nawras. The company was awarded the second fixed licence in Oman in 2009, and launched its international gateway in April 2010, its corporate fixed and broadband services in May 2010, and its residential fixed and broadband services in June 2010. Since 2010, Ooredoo has been an integrated services telecommunications operator and is currently serving over 2 million customers across the Sultanate.

Delivering omnichannel experiences

Customers know that brands capture and analyse vast amounts of data to understand their lifestyles, interests and purchase habits. Research shows that, while customers don't expect omnichannel perfection, they do expect increasingly personalized experiences to be delivered where, when and how they want.[18] This means it's the brand's responsibility to have a single view of the customer, then build consistent and cohesive experiences that let them glide between channels in a single seamless sweep. To do this, brands need to unify previously discrete experiences that could span mobile, tablet, desktop, retail or more into one intuitive experience that helps a customer get a 'job' or 'jobs' done.

But building omnichannel experiences is easier said than done. Forty per cent of brands agree that their customer experience is inconsistent across channels,[19] and 37 per cent of executives state that greater digital and physical alignment was a brand experience priority for 2017.[20]

Figure 5.4 provides an omnichannel experience example for Evelyn, a tech-savvy, socially connected student who wants to book an airline ticket. This chart illustrates how experiences delivered on each channel combine and complement each other to form a greater whole. One customer journey could entail:

- general conversation with friends at a party about forthcoming travel;
- conducting a preliminary and casual search on a mobile travel app;
- picking up more detail from a retail store as she is passing by whilst shopping with friends;
- conducting a more detailed search online (desktop) to compare prices;
- calling customer services to clarify some points she is unclear about;
- obtaining social proof via blogs or sites like TripAdvisor on mobile;
- purchasing an airline ticket online.

Figure 5.4 Buying an airline ticket: an omnichannel experience example

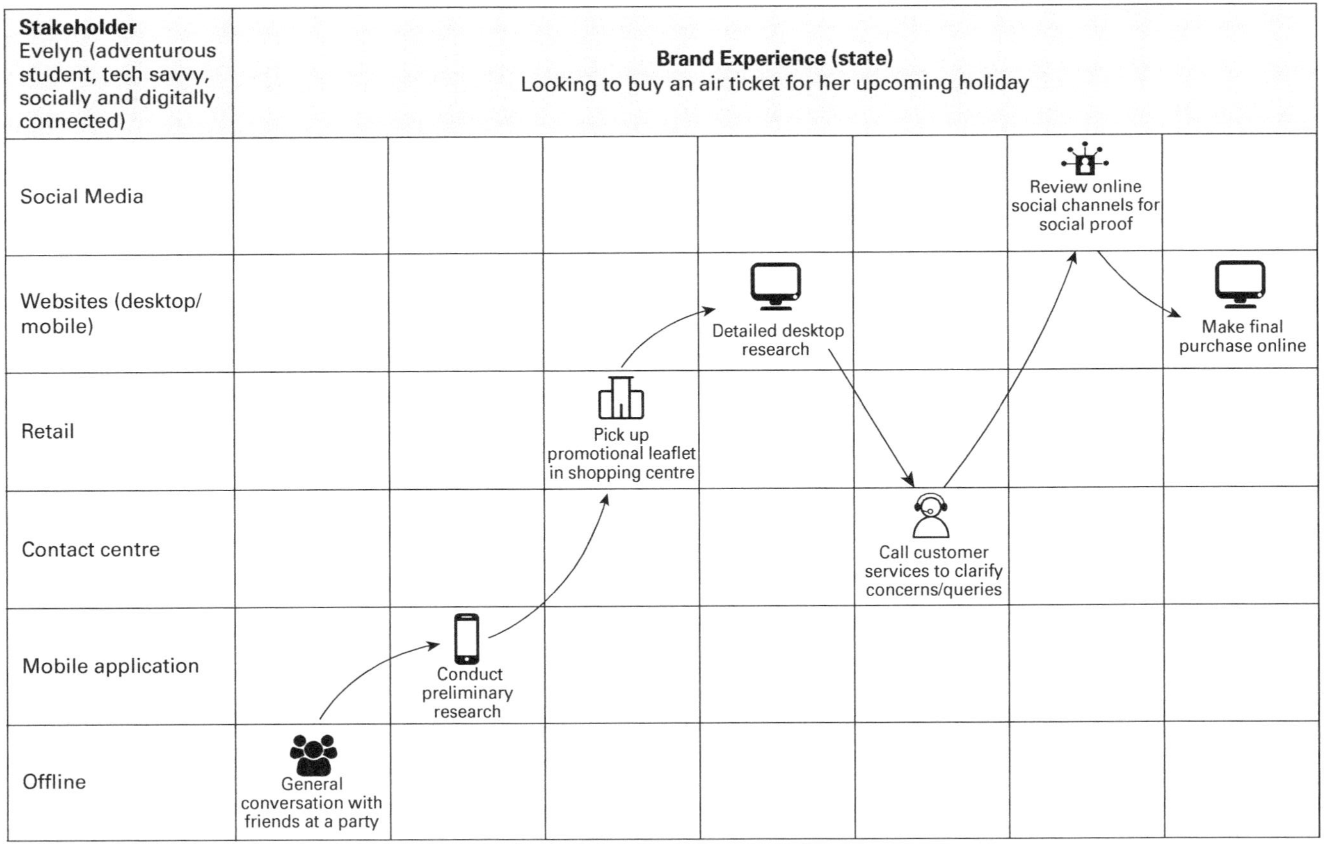

Stakeholder
Evelyn (adventurous student, tech savvy, socially and digitally connected)

Brand Experience (state)
Looking to buy an air ticket for her upcoming holiday

Social Media					Review online social channels for social proof	Make final purchase online
Websites (desktop/mobile)			Detailed desktop research			
Retail		Pick up promotional leaflet in shopping centre				
Contact centre				Call customer services to clarify concerns/queries		
Mobile application	Conduct preliminary research					
Offline	General conversation with friends at a party					

Conversely, the customer journey, leading to getting the same job done, could be:

- picking up more detail from a retail store as she is passing by whilst shopping with friends;
- carrying out a preliminary and casual search online (mobile);
- calling customer services to clarify some points she is unclear about;
- general conversation with friends at a party about forthcoming travel where she seeks social proof;
- conducting a more detailed online (desktop) search to compare prices;
- obtaining further social proof via blogs or sites like TripAdvisor on mobile;
- making the final purchase from the airline's website or by visiting a retail store.

This scenario represents the ideal situation where a stakeholder progresses through one touchpoint to the next. In reality, omnichannel experiences are more iterative, fragmented and complex. They are not always linear, and touchpoints can be experienced in parallel – a trend which is particularly pronounced for Gen Z. For example, a customer may call your customer services team, go to your mobile app before visiting your retail store, have a think, then buy online or via your app. In another scenario, a customer could be in-store, reading an online review on a third-party site whilst their friend sees if anyone in their social network has bought the product under consideration. The challenge is to understand where stakeholders are in the overall journey and understand what 'job' they are trying to achieve at that moment, irrespective of which route they take, to prompt progression along your experience. Using customer journey maps provides one solution and this will be covered in Chapter 16 when we look at service design.

Luxury retail brands have been quick to grasp the importance of delivering omnichannel experiences. At Burberry's Regent Street store, RFID tags[21] are woven into selected products to trigger bespoke multimedia content relevant to the products, mirrors turn into screens with runway footage and exclusive video, satellite technology enables the live streaming of events in-store, and employees use iPad apps to tailor the customer experience. Tiffany used Snapchat to create a buzz and attract consumers when it reopened its refurbished Beverly Hills store. Their snaps took viewers on a virtual tour and showcased the opening party graced by A-listers including Reese Witherspoon, Kate Hudson and Halle Berry.

> Customers trusted banks that were in the top quartile of delivering consistent customer journeys 30 per cent more than banks in the bottom quartile.[22]

In the beauty market, Sephora combines cross-channel touchpoints throughout the entire customer journey with admirable finesse. In-store, the brand provides customers with online make-up tutorials at stations called the 'Beauty Workshop',[23] whilst the use of 3D facial recognition on its app and website allows users to view themselves moving in real time with the digital makeup. Post purchase, customers receive a branded delivery tracking page to display the status of their order, which also provides recommendations and educational content to keep them engaged and excited about their purchases.

Cosmetics brands such as SK-II and L'Oréal have been quick to capitalize on Chinese consumers' love of purchasing items while travelling overseas. SK-II's Chinese website provides details of duty-free shops where its products can be bought abroad, and links to interactive Baidu maps that show where the shops are. They also list duty-free shops that allow products to be reserved for in-store collection. L'Oréal Travel Asia Pacific offers online reservations for airport pick-up for brands such as Biotherm and Urban Decay.

The #showyourcolor campaign for Beats by Dr Dre was another omnichannel masterclass. The campaign started with television advertisements featuring celebrities posing with their Beats to raise awareness. Consumers were then invited to the Beats Facebook page to design a custom 'profile cover' using the TV ad design: the most creative designs won prizes. Beats also took over Times Square for one day by allowing pedestrians to take photos in a modified photo booth posing with Beats products. Their photos and captions were beamed on one of three digital billboards in Times Square. The #showyourcolor campaign boosted Beats by Dr Dre's Instagram followers by 76 per cent and YouTube subscriber numbers by 57 per cent.

As impressive as these examples are, the world's most valuable brands like Amazon and Microsoft have progressed to a deeper level of omnichannel integration by building 'ecosystems'. These fuse experiences under or closely connected to their master brand. Amazon Prime gives subscribers access to unlimited delivery on Amazon orders, unlimited film and TV episode streaming (Prime Video), music streaming (Prime Music), everyday essential food delivery (Amazon Pantry) and clothes (Amazon Wardrobe) for £79 per year. In Microsoft's consumer portfolio, Windows, Surface and Xbox integrate to deliver a seamless customer experience as part of a connected ecosystem. Chinese internet giant, Tencent, is building an ecosystem which encompasses an instant messaging app (QQ), a social network (WeChat), online payment (Tenpay), gaming, and music streaming (QQ Music). The connected experiences these ecosystems deliver further embed customers with the brand by helping them to get a simple job done – make their lives easier.

What's next for omnichannel experiences? Two areas are emerging: virtual and augmented reality (VR and AR), and the Internet of Things (IoT). As part of its 50th birthday celebration, Audi created 'A Drive Back in Time'. This was a virtual reality experience where passengers could take a drive down memory lane and see what Singapore was like in 1965. A *Game of Thrones* experience takes the audience inside the world of *Game of Thrones* where they can move around and interact in a branded virtual world armed with a bow and arrow. Google Daydream has a mobile clicker which is connected to the headset to give people greater control over the experience they are engaging with. Early findings indicate that in comparison to classic 2D or even 360-degree experiences, VR delivers more emotionally engaging experiences over longer durations.[24]

With the advent of the Internet of Things, customers will increasingly seek out brand experiences that blend physical and digital seamlessly. Customers will expect brands to build brand experiences which connect homes, cars, work, other physical spaces and objects. For example, BMW, in partnership with Garageio, has launched a suite of apps that will automate tasks such as adjusting your central heating so the temperature's just right when you arrive home, opening your garage door as you pull up, and closing it when you leave. These developments provide new avenues of opportunity for brand building experiences.

Conclusion

To build relevant brand experiences you need to consider the mechanics of brand experience delivery. This entails giving thought to how you create an emotional connection, facilitate co-creation and deliver omnichannel experiences. Considering the mechanics of delivery will encourage you to think about important details associated with the Brand Experience Environment that should inform how you develop and define your Brand Experience Essentials.

This chapter is accompanied by Toolkits 5.1, 5.2 and 5.3.

Endnotes

1 Hargrave, S (2017) 'Emotion is the new currency of experience', Adobe's VP of strategy tells summit participants, CMO, 11 May [online] http://bit.ly/wavelength-emotion

2 Puett, M (2016) *The Path: What Chinese philosophers can teach us about the good life*, Simon & Schuster

3 Damasio, A (1995) *Descartes' Error: Emotion, reason and the human brain*, Avon, New York; Damasio, A (1999) *Feeling of What Happens: Body and emotion in the making of consciousness*, Harcourt Brace, Orlando, FL

4 Ariely, D (2009) *Predictably Irrational: The hidden forces that shape our decisions*, HarperCollins

5 Kahneman, D (2012) *Thinking, Fast and Slow*, Penguin

6 Magids, S, Zorfas, A and Leemon, D (2015) The new science of customer emotions: a better way to drive growth and profitability, *Harvard Business Review*, November

7 Heath, R, Brandt, D and Narin, A (2006) Brand relationships: strengthened by emotion, weakened by attention, *Journal of Advertising Research*, **46** (4), pp 410–19

8 Pringle, H and Field, P (2008) *Brand Immortality: How brands can live long and prosper*, Kogan Page

9 Brandt, D (2016), What's next: emotions give a lift to advertising, Nielsen [online] http://bit.ly/wavelength-nielsen

10 KPMG Nunwood (2017) B2B customer experience: winning in the moments that matter [online] bit.ly/wavelength-kpmgnunwood

11 Leek, S and Christodoulides, G (2012) A framework for generating brand value in B2B markets: the contributing role of functional and emotional components, *Industrial Marketing Management*, **41** (1), pp 106–14

12 Nathan, S and Schmidt., K (2013) From promotion to emotion: connecting B2B ustomers to brands, *Think with Google* [online] http://bit.ly/wavelength-google

13 See http://bit.ly/wavelength-ge

14 See http://bit.ly/wavelength-cat

15 Vargo, S L and Lusch, R F (2004) Evolving to a new dominant logic for marketing, *Journal of Marketing*, **68** (1), pp 1–17

16 Accenture (2016) Seeing beyond the loyalty illusion: it's time you invest more wisely [online] http://bit.ly/wavelength-loyalty

17 Michael, I et al (2012) The IKEA effect: when labor leads to love, *Journal of Consumer Psychology*, July

18 CMO Council (2017) The customer in context: understanding the real expectations of today's connected customer [online] http://bit.ly/wavelength-CMO-Council-Context

19 Accenture Interactive (2016) Expectations vs experience: the good, the bad, the opportunity [online] http://bit.ly/wavelength-accenture

20 CMO Council (2016) Connected interaction to power brand attraction: how marketing is transforming to create more connected customer engagements [online] http://bit.ly/wavelength-omnichannel

21 An RFID tag is a device that uses radio frequencies to automatically identify and track objects.

22 Pulido, A, Stone, D and Strevel, J (2014) *The Three Cs of Customer Satisfaction: Consistency, consistency, consistency*, McKinsey

23 Milnes, H (2015) Sephora's new retail store will take cues from YouTube, *Digiday* [online] http://bit.ly/wavelength-sephora

24 YuMe and Nielsen (2016) Groundbreaking virtual reality research showcases strong emotional engagement for brands, *Business Wire*, 9 November [online] http://bit.ly/wavelength-VR

Adopting a data-driven approach

In the previous chapter I outlined the role fine-tuning your perspective plays as part of the Brand Experience Environment. This entails creating an emotional connection, facilitating co-creation and delivering omnichannel experiences. This chapter covers the fourth (and final) element of the Brand Experience Environment: adopting a data-driven approach.

As data plays an increasingly critical role in the development and delivery of brand experiences, I will outline the importance of:

- obtaining robust insights (quantitative and qualitative);
- measuring holistically.

This will help you deliver a stronger business case in the boardroom for building brand experiences, providing you with a credible, informed and defensible position in senior management and executive circles. It will also mean the brand experiences decisions you make are based on more objective insights rather than individual anecdotes.

Obtaining robust insights

Based on my experience, numbers tend to be well received in the boardroom. But, budget and time permitting, employing a mixed-methods approach that combines quantitative and qualitative methods is best. This compensates for each approach's weaknesses, provides a more rounded perspective and helps to verify, or challenge, your results as you'll be embracing multiple prongs of attack.

Quantitative insight

Quantitative data collection often reminds me of the Clint Eastwood classic western film *The Good, The Bad and The Ugly*. Some data collection is good but, regrettably, most is bad and ugly. Specific problems relate to inadequate sampling methods, in addition to biased questions, scales or responses. This is problematic because even the most talented quantitative data analysts can't cure bias. For a very practical and thorough overview of how to address such issues I recommend reading Dillman and colleagues' book on survey design.[1]

Once quantitative data has been collected via a survey or other means, you can use advanced statistical methods to add scientific rigour to your brand experience-building endeavours. Table 6.1 describes some of the statistical methods you can use, shows how they can help, and provides practical examples to fire your imagination. Please note these methods can be used in a variety of ways, so the examples given are purely illustrative.[2]

Most of the methods outlined in Table 6.1 use 'inferential statistics' which help you 'infer', with levels of statistical confidence, how well your data (the 'completed sample') represents the people you are interested in (the population).[3] This compensates for a major weakness in most data analysis where insights tend to be based on the completed sample with no regard for the population. Being able to infer from the completed sample to the population, with levels of statistical confidence, is important; it will give you a more complete and rounded perspective on the brand experience picture and so reduce your exposure to brand investment risk.

You don't have to be able to apply these methods yourself, but if you're aware of them you can select and brief external research agencies or internal research teams in a more robust, rigorous and focused way. You'll also be able to identify more competent external agencies by asking questions about statistical methodologies. Using such methods will also help you command more respect and give you clout in the boardroom. This is always a good thing, especially when it comes to looking for budgets from chief financial officers who tend to have a strong grasp of, and bias towards, statistical matters.

Multinational hotel company, InterContinental Hotels Group (IHG), used a data-driven approach to inform its brand experience-building efforts.[5] From 240 attributes associated with a hotel stay they identified about 20 per cent of features would add no significant value to the guest

Table 6.1 Using advanced statistical methods to build brand experiences

Method	This can help you	Practical application
Regression	Identify which variables influence an outcome of interest.	Identify which brand experience touchpoints drive performance metrics such as revenues, relevance, advocacy or willingness to pay a price premium. Regression will help you identify the touchpoints that matter so you can focus your efforts on those. At Wavelength, we used regression to help a corporate finance firm identify which values drove brand equity metrics.
Structural equation modelling	Understand the causal relationship between variables and an outcome of interest.	Establish if relative satisfaction drives loyalty (or vice versa) in the context of revenues. Once you understand the causal relationship that drives revenues, you can focus your efforts on those areas to start the sequence of events.
Bayes net modelling	To understand and identify variables, and the interaction between those variables on an outcome of interest.	Understand which variables drive an outcome of interest such as sales, relevance or willingness to pay a price premium. Bayes net is considered by many brand scientists to be a better way of modelling 'driver analysis' than regression and structural equation modelling because it mitigates problems of multicollinearity (when two predictor variables are highly correlated) and accounts for interaction effects between variables in the analysis. The visual presentation also tends to be well received in the boardroom.
Conjoint analysis	Optimize touchpoint design to drive choice.	Establish optimal serviced design at a given touchpoint. For example, should your mobile site have phone, email, live chat and Skype support? It may be that email and live chat support suffice. This streamlines the experience, reduces costs, speeds up delivery times and simplifies customer service support.
Cluster analysis	Objectively identify segments.	Understand how many segments you have and what they look like. You may think you have four discrete segments. Cluster analysis will help you determine if that is true. At Wavelength, we helped an exclusive lifestyle club identify segments and now they shape the experiences they design and deliver around these.

(continued)

Table 6.1 (Continued)

Method	This can help you	Practical application
Exploratory factor analysis	*Identify the underlying benefits that drive choice.*	*Identify salient brand experience benefits.* Wavelength worked with a property developer in the Middle East. An ideation workshop identified a long list of benefits associated with the development. Using exploratory factor analysis we demonstrated that the long list of benefits could be accounted for by four factors: environmental aesthetics; sense of community; local amenities; and status. These four factors shaped subsequent brand communications.
Multidimensional scaling	Identify which brands are perceived as being similar to yours.	*Measure the (Euclidian) distance between your brand and competitors' brands in respondents' minds.* This will help you objectively demonstrate which brands are perceived as being similar. However, multidimensional scaling does not help you understand *in what way* your brand is similar to others included in your analysis. Multidimensional unfolding does this.
Multidimensional unfolding	*Identify which brands are perceived as being similar to yours and in what way they are similar/assess internal and external alignment.*	*Identify your competitors based on brand associations.* The diagrams below share an anonymized Wavelength client example that was part of a brand experience-building project completed in the educational sector.[a] The diagram shows that employees thought: • Brands BMC, SOL, BC, JCC and UCB are perceived as being similar because the black dots are in close proximity. • These brands tended to be professional, academic and inspiring (the crosses which are closest to these brands). • CCB has no brand associations • SBC was student focused and vocational. This was our client.

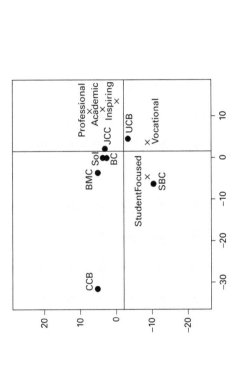

We conducted the same analysis with existing and prospective students. This highlighted how employees' views were not aligned with existing or prospective students due to the divergent brand and brand association perceptions held.

(continued)

Table 6.1 *(Continued)*

Method	This can help you	Practical application

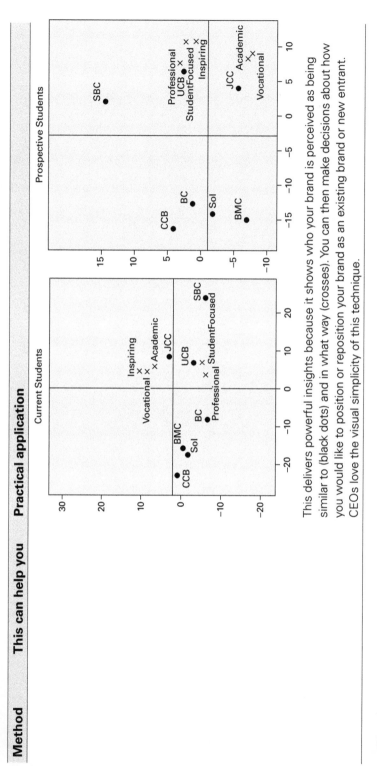

This delivers powerful insights because it shows who your brand is perceived as being similar to (black dots) and in what way (crosses). You can then make decisions about how you would like to position or reposition your brand as an existing brand or new entrant. CEOs love the visual simplicity of this technique.

a This project was delivered in partnership with Birmingham-based agency Traffic Marketing & Communications Ltd, http://www.thisistraffic.co

experience, 40 per cent would add between US $0.10–0.50 per guest night, and 40 per cent would add US $0.50–$2 per guest night. While the impact of each individual feature is small, aggregated across nearly 4,000 hotels with half a million rooms and over 100 million guest nights per annum, a few dollars difference per night stayed has the potential to make a substantial revenue contribution. From the initial pool of 240 experience features, IHG combined salient features to create 'moments of truth' that represented signature moments in the guest experience. Moments of truth implemented in September 2016 were:

- the optimized breakfast experience: worth $1.50–4 per night stayed;
- the perfectly prepared bathroom: worth $3–7 per night stayed;
- a productive room: worth $3–7 per night stayed;
- first impressions and first 10 minutes of the restaurant: worth $4–7 per night stayed, for guests who choose to use the restaurant;
- a perfect welcome and arrival: worth $3–6 per night stayed.

In his Expert Insight, Álvaro Gallart outlines how he used a data-driven approach to building brand experiences at Barranquilla Zoo, Columbia, whilst Ben Loeb's Expert Insight outlines how the experiences built by Microsoft are driven by data.

EXPERT INSIGHT 6.1 Using brand insight to improve Barranquilla Zoo's brand experience

Álvaro Gallart, Brand Equity Consultant, assigned by Barranquilla Zoo

Barranquilla Zoo has a long-standing reputation of devotion to conservationism and scientific contribution, making it an admired brand among citizens. Serving a total population of 1.8 million inhabitants, Barranquilla Zoo is operated by a private foundation with no significant government funding, so visitor revenues cover most of the operational expenses. The zoo has about 300,000 visitors per year with about 65 per cent belonging to low-income groups, for whom a visit to the zoo represents a sizeable family expense.

Barranquilla Zoo is home to 140 species (more than 500 animals on two hectares of land). Facilities were ageing and because of the natural growth of the city, the zoo has been surrounded by large residential areas, so expansion was not possible. The zoo needed to identify a new location, presenting the

Figure 6.1   Adopting a data-driven approach to building brand
experiences at Barranquilla Zoo

The Barranquilla Zoo Market Research Programme was deployed by blending a series
of seven different studies, well articulated, to deliver reliable and conclusive results

ROUTE TO RESULTS

On-premises Survey
(252 personal interviews)
Update visitors profile,
current perceptions and
opinions

Opinion Leaders Assessment
(40 in-depth interviews)
Assessing perceptions and qualified opinions
regarding the Zoo relocation

Optimal Location Study
Composed Statistical Model:
P-Median & MCLP (Maximal
Covering Location Problem)
Evaluate the new location options
according to users' home locations
across the city, to identify the 'best
accessible option'

Users in-depth interviews (8 Focus Groups)
Understanding actual perceptions, new location
options evaluation and preference, new facilities
expectations and desires

Home interviews (Sample: 457)
Barranquilla and metro area, to measure location
options preference and expectations/desires
from new facilities

Visitors New Zoo Design Survey
(on premises personal/ family
interviews)
Visitors allowed to prototype species
exhibition design, according to visit
desired experience **(300 active**
interviews were conducted)

Before I die... poll
Using candy chang's idea from the book *Before I die
I want to...* A series of boards were deployed on site,
asking also 'Barranquilla Zoo is missing...'
(1924 responses were obtained for the Zoo topic)

CONCLUSIVE RESULTS

management with a good opportunity to reconsider the visitor experience it delivered. An insight-driven approach to visitor experience design was adopted.

Our insights revealed a 'satisfaction gap' concerning the actual facilities and the actual experience. This insight informed three principles that shaped the new design of the visitor experience:

- more/better/vivid learning about animals, habitats and ecosystems;
- involve visitors in new activities like helping to feed animals at the farm;
- provide entertainment for the family group.

This resulted in the following changes at the zoo. The exhibition was changed to show collections by habitat. Educational materials and signalling became better, and included interactive pedagogical files to deliver a more engaging experience. Activities were improved by allowing visitors to learn and interact with minor species with properly conducted shows. A number of customer experience innovations were also launched, such as working on the farm, taking care of parrot land, a new approach for school group visits, night safari visits, and family shows. Social media content and conversations were enhanced by news about animals, habitats, conservational issues and ecosystems, while inviting people to visit and enjoy the new experiences at the zoo.
'Zoológico de Barranquilla' staff now conduct periodical surveys to measure brand experience satisfaction and ensure that the brand delivers value according to visitor expectations. This has become an important part of delivering a relevant visitor experience.

As a private foundation, 'Fundación Botánica y Zoológica de Barranquilla' is an environmentally devoted organization, leading and supporting initiatives on conservationism, research and education, to create awareness and inspire positive attitudes and behaviours in the community towards the biodiversity of the Caribbean coast region in Colombia.

EXPERT INSIGHT 6.2 How Microsoft measures brand experiences

Benjamin Loeb, Senior Market Research Manager, Microsoft, United States

At Microsoft, we directly or indirectly interact with millions of people each day. Customer interactions can range from an individual using our technology or contacting our customer support to Microsoft's actual marketing efforts such as PR, social media, or advertising. Each of these moments is an opportunity to build a Microsoft fan or lose a customer, so it's critical that we measure these experiences and act.

Thinking about the first scenario of someone using our technology, some experiences we need to understand and measure would be the usage of and satisfaction with the technology. Usage is critical because for us to remain relevant and maintain market share, customers need to use our products and enjoy the experience they deliver. We can measure usage in terms of time spent, such as time on Xbox Live, or accessing a specific feature, such as power users using a specific feature within Outlook. Satisfaction is typically measured through surveys and this helps inform whether a customer is having a good experience or may be at risk of leaving.

A customer contacting customer support is likely encountering a product or user experience issue so is seeking help. When you're a company as big as Microsoft, customer support issues can range from a gamer struggling with their Xbox to an enterprise customer having issues with their cloud infrastructure. Both scenarios are equally important customer experience opportunities for Microsoft. The frustrated gamer might leave for a competitor should their experience be a poor one. A cloud issue might be a business risk for the customer as well as for Microsoft. Therefore, effective measures of customer support experiences, ie time to resolution or satisfaction with the technician, are critical.

Measuring outbound marketing requires understanding whether a tactic was effective, efficient and positive. Was it worth it? Determining this means measuring the return on investment (ROI). Every marketing effort has a cost and not all marketing efforts will have a positive ROI. Aligning marketing goals directly to the balance sheet or to a business-specific metric such as market share, sales or usage, can make fighting for marketing dollars a little bit easier – when you can demonstrate a positive return.

Microsoft (Nasdaq 'MSFT' @microsoft) is the leading platform and productivity company for the mobile-first, cloud-first world, and its mission is to empower every person and every organization on the planet to achieve more.

The advent of 'Big Data'

Big Data is a topic that is never far from the senior executive agenda and is increasingly moving into the brand marketing mainstream. Whilst the definition and scope of the topic are debated, my view is that Big Data entails obtaining, aggregating and analysing large, often complex data sets that feed into subsequent decision making. For example, cookie tracking and 'data management platforms' aggregate data so it's possible to observe individual behaviour, at scale, then use these insights to create real-time, personalized experiences. This can compensate for some of the generalizations required to develop customer personas (see Chapter 3).

Whilst this book doesn't focus on Big Data I have included some examples to show how it is being used to help brands define and refine the experiences they build.

For the launch of *Pan*, Warner Brothers unified a variety of data sources spanning social media exposure and activity, postcode and TV channel exposure into a single, integrated Big Data set. Based on the insights this delivered, different messages and creative executions were crafted for certain groups based on appeal and relevance.

Verizon, the US telecommunications brand, combined data from search, social and display advertising along with machine learning, segmentation, consumer insights and behavioural economics to model consumer behaviour.[4] This fed into the creation of dynamically generated messages that were based on the data and associated algorithm so as to deliver a personalized messaging experience. Doing so resulted in an incremental sales conversion uplift of 117 per cent and a decrease in the cost of new line activation of just under 20 per cent compared with the control group.

Many Big Data approaches are beyond the reach of most small- to medium-sized enterprises but Australian firm Narellan Pools has bucked this trend.[6] The initial stage of their work entailed exploratory qualitative research which revealed that the first 'dive in' moment was a powerful motivator for buying. Next, they conducted an extensive data mining exercise where they analysed five years' worth of data spanning sales leads, sales, conversion rates, promotional plans, website analytics, consumer confidence, interest rates, search volumes for pools and annual weather trends. They discovered that certain weather conditions acted as a tipping point for people moving from wanting a pool to buying one. The occurrence of these weather conditions activated programmatic media spend for pre-roll adverts, banner adverts, search, and social adverts. The campaign increased sales leads by 11 per cent, sales by 23 per cent, and reduced their media budget by 30 per cent.

Numbers tend to talk in the boardroom, as their perceived objectivity provides credence, but they only paint part of the picture. As the Narellan case illustrates, qualitative data can play an important role in helping you obtain a more rounded brand experience-building perspective so it shouldn't be overlooked.

Qualitative insight

Qualitative insight provides data that can be more contextually relevant, richer and more nuanced than quantitative methods. It's also particularly useful when conducting research on topics that are sensitive, or have a strong social or cultural dimension, in addition to situations where the words used have particular importance or meaning so need to be carefully understood in context.

One of Wavelength's healthcare clients wanted to explore the anxieties patients experienced about particularly delicate subjects to understand how they could be mitigated or better managed. One-to-one interviews with family members in attendance were used to understand this topic in an empathetic and sensitive way. A youth brand client wanted to understand the culture and associated language used by their target customers so this could be incorporated into subsequent brand communications and experiential events. To address these issues, we used advanced text analytics and video diaries taken by mobile phone. Being sensitive to such subtle insights can make all the difference when building brand experiences, and this is where qualitative methods shine in comparison to quantitative methods. Table 6.2 shares qualitative methods you can use, together with examples of how they can help you build brand experiences.[7]

One criticism frequently levelled at qualitative data is subjectivity. Bias can creep into the creation of questions, conducting the research and data analysis. To address this, it's wise to validate your findings via 'triangulation'. This entails using other methods (qualitative and, ideally, quantitative) to check whether the same findings emerge. Doing this will build trust and inspire confidence in your insights as they will have a more rounded, robust and scientific feel. The small sample sizes associated with most qualitative research also tend to be problematic in the boardroom. Whilst the argument is valid, to some extent, your response should outline how qualitative methods provide perspective based on rich, contextual insights in ways quantitative methods cannot. Failing that, you can also back up your argument by citing brands such as Lego who used qualitative methods to re-focus their brand.[8]

Irrespective of the approach adopted it is important to appreciate that qualitative and quantitative data are not better or worse than each other. It's a case of understanding which approach is the most appropriate to your research goals, whilst keeping in mind that the best results are usually obtained by mixing quantitative and qualitative methods in, for example, the following combination:

Table 6.2 Using qualitative methods to build brand experiences

Method	This can help you	Practical application
Ethnography[a]	Appreciate the cultural context within which decisions are made.	Assess how snowboarders use your equipment on the slopes. This would entail building a relationship with them, joining their community and participating in their activity so you can observe and obtain insights from their perspective. Another option is to ask riders to take video diaries with their mobile phones throughout their day then share these with you. At Wavelength we have used this with a few clients and the stream of consciousness produced tends to be a revelation.
Customer visits	Discover the problems and challenges customers face in their environment (tends to have B2B focus).	Visiting a client's premises with a topic-based discussion guide so you can understand some of the frustrations your clients encounter with your brand experience. Customers tend to reveal more in familiar surroundings than they would over the phone, on a survey or in a focus group. If possible, it's useful to walk around the customer's environment, eg office, factory, shop, so you can contextualize their views. The insights you obtain can feed into subsequent touchpoint designs that aim to solve 'customer' frustrations. The key is to ask open-ended questions then keep your eyes open and ears close to the ground.
Focus groups	Explore perceptions, opinions, beliefs and attitudes towards your brand experience in addition to understanding language used in connection with your brand experience.	Investigate how your brand experience is perceived, which touchpoints require more attention, or better understand the everyday language associated with your brand experience. The presence of dominant personalities, 'herding mentality' and bias need to be addressed, as best as possible, in focus groups. At Wavelength, with client consent, we like to include a 'devil's advocate' in the focus group. Their brief is simple: constructively challenge, clarify and explore views expressed by the group in subtle ways. This is achieved with statements such as 'Hmmn, I'm not so sure about that because there was this one time that…' or by posing questions such as 'Ohhh. OK. I kind of see what you mean but does it always work like that?' Adopting this approach will help you understand if focus group participants are saying what they really think, something to make themselves look good, what they think you want to hear, or the first thing that comes to mind (as they want to leave the room as soon as possible). None of these are particularly useful. To be ethical, reveal the devil's advocate to the group at the end of the session. The devil's advocate doesn't need to be a specialist market researcher, just someone who fits the focus group profile.

(continued)

Table 6.2 (Continued)

Method	This can help you	Practical application
Lead user analysis	*Draw on expert knowledge of advanced users to enhance the experiences you build.*	*Understand if the experiences you build have alternative applications.* Sometimes your expert customers or 'power users' might find new applications for your products that are different from the ones initially intended. Other customers could benefit from their experience and insight, and what you learn could enable you to identify new markets. Wavelength worked with a laser manufacturer who acknowledged that many of their clients knew more about applied laser use than they did. Lead user analysis was incredibly useful to them.
Stakeholder advisory panels	*Incorporate the views of key stakeholders into brand experience design at an early stage.*	*Have customer or local community advisory boards.* Understand local community concerns regarding factory expansion so you appreciate their views and, where appropriate can involve them in parts of the facility planning. Having a 'customer advisory board' will help you understand the 'voice' of your most valuable or demanding customers. The key is to select objective and focused people so the conversations are constructive and stay on track. It's also important that executives with relevant authority are in the room so they can hear the 'voice' of their customer or other stakeholders first-hand. This can be an illuminating moment.

a For an interesting read on how Big Data and Thick Data (qualitative methods such as ethnography) should combine Tricia Wang's article is worth a read: http://bit.ly/wavelength-thick-data

1 An exploratory qualitative stage, to gain a contextual understanding of the key insights, trends, themes and language associated with the topic.

2 A quantitative stage to validate the views expressed during the previous qualitative stage with a larger completed sample.

3 A final qualitative stage to 'sense check' if the experiences you are going to build are relevant and resonate with stakeholders in a meaningful way. This sense check should be based on the preceding qualitative and quantitative insight.

If adopting this approach overwhelms you, it's a good idea to involve someone with relevant experience, or work with an external agency.

A note on biometrics and neuroscience

While qualitative research is often criticized for its subjective nature, quantitative methods are also prone to bias. As a result, some brands with deeper pockets are increasingly using biometrics and neuroscientific methods to enhance the objectivity of their insight before substantial brand experience investments are made.

Biometrics measure heart rate, skin response, eye movement and pupil dilation. To measure viewers' reactions to pre-release screenings of *The Revenant*, 20th Century Fox used wristbands to monitor heart rate variability, perspiration levels, temperature and movement. The data identified moments when the audience was most engaged and emotionally affected by the film. Neuroscience entails using advanced research methods such as MRI (magnetic resonance imaging) and EEGs (electroencephalogram) to measure the brain's electrical activity. Both methods can help identify brand experience touchpoints that generate the strongest emotional response.

This is an emerging area of brand research, so if you're thinking of making large brand experience investments, it warrants closer investigation, with expert guidance. If you would like to read more around the application of neuroscience I would recommend Professor Zurawicki's book *Neuromarketing*,[9] whilst the work of Professor Gemma Calvert is also well worth a look.[10]

Measuring holistically

Brands tend to focus on financial metrics because money talks. Whilst understandable, financial metrics have limitations. They are retrospective, have short-term horizons and account for only part of the brand experience measurement equation. A more informed, holistic approach incorporates employee, brand, and financial metrics.

Because employee and brand metrics drive financial performance (this relationship is explored in more detail in Chapter 19), adopting this approach delivers powerful cause-and-effect insights. This has important implications for where you should focus your efforts to drive brand experience performance. This is something you'll learn more about later in the book, but at this stage I just want you to register the importance of measuring brand experiences holistically and this entails taking employee, brand and financial measurements.

Conclusion

This chapter has outlined how adopting a data-driven approach to building brand experiences is an important element of the Brand Experience Environment. Informed managers and executives obtain robust qualitative and quantitative insights to shape the development and definition of their Brand Experience Essentials.

The perceived objectivity of quantitative methods means they tend to be well received in the boardroom, but I would also encourage you to obtain qualitative data. This will give your insights a more rounded and contextually richer feel. It will also help you 'hear' the voice of your customer, or other stakeholders, more clearly. I also advocated adopting a holistic approach to measuring brand experiences. As I will outline later in the book (Part Four), adopting this approach is wise, because it allows you to determine cause and effect relationships and also compensate for some of the limitations associated with using financial metrics.

Adopting a data-driven approach is the fourth and final element of Brand Experience Environment. The next (brief) chapter will summarize what we have covered in Part One of this book.

This chapter is accompanied by Toolkits 6.1 and 6.2.

Endnotes

1 Dillman, D A, Smyth, J D and Christian, L M (2014) *Internet, Phone, Mail, and Mixed-Mode Surveys: The tailored design method*, revised 4th edn, John Wiley & Sons

2 To learn more about these and other methods consult Hair Jr, J F and Black, W C (2013) *Multivariate Data Analysis*, Pearson

3 For an accessible overview of 'inferential statistics', Field, A (2013) *Discovering Statistics using IBM SPSS Statistics*, Sage Publications, is a good place to start

4 Warc (2016) Verizon Wireless: DecisionIQ, Direct Marketing Association (US), Silver, DMA International ECHO Awards [online] warc.com

5 Caldwell, L and Seear, L (2016) Behavioural economics gets real for IHG: probably the largest implicit market study in history, for one of the world's best-known hotel brands, ESOMAR Conference papers, Congress, New Orleans, September 2016

6 Brown, L (2016) Narellan Pools: Diving into big data for Narellan Pools, Institute of Practitioners in Advertising, Gold, Best Small Budget, IPA Effectiveness Awards, 2016 [online] warc.com

7 To learn more about qualitative data analysis, Maxwell, A (2012) *Qualitative Research Design: An interactive approach*, Sage Publications, is a good place to start

8 Madsbjerg, C and Rasmussen, M B (2014) An anthropologist walks into a bar... *Harvard Business Review*, March [online] http://bit.ly/wavelength-lego-qualitative

9 Zurawicki, L (2010) *Neuromarketing: Exploring the brain of the consumer*, Springer, Berlin

10 To learn more about how brands affect our brains, BBC's Technology Superbrands is a great watch: http://bit.ly/wavelength-superbrands (from 9 minutes 45 seconds)

Summary: 07
Brand Experience
Environment

In Part One of this book, I introduced the Brand Experience Environment. This comprises four elements:

- *Understanding your stakeholders*: profiling stakeholders; helping stakeholders get 'jobs done'; encouraging stakeholder engagement; managing stakeholder expectations.

- *Fine-tuning your perspective*: embracing transparency; adopting a holistic mindset; competing primarily through value not price; having patience; accepting a loss of control.

- *Considering the mechanics of delivery*: creating an emotional connection; facilitating co-creation; delivering omnichannel experiences.

- *Adopting a data-driven approach*: obtaining robust insights; measuring holistically.

The Brand Experience Environment is important because it provides context that will help you define and develop relevant Brand Experience Essentials (Part Two).

The order in which the Brand Experience Essentials are presented does not imply relative importance. It is not suggested that understanding stakeholders is more important than adopting a data-driven approach. Similarly, stakeholder profiling is not more or less important than embracing transparency. Every organization is unique, and some elements of the Brand Experience Environment will, inevitably, feel more relevant to yours. The specific characteristics of your organization and market, and the resources and competences available to you will determine their relative importance and influence. A mixture of experience, insight and practicality should help you find the right balance.

I have developed the Brand Experience Environment based on more than two decades of global brand experience spanning consulting, insight and executive education. The model is also underpinned by extensive practitioner-oriented thought leadership and peer-reviewed academic research. Other factors could be considered as part of a Brand Experience Environment but in the name of focus, practicality and compromise are required. One size does not fit all, so if you feel other elements should be included, by all means consider them when defining your Brand Experience Essentials. I would be keen to hear what they are.

This chapter is accompanied by Toolkit 7.1.

PART TWO
Brand Experience Essentials

Figure P2.1   The Brand Experience Blueprint: time to focus on the Brand
Experience Essentials

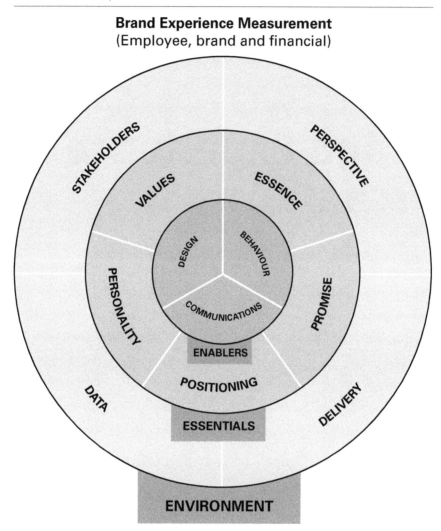

The Brand Experience Essentials comprise:

- brand values;
- brand essence;
- brand promise;
- brand positioning;
- brand personality.

Reading about the Brand Experience Essentials in Part Two will:

- encourage you to focus on the substance and not trappings of building brand experiences;

- help you construct the blocks on which your brand experiences will be built;

- help you scale the brand experience-building process because you will have guiding principles that facilitate the delivery of cohesive and consistent brand experiences to more people;

- accelerate the speed at which you can deliver brand experiences, because your organization will have a shared understanding of your 'brand';

- provide an underlying logic you can call on when you bring your brand to life through Brand Experience Enablers (Part Three).

To increase the relevance of your Brand Experience Essentials, you need to develop and define them in the context of the Brand Experience Environment. At the start of each chapter in Part Two, some illustrative questions are posed that will help you do this. These are summarized in Table P2.1.

Please remember that connecting the Brand Experience Environment and Brand Experience Essentials is not a check-box exercise. There's no need to map every Brand Experience Essential onto every part of the Brand Experience Environment. The relative importance of each Brand Experience Environment element depends on a variety of factors including organizational sector, size, resources, attitude to risk, culture, objectives and a host of others determined by the specific nuances of your organization and the characteristics of its market.

Table P2.1 Connecting Brand Experience Environment and Essentials: questions to ask yourself

	Values	Essence	Promise	Positioning	Personality
UNDERSTANDING YOUR STAKEHOLDERS					
Profiling stakeholders	How confident are we that our values resonate with stakeholders in relevant ways?	How does our essence encourage us to build experiences that are relevant to our stakeholders?	Which of the benefits we deliver are relevant to our stakeholders, and which are simply convenient for us to deliver?	How relevant is our positioning to our stakeholders?	How do we use our personality to help our stakeholders identify with our brand in ways that are relevant to them?
Helping stakeholders get 'jobs done'	To what extent do our values help stakeholders get relevant jobs done?	To what extent does our essence guide us to build experiences that help stakeholders get relevant jobs done?	Which parts of our brand experience deliver benefits that help stakeholders get relevant jobs done?	In what ways does our positioning help our stakeholders get relevant jobs done?	In what ways does our personality help our stakeholders get jobs done, eg demonstrate membership of a relevant group?
Encouraging stakeholder engagement	In what ways do our values encourage our stakeholders to engage with our brand?	How does our essence direct us to build engaging experiences for all of our stakeholders?	In what ways do our experiences deliver benefits that originate from stakeholder engagement?	How does our positioning encourage stakeholders to engage with our brand experiences?	How do we use our personality to encourage stakeholders to engage with our brand experiences?

Managing stakeholder expectations	Realistically, to what extent can we deliver on our values across our entire brand experience?	How realistic is our essence?	Where do we overpromise and under-deliver the brand benefits we communicate?	In what ways does our positioning accurately represent the experiences we deliver?	To what extent is our personality a fair reflection of who we really are or are working towards becoming?

FINE-TUNING YOUR PERSPECTIVE

Embracing transparency	To what extent will our values stand up to public scrutiny?	How does our brand essence guide us so we can factor transparency into the experiences we build?	To what extent are we honest about the benefits we deliver?	Could we defend our positioning if its underlying logic was challenged by our stakeholders?	If our brand was a person, to what extent would it conduct itself in an open and transparent way, with integrity?
Adopting a holistic mindset	How relevant do we think our values are to all our employees?	Which parts of our organization understand what our brand essence means to them in practical terms?	How do we engage people in departments that we need to contribute to delivering our brand promise?	Which parts of our organization understand the role they play in delivering our brand positioning? Which parts don't?	To what extent does everyone in our organization understand the role they play in bringing our brand personality to life?

(continued)

Table P2.1 (*Continued*)

	Values	Essence	Promise	Positioning	Personality
Competing primarily through value not price	In what ways do our values deliver relevant stakeholder value?	In what ways does our essence guide us to build experiences that deliver relevant stakeholder value?	In what ways are the benefits we deliver primarily based around value rather than price?	To what extent is our positioning focused primarily on value rather than price?	Which traits associated with our personality help us compete primarily through value rather than price?
Having patience	Which of our core values will stand the test of time?	How does our essence provide us with the long-term latitude to build new brand experiences?	Which of our brand experience-related benefits have longevity?	In what ways has our positioning been developed with long-term (however defined) relevance in mind?	Which of our stakeholders will identify with our personality in the future?
Accepting a loss of control	How do our values direct but not dictate the experiences we build?	To what extent do our social media team and/or the influencers we work with understand how their role(s) and our essence intersect?	Which of the brand experience benefits we deliver give our stakeholders a sense of control?	To what extent do we use social media monitoring to gauge and, if necessary, guide conversations (as best as possible) in a way that aligns with our desired brand positioning?	What steps do we take to work with 'influencers' who embody our personality?

CONSIDERIG THE MECHANICS OF DELIVERY

Creating an emotional connection	Which of our values help us connect emotionally with our stakeholders?	How does our essence help us deliver experiences that foster the emotional connection we want to create?	Which of the benefits we deliver reinforce the emotional connection we want to create?	How does our positioning align with the emotional connection we want to create?	How do we use our personality to help us create the emotional connection we want to make with our stakeholders?
Facilitating co-creation	How do our values encourage co-creation?	To what extent do we give stakeholders opportunities to co-create personalized experiences that sit within the scope of our essence?	How do the experiences we build provide our stakeholders with the context, tools and knowledge they need to realize the co-created benefits we can deliver?	What type of role does co-creation play in our positioning?	In what ways does our brand personality actively encourage co-creation?
Delivering omnichannel experiences	How consistently do we deliver our values across different channels?	How do we use our brand essence to help us select relevant channels for the brand experiences we build?	How do we map the benefits we deliver to their most relevant channel?	How aligned is the positioning of our brand experiences within and across all channels?	How do we express our personality across all channels?

(continued)

Table P2.1 (*Continued*)

	Values	Essence	Promise	Positioning	Personality
ADOPTING A DATA-DRIVEN APPROACH					
Obtaining robust insights	How do we establish which of our values drive the performance of our brand experiences?	How do we use data to help us objectively assess how relevant our existing/planned brand experiences are to our brand essence?	How do we obtain data to demonstrate which benefits drive key performance metric such as revenues, choice, price premiums and word of mouth?	To what extent do we make positioning decisions based on data-driven insight not anecdote?	How do we obtain insights that help us understand if our personality is perceived as more or less relevant to certain stakeholder groups?
Measuring holistically	How do we assess which of our values are more or less relevant to employees, customers or other stakeholders?	How do we measure the extent to which our employees, clients or other stakeholders *intuitively* understand what our essence is?	In what ways do we measure the value our benefits deliver to employees, clients or other stakeholders groups?	How do we know if perceptions of our brand positioning amongst employee, client and other stakeholders groups are aligned?	To what extent is our personality interpreted in the same way by employees, customers and other stakeholders?

Brand values 08

This chapter clarifies what brand values are then outlines why brand values are important when building brand experiences. It also provides practical advice on how you can create great brand values. Reading this chapter will give you a deep yet pragmatic understanding of how you can develop and define brand values that support your brand experience-building efforts.

As you progress through the chapter I encourage you to think about how brand values connect with the Brand Experience Environment. This will promote the development and definition of more relevant brand values. You can do this by asking yourself the illustrative questions outlined in Table 8.1.

What are brand values?

Brand values can be dismissed as brand management jargon and treated with suspicion or, worse still, disdain. This is problematic because it means a key Brand Experience Essential could be overlooked. To address this it's useful to discuss brand values using practical everyday English. You can achieve this by asking, 'How would you describe your brand in four or five words?' This is a straightforward question most people can answer. Responses tend to provide good approximations for values such as 'active', 'ambitious', 'fun' and 'diligent'. You can then refine these into your final brand values.

Table 8.1   Connecting brand values and the Brand Experience Environment: questions to ask yourself

Connecting your brand values with the brand experience environment	
Understanding your stakeholders	
Profiling stakeholders	• How confident are we that our values resonate with stakeholders in relevant ways?
Helping stakeholders get 'jobs done'	• To what extent do our values help stakeholders get relevant jobs done?
Encouraging stakeholder engagement	• In what ways do our values encourage our stakeholders to engage with our brand?
Managing stakeholder expectations	• Realistically, to what extent can we deliver on our values across our entire brand experience?
Fine-tuning your perspective	
Embracing transparency	• To what extent will our values stand up to public scrutiny?
Adopting a holistic mindset	• How relevant do we think our values are to all our employees?
Competing primarily through value not price	• In what ways do our values deliver relevant stakeholder value?
Having patience	• Which of our core values will stand the test of time?
Accepting a loss of control	• How do our values direct but not dictate the experiences we build?
Considering the mechanics of delivery	
Creating an emotional connection	• Which of our values help us connect emotionally with our stakeholders?
Facilitating co-creation	• How do our values encourage co-creation?
Delivering omnichannel experiences	• How consistently do we deliver our values across different channels?
Adopting a data-driven approach	
Obtaining robust insights	• How do we establish which of our values drive the performance of our brand experiences?
Measuring holistically	• How do we assess which of our values are more or less relevant to employees, customers or other stakeholders?

Why give a brand values?

Values influence behaviour

Values influence our beliefs and beliefs influence our behaviour.[1] Whether you like it or not, the ultimate aim of brand experiences is to influence behaviour. Buy, pay, recommend, travel, eat, drink or give are examples of things they encourage us to do more (or, sometimes, less) of. This means that if you want to influence behaviour you have to connect with stakeholders at a values level to compel behavioural change. Under Armour's campaign, 'I Will What I Will', embodies values of being active, confident and competitive. The campaign encourages customers to use willpower to do things that help them accomplish their goals. It's the customer connecting with the brand values that, ultimately, triggers a particular behavioural response.

Values can make your brand magnetic

If your brand values resonate with stakeholders they will identify with, and be drawn to your brand. Toyota Prius consumers (not Uber drivers!) are drawn to the brand because they buy into its values of being progressive, tech-savvy, prudent and environmentally aware.[2]

Prospective employees will be drawn to your brand if they can identify with your values. Building this type of 'employer brand' is particularly important for many of the Millennial generation who seek to work for organizations with a clear moral compass. Online influencers are also becoming an increasingly important stakeholder group. Research[3] outlines how 42 per cent of influencers feel that alignment with a brand's core values is the most important factor when approached with a brand partnership opportunity.

Just like a magnet, values have the potential to push someone away. If someone doesn't identify with your values this could deter them from engaging with the experiences you build. Versace customers will be drawn to extrovert, gregarious and bold brand values but Armani customers won't, given that they tend to be drawn to more refined, timeless and understated values.

'When positive, heartfelt values are instilled in your team, they will be empowered, they will feel appreciated and know they are part of a bigger mission than just making money. This will come across in the way they treat your customers, who in turn will prove to be more loyal to your brand and service. And, in the end, this will reflect positively on your profits too.'

Sir Richard Branson, Founder, Virgin Group

I highlighted the importance of identifying stakeholders' values when I explained stakeholder profiling in Chapter 3. This helps you assess whether your brand values will resonate with, and so have relevance for a given stakeholder group. This is important because research has shown that aligning brand and consumer values drives customer satisfaction, trust, affective commitment, and loyalty.[4] The key point is to define brand values that you feel realistically reflect your business now or ideally, then assess how aligned this is with your respective existing and/or ideal stakeholders.

At Wavelength we helped build the UK Sepsis Trust brand. Part of the project entailed assessing which brand values were more or less relevant to certain stakeholder groups (see Figure 8.1). Understanding how the values acted as a common denominator provided the basis for subsequent brand communication and experiential events that were tailored with segment values in mind. For example, 'Roger' is drawn to a brand that is expert

Figure 8.1   Aligning segment and brand values: client example from The UK Sepsis Trust

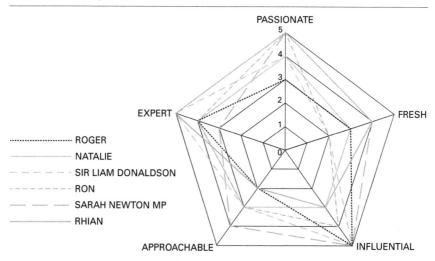

and influential. Establishing himself as a thought leader and building his personal brand were key 'jobs' Roger wanted to get done, so these values appealed. As a result, Roger received technical papers and thought leadership content that would resonate with those values. This contrasts with Rihan, who is drawn to the values of being expert, passionate and fresh, which means she is keen to learn more about Sepsis and help others do the same. The brand values co-exist, but certain facets of the brand, through its values, were exposed more prominently when the brand engaged with certain stakeholder groups in order to amplify appeal and increase relevance.

In her Expert Insight, Gemma Saunders outlines the role defining and developing brand values played in helping Gleeson Recruitment retain and attract relevant talent. This is particularly relevant for service sector SMEs who can struggle to articulate then use their values as a platform for subsequent growth.

EXPERT INSIGHT 8.1 How a recruitment firm used their values to scale their business

Gemma Saunders, Associate Director, Head of Human Resources, Gleeson RG

Gleeson RG directors' ambitious growth plans created a number of challenges. These included delivering a consistent client experience, retaining Gleeson's much-loved family feel and expressing everyone's tacit understanding of our values consistently. These challenges made us realize we needed to articulate our values as a platform for subsequent growth.

To do this we embarked on a two-stage project. During the first stage every employee attended a series of highly-facilitated workshops with the output being distilled into ten 'values'. The second stage of the project entailed the creation of a 'Gleeson Experience Survey'. This was completed by every employee and helped identify which 'values' they felt best represented Gleeson.

The 'values' that employees felt best represented Gleeson most accurately were: fun, family-oriented, flexible and supportive. These were also intuitively appealing as we felt they represented the business in a way we all understood but had never really spoken about. The directors also added 'collaborative' as they felt it was fundamental to business success.

We use these values during recruitment, to inform our employer branding strategy and guide the social responsibility initiatives we support. If we had not taken a step back to clearly define our values none of these things would be possible.

Gleeson Recruitment Group are a medium-sized recruitment business who recruit at all levels within finance and accountancy, human resources, engineering and supply chain, IT, sales and office support.

Much has been said about the Millennial generation and their unique characteristics. I do wonder if these differences have been exaggerated. Values can span generations and act as a powerful force which brings people together. Some time ago Wavelength worked with an active outdoor lifestyle brand. We held focus groups with people ranging from their teens through to their late 60s who shared a love of winter sports, running, fitness and cycling in extreme conditions. It was noticeable how the younger people in the groups looked up to and admired the more senior participants. The ethnographic study that comprised part of the same research delivered the same insight: their values, which the brand aligned with, acted as a common denominator for the group.

Brand values help stakeholders express their values

For example, 'I drive a Toyota Prius to show I'm progressive, tech-savvy, prudent and environmentally aware.' In this sense, the brand, or more specifically, the values that underpin the brand, become a means of self-expression that help Prius drivers make a statement to the world about their values. This is powerful because when this happens the brand (underpinned by its values) acts as a cue which signals the communities an individual belongs or aspires to belong to. Burton and Billabong have utilized this knowledge to great effect with snowboard and surf communities.

Values guide the use of Brand Experiences Enablers

If a brand is shaped around values of being refreshing, bold and funky, then it needs to express these values through relevant employee behaviour, communications and design, ie Brand Experience Enablers. In practical terms, this means this brand would locate an experiential event in the heart of pop-up shops with a cool DJ spinning funky vinyl on Technics 1200 turntables. The backdrop would use bold and vibrant colours, and the employees would be 'hipsters' or 'fashionistas'. Collectively, these combine to enable the brand values.

By clearly defining your brand values, you'll have guiding principles in place to guide your use of the Brand Experience Enablers that facilitate the delivery of more consistent and cohesive experiences, at scale. We will cover this point in more depth in Part Three of the book.

The Expert Insight provided by Dr Ron Daniels details how the UK Sepsis Trust's values guide and contribute to the life-saving work it does.

EXPERT INSIGHT 8.2 How brand values help guide the UK Sepsis Trust's life-saving work

Dr Ron Daniels BEM, Chief Executive Officer, The UK Sepsis Trust

In five years, the UK Sepsis Trust has grown into an established national charity with professional and celebrity support, coupled with influence in Westminster (the home of the UK Parliament) and Whitehall (where the UK's Civil Service leadership is based).

Articulating our values has been key to our success. We considered ourselves *influential, approachable* and *expert,* but to differentiate ourselves we felt we needed to be *fresh* and *edgy.* Coupled with a user segmentation exercise we set about mending sepsis through the UK Sepsis Trust shaped by these five values.

Our employees and executive team all joined us on this journey and we have our values on our walls to this day. Every new output is tested against them. This could be new creative work, a fundraising event, communications or how we respond to a given issue.

The results:

- The Secretary of State for Health and the Medical Director of the NHS are united in their announcements that 'sepsis is a condition whose time has come'.

- Public Health England has distributed 1.6 million of our leaflets, and national news outlets wait for our stories. Television dramas display our posters.

- At least 25 million more people are now aware of sepsis than when we started – with an advertising budget of zero.

- The chance of surviving sepsis has increased from 60 per cent to 80 per cent which means we are saving thousands of lives every year.

Through strategy coupled with focused brand-building initiatives that are guided by our values, we are well on our road to mending sepsis in the UK and further afield.

Every year in the UK 250,000 people are affected by sepsis, 44,000 people die because of sepsis and 40,000 suffer permanent, life-changing after-effects. The UK Sepsis Trust has a clear mission to save lives and improve outcomes for survivors of sepsis by instigating political change, educating healthcare professionals, raising public awareness, and providing support for those affected.

Values give a brand an opinion

According to Edelman:[5]

- 67 per cent of respondents bought a brand for the first time because they agreed with its position on a controversial topic;
- 23 per cent of respondents will pay at least a 25 per cent premium for a brand that supports their position;
- 48 per cent of respondents will advocate for your brand, defend it and criticize its competition if it speaks up compared to staying silent;
- 57 per cent of respondents buy or boycott brands based on a brand's position on a social or political issue.

Brands who voice a credible, authentic and authoritative opinion are powerful because when people agree with, or are intrigued by their point of view, they are drawn in.

During Ramadan 2016, Coca-Cola tackled the prickly topic of stereotyping and labelling people based on appearance in the Middle East. They invited six strangers to an Iftar (Ramadan meal where people break their fast at dusk) in a pitch-black room, and encouraged them to speak about their life and interests. When the lights were turned on each participant received a box with two cans, absent of Coca-Cola branding, with the words 'Labels are for cans, not people'. This became Coca-Cola's second-most-viewed video, delivering over US $30 million in earned media with a $50,000 spend.[6]

Kenco uses its 'Coffee vs Gangs' to express an opinion on how a career in coffee provides an alternative to gang life. Salesforce made its opinion clear on LGBT (lesbian, gay, bisexual and transgender) legislation via #WelcomesAll. In India, Brooke Bond Red Label tea positioned itself as an ally of the transgender cause by partnering with the transgender community to launch Six Pack, India's first transgender band. Their videos generated over 7.5 million YouTube views and contributed to a 1 per cent increase in the brand's market share in urban India.[7] Unilever uses brands like Axe/Lynx and Knorr to express opinions that challenge gender stereotypes by using hashtags like #loveatfirsttaste and #unstereotype. Its sustainable living brands, including Dove and Hellman's, have grown twice as fast as others in the company's portfolio.[8] Dove's opinion is that natural beauty should be a source of confidence and inspiration, not anxiety for women. Always, the producer of feminine hygiene products, confronts degrading gender stereotypes head-on and promotes teenage confidence and self-esteem via its #LikeaGirl hashtag.

The opinions these brands share on issues they feel are important to them are shaped by their values. Customers and other stakeholders can then make an informed decision on whether the brand is relevant to them.

How to create great brand values

Managers and senior executives that do a great job of creating brand values articulate values that are unique, specific, active, deliberate and balanced.

Unique values

Unique values facilitate the delivery of unique brand experiences. Some time ago Wavelength worked with a large government-backed savings bank in Southeast Asia. During our work, a value of being 'humble' emerged as being important. This struck me as refreshingly different in comparison to most financial services brands that have a strong commercial edge. Being 'humble' was tested locally and resonated deeply with local market sensitivities. Similarly, we worked with a healthcare brand who understood the importance of being 'attentive'. I felt this got to the heart of what you would want a healthcare brand to be. In a subtle way, it also goes further than the usual values of being 'patient-focused' or 'caring' which can sound a little clichéd at times.

Contrast these examples with values such as 'quality', 'innovation' and 'professional'. These kinds of values are depressingly common and generic. This is problematic because, when enabled through behaviour, communications or design, they won't result in unique experiences that differentiate you in the market.

Specific values

Values need to be specific so your brand is brought to life in the way you intend. Specific values reduce ambiguity and narrow the scope for all sorts of internal and external misunderstanding. If you have specific values, this will:

- help human resources colleagues recruit people whose values align with your desired brand experiences;
- help internal and external communications deliver communications that reflect your values;
- help you to create clear and accountable briefs for your agencies, which will give you a more defensible position should their design work disappoint you.

Let's consider the 'values' of quality, innovation, and professionalism further. The scope and room for interpretation of such 'values' is broad and this is problematic. Your colleagues' or agency's understanding of 'quality', 'innovation' or 'professionalism' may be drastically different to yours. Unfortunately, that doesn't tend to become apparent until it's too late. That could be an expensive mistake in terms of hiring the wrong recruit, communications that miss the mark, or disappointing creative work.

Active values

Framing your values actively means they focus on cause, not effect, in order to encourage behavioural change. 'Quality', 'innovation' and 'professionalism' are not values; they are behavioural outcomes that stem from values. You could reframe:

- 'quality' as 'meticulous': being meticulous could result in the quality of in-store service or online user experience delivered being enhanced in very specific ways;
- 'innovation' as 'progressive': being progressive could result in more innovative and forward-thinking brand experience-building processes being developed;
- 'professional' as 'dedicated': being dedicated could result in more professional customer service which ensures all customer enquiries are addressed.

'Teamwork' is another classic example. This is a behavioural outcome of values such as being 'empathic', 'emotionally intelligent' or 'collaborative'. If you focus on the behavioural outcome, not the value, you won't get to the root of things. As a result, you'll struggle to foster the behaviours you seek to encourage.

The importance of defining 'active' values will become more apparent when we explore employee behaviours in Brand Experience Enablers (Part Three).

Deliberate values

You need values that are related, but do not overlap. That way, they serve a unique purpose, but don't become repetitive and so redundant. Your values should act like a family of close brothers and sisters but you want to avoid identical twins (apologies to my lovely twin cousins!).

A brand ideation session for a corporate law client teased out preliminary values of being 'insightful', 'honest', 'supportive', 'diligent' and 'sociable'. Can you spot the odd one out? It is unlikely you would select a corporate law firm because they're sociable. That's not what they're paid to be and it doesn't feel related to the other values. They wanted to convey they are easy to do business with and were non-threatening. We reframed this as 'approachable'. Problem solved.

At the other extreme, overlap can be an issue. An urban fashion brand client had values of being 'confident', 'inventive', 'vibrant' and 'fun'. Being 'vibrant' and 'fun' overlap so we traded in 'fun' for 'selfless' to give the brand more empathy. A youth brand that is confident, inventive, vibrant and selfless was relevant to the goals and sensitivities of the Millennial generation.

To create deliberate values, I would encourage you define them carefully. Doing so will facilitate clarity and prevent overlap. Until you have defined your values the extent to which they align or overlap may not be apparent. It may sound academic, but will be time well spent.

I have seen some pretty terrible brand values which cause confusion, and unnecessary costs, when it came to using Brand Experience Enablers. I have also seen really good ones, so I wanted to share some to spark your imagination (see Figure 8.2). Please bear in mind they are illustrative, so some will be more relevant to your brand context than others. As you can see, these values feel quite unique and specific. They're also framed actively, so will encourage behavioural change.

Until you start to develop your brand values it will be hard to assess how deliberate they are – but remember, values should be close brothers and sisters, not identical twins.

Figure 8.2   Examples of brand values

> Approachable, aspirational, bold, candid, caring,
> commercially driven, concise, considerate, courageous,
> curious, decent, dependable, diligent, down to earth,
> dynamic, educational, emotionally intelligent, empathetic,
> energetic, engaging, focused, fun, hard-working, helpful,
> humble, inquisitive, insightful, meticulous, objective,
> ostentatious, outgoing, passionate, personable, practical,
> principled, realistic, rebellious, responsible, sensitive,
> succinct, traditional, trendy, unconventional, understated,
> vibrant, welcoming and witty.

Balanced values

Once you've created values that are unique, specific, active and deliberate, you need to come up for air and reflect on how balanced your values are. To do this you need to explore your values from core, peripheral, functional and emotional perspectives.[9]

Core values do not change. They're the bedrock of your brand and are about staying true to your roots. It's likely that a value of being 'socially responsible' has, and always will be core to The Body Shop brand.

Peripheral values may be modified or removed in exchange for other values so the brand can retain relevance. It could be argued Bentley's brand has become less 'refined' and more 'bold' through the launch of models like the Continental GT and more recently the Bentayga.

Functional values concern the practical facet of a brand. For instance, being 'reliable' is primarily a functional value. Whilst powerful brands develop a strong emotional response the importance of function should not be overlooked. There's no point having a Ferrari that never starts or a Gucci handbag that falls apart. Even the most luxurious brands need functional values.

Emotional values allow the brand to connect with the target market in deeper and more emotive ways. Procter & Gamble aimed to show it was 'supportive'[10] with its 'Proud Sponsor of Mums' campaign during the London 2012 Olympics.

It's important your brand values have 'balance'. If all your values are core your brand may lose relevance as the market evolves. If all your values are peripheral your brand will be a moving target, so stakeholders won't know

Table 8.2   Core, peripheral, functional and emotional values matrix

	Core	Peripheral
Functional		
Emotional		

how to relate to you. If all your values are functional, you won't appeal to stakeholders' emotions, and if all your values are emotional your brand may not deliver the basics. For these reasons it's a good idea to have at least one value in each box of Table 8.2. This will help you manage the difficult balancing act of appealing functionally and emotionally to your customers today, tomorrow and in years to come.

Hyundai has taken a strategic approach to building driving experiences around its brand values. The brand initially established its core and functional values by selling reliable cars. Extensive mileage and body warranties provided credible reasons to believe. With time, Hyundai built on these core and functional values and moved the brand into a more emotive space. This is reflected through Hyundai's updated tagline of 'New Thinking. New Possibilities', which has aspirational, emotive undertones. It's debatable if Hyundai could have enjoyed such success if had not established its functional credentials as a platform for more emotionally oriented brand growth.

It may sound like semantics, but defining values that are unique, specific, active, deliberate and balanced will pay dividends when it comes to delivering your brand experiences through Brand Experience Enablers.

Conclusion

This chapter has outlined what brand values are, why they're important and how you can go about defining great brand values. Carefully articulating your brand values will save you time, money and possibly even heartache further down the line. If you've thought through your values you'll be able to brief agencies accurately and constructively challenge design or communications work you feel isn't 'on brand'. If your values are clearly defined, HR will be well placed to recruit people who can deliver the desired brand experience in a natural and authentic way. In clearly defining your values, you have laid the cornerstone for building your brand experiences.

This chapter is accompanied by Toolkit 8.1.

Endnotes

1   Rokeach, M (1973) *The Nature of Human Values*, The Free Press, New York; Rokeach, M (1968) *Beliefs, Attitudes, and Values: A theory of organization and change*, Jossey-Bass

2   These are assumed values.

3   Business Wire (2016) TapInfluence unveils no. 1 thing motivating social influencers when working with brands, and it's not money, 10 November [online] http://bit.ly/wavelength-social-influences-values

4   Zhang, J and Bloemer, J M (1998) The impact of value congruence on consumer-service brand relationships, *Journal of Service Research*, **11** (2), pp 161–78

5   2017 Edelman Earned Brand Study [online] http://bit.ly/wavelength-endelman

6   Rais, T and Kearney, E (2017) Coca-Cola: Finding Light in the Dark, WARC Prize for MENA Strategy, Gold, 2017 [online] www.warc.com

7   Dasgupta, R and Tomar, C (2016) Brooke Bond Red Label: Happiness that truly went viral! WARC Prize for Asian Strategy, Entrant [online] www.warc.com

8   Oliver, L (2017) Brands get political for good causes, Raconteur, 6 July [online] http://bit.ly/wavelength-opinion

9   de Chernatony, L (2006) *From Brand Vision to Evaluation: The strategic process of growing and strengthening brands*, Butterworth-Heinemann

10   This is an assumed value.

Brand essence 09

The previous chapter outlined what values are, why they are important and provided practical advice on how to create great brand values. This chapter addresses brand essence. The first section clarifies what brand essence is, before outlining why it's important when building brand experiences. It also:

- provides tools and techniques to help you define your brand essence;
- clarifies the difference between brand essence and tagline.

Understanding more about brand essence will help you appreciate how you can scale your brand experience-building efforts in both existing and new markets by using your own and third-party resources. Whilst reading this chapter I encourage you to consider brand essence in the context of the Brand Experience Environment. Thinking about the illustrative questions posed in Table 9.1 will help you do this.

Table 9.1 Connecting brand essence and the Brand Experience Environment: questions to ask yourself

Connecting your brand essence with the brand experience environment	
Understanding your stakeholders	
Profiling stakeholders	• How does our essence encourage us to build experiences that are relevant to our stakeholders?
Helping stakeholders get 'jobs done'	• To what extent does our essence guide us to build experiences that help stakeholders get relevant jobs done?
Encouraging stakeholder engagement	• How does our essence direct us to build engaging experiences for all of our stakeholders?
Managing stakeholder expectations	• How realistic is our essence?

(continued)

Table 9.1 *(Continued)*

Connecting your brand essence with the brand experience environment	
Fine-tuning your perspective	
Embracing transparency	• How does our brand essence guide us so we can factor transparency into the experiences we build?
Adopting a holistic mindset	• Which parts of our organization understand what our brand essence means to them in practical terms?
Competing primarily through value not price	• In what ways does our essence guide us to build experiences that deliver relevant stakeholder value?
Having patience	• How does our essence provide us with the long-term latitude to build new brand experiences?
Accepting a loss of control	• To what extent do our social media team and/or the influencers we work with understand how their role(s) and our essence intersect?
Considering the mechanics of delivery	
Creating an emotional connection	• How does our essence help us deliver experiences that foster the emotional connection we want to create?
Faciltating co-creation	• To what extent do we give stakeholders opportunities to co-create personalized experiences that sit within the scope of our essence?
Delivering omnichannel experiences	• How do we use our brand essence to help us select relevant channels for the brand experiences we build?
Adopting a data-driven approach	
Obtaining robust insights	• How do we use data to help us objectively assess how relevant our existing/planned brand experiences are to our brand essence?
Measuring holistically	• How do we measure the extent to which our employees, clients or other stakeholders *intuitively* understand what our essence is?

What is brand essence?

Professor Kevin Lane Keller from Tuck Business School, Dartmouth College, refers to brand essence or 'brand mantra' as the 'heart and soul' of a brand

and outlines how brand essence is an articulation of what a brand fundamentally represents.[1] Nike's brand essence is 'authentic athletic performance' and Disney's is 'fun family entertainment'. I like to think of brand essence as the core idea or premise that underpins and informs everything the brand does. As brand essence is quite abstract, it might be easier to consider it as two or three words that sum up 'what your brand is all about'. So, Nike is all about 'authentic athletic performance' and Disney is all about 'fun family entertainment'.

Why is brand essence important?

Brand essence serves a number of purposes. It helps employees understand the fundamental premise or core meaning that underpins your brand. This provides focus for internal brand education and facilitates alignment. Brand essence can even be used to guide your approach to acquiring other brands or selecting the channels through which you deliver your brand experiences. More importantly, because brand essence is closely linked to brand positioning it also provides a useful internal litmus test for your brand experience strategy that helps you evaluate which categories or markets your brand should and should not move into. *Should we stay in snowboarding or move into skiing as well? Should we launch a private banking service in addition to a traditional retail banking offer?* This is where I feel brand essence can make a unique and particularly useful contribution to your brand experience-building endeavours compared to other Brand Experience Essentials. It provides a 'sense check', scope or boundaries for the experiences you should and shouldn't build. The benefits that brand essence can bring is best illustrated by example.

Nike operates in athletics, basketball, tennis, football, rugby, golf, etc. The experiences Nike wraps around its products express 'authentic athletic performance'. The company could open a chain of sports academies as long as they conveyed 'authentic, athletic performance'. At these academies, you would expect to see athletes giving every last ounce of energy to make that shot or tackle. It would be all about competition, winning and being the best you can be, rather than, say, social participation. Nike has moved into snowboarding and skateboarding with limited success. That doesn't fit with authentic athletic performance. Cool and hip lifestyle brands like Burton, Vans and Volcom thrive in these markets.

Disney is in amusement parks, films, toys, games, holidays, etc. Their products or experiences convey 'fun family entertainment'. Disney could roll out a chain of themed restaurants that majored on 'fun family entertainment' to compete with the likes of Denny's. Imagine being welcomed to a restaurant by Daffy Duck and served by Mickey Mouse. Fun entertainment for the family. Conversely, if Disney launched a chain of boxing clubs for kids, it's debatable if that would sit within their essence. Boxing doesn't tend to be about fun family entertainment – at least in the way that fits with Disney's brand.

Let's assume Red Bull's brand essence is 'adrenaline-fuelled extreme fun'. This explains why Red Bull has an F1 team, sponsors extreme sports and conducts stratospheric public relations stunts. Being associated with these types of experience sits perfectly within the scope of Red Bull's brand essence. If the company wanted to, it could open a theme park with the most extreme roller coasters on the planet. This would fit within the scope of their essence.

Comparing British Airways with Virgin highlights the importance of brand essence. British Airways have tried in vain to move into other markets including holidays, hotels, car rental and holiday-related experiences. They've struggled because their brand was built around the category of flying. This created restrictive brand associations that anchored the brand as an airline, hindering growth in new categories. Contrast this with Virgin's brand-driven strategy where they aren't shackled by product category chains. Their brand acts as a powerful platform for growth whilst their brand essence marshals the markets they should and should not enter.

The following examples illustrate how brand essence can accelerate cost-effective, brand-driven growth:

- Although your brand essence polices which categories and/or markets you should or shouldn't take your brand into this doesn't mean you have to manage the experiences that sit under your brand. You can screen potential white-label or third-party offers based on how well they align with your brand essence, then outsource operational delivery to them. A Nike Sports Academy could be run by an established sports centre brand with relevant operational expertise. Nike would provide clear guidance on how the sporting experiences should be provided, so they deliver 'authentic athletic performance'. Then they can leave the experience execution to their specialist partner, in line with clearly articulated Terms and Service Level Agreements, brand guidelines and so forth.

- Adopting a brand essence-driven approach gives limited exposure to research and development costs, capital expenditure investment and so forth. The AA (Automobile Association) was founded in 1905 to provide road assistance. It now offers a range of other services including insurance and heating breakdown cover that help you when things go wrong. These fit with their car breakdown heritage. The AA does not underwrite insurance policies or repair broken boilers itself, but offering these services through partners, under their brand, sits nicely within the scope of their brand essence.

- Small and medium-sized enterprises can also benefit from understanding and embracing their brand essence. At Wavelength we worked with niche luxury brand, StaaG, on their brand essence. Doing this helped the brand move beyond the confines of its original polo shirt category and flourish in a number of other luxury categories including overnight travel bags, belts and jewellery, which are handmade in England by artisan craftspeople. StaaG's brand essence has also guided other decisions in relation to travel photography awards, its relationships with the University of the Arts London, and the content it produces in its StaaG heritage sports handbooks, which sit comfortably with their lifestyle brand.

When organizations understand brand essence it can revolutionize their business model. They realize that the main sources of value they offer don't lie in physical functional goods, but in intangible assets including brands and experiences. So, instead of investing heavily in capital expenditure projects, organizations are increasingly investing in intangible assets such as brands whose operational delivery is outsourced, with decisions being filtered through a clearly defined brand essence. This is a trend that has developed over the past 40 years, with the sources of value for S&P 500 countries being inversed during that time (Figure 9.1).

Figure 9.1 Tangible and intangible assets for S&P 500 (1975–2015)

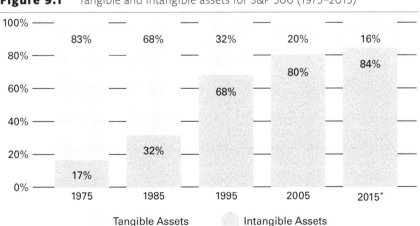

SOURCE Ocean Tomo LLC, 2015 Annual Study of Intangible Asset Market Value, 3 May [online] bit.ly/wavelength-ot

How to define your brand essence

Brand consultants will encourage you to use methods such as 'laddering' to tease out your brand essence. This entails progressing from functional brand features to higher-order emotional benefits.[2] Laddering can be effective if someone in the room keeps context and a sense of reality. Some brands' ladders reach for the heavens and end up losing relevance in the real world. Experienced consultants will prevent you from moving from this world to the next before your time has come.

A more hands-on and structured approach to formulating your brand essence entails considering your essence in three parts:[3]

- *Brand functions*. This entails defining the nature of the experience being provided. Nike focuses on *performance*, Disney on *entertainment*.
- *Descriptive modifiers*. This part of the essence clarifies the type of experience being delivered. For example, Nike isn't just offering performance, but *athletic* performance, whilst Disney is focused on *family* entertainment.
- *Emotional modifiers*. These outline how the brand delivers value or a benefit. Nike is *authentic* and Disney is *fun*.

When working with clients, I find it useful to start with brand function, move to the descriptive modifier then look at the emotional modifier. Using this method provides structure, and a sequence that starts with the big picture and becomes increasingly focused and emotive. It's also useful to think of 'emotional modifiers' and 'descriptive modifiers' as adjectives and 'brand functions' as a noun.

I have developed another approach to articulating brand essence. Because it's practical and intuitive, clients find it particularly useful. It entails completing the following sentence:

> 'If I was asked to sum up our brand in two or three words I'd say it's all about _____/_____/_____' (eg authentic athletic performance, fun family entertainment etc).

Combining the more structured approach with this sentence completion method works well. The former provides an overarching template and framework to guide your initial thoughts. And the sentence completion method helps you sense-check if the two or three words you have identified sum up the heart and soul of your brand. If you try to start with the sentence completion method you may find it lacks the structure and direction required to develop and focus your thinking.

Some examples of client brand essence have been included in Table 9.2, which also shows how a clearly defined brand essence creates new business opportunities.

Table 9.2   Brand essence driving business growth: Wavelength Marketing client examples

Previous products/lines of business	Brand essence	Additional products/lines of business enabled by brand essence
Flat pack furniture (especially tables/ chairs)	Clever compact design	Interior design and consulting for high-net-worth individuals that live in major cities in emerging markets, eg Jakarta, Delhi, Brasilia and luxury yacht manufacturers that value 'clever compact design' due to the premium space commands.
Outdoor clothing (for particularly harsh and demanding terrain)	Active outdoor excellence	Food supplements, flasks, watches, educational seminars, personal development programmes etc, that help you achieve 'active outdoor excellence'.
Natural cosmetics	Balanced scientific beauty	Food, consulting services and well-being educational programmes that provide 'balanced scientific beauty'.

Is a brand essence a tagline?

No. Brand essence and tagline are related but distinct. Amongst other things, brand essence establishes the scope or boundaries for the markets your brand should and should not move into. This means it's an internal brand strategy tool you should use to filter any moves into new categories or markets. A brand tagline is another tool you can use to express your brand in conjunction with other design cues such as your logo, name and colour palette. For example, Nike's 'Just Do It' tagline helps convey 'authentic athletic performance' and connotes winning, which lies at the core of the brand and the associated experiences it delivers.

Conclusion

This chapter explored what brand essence is, why it is important and how, amongst other things, it provides boundaries for the markets your brand should and should not enter. When managers and executives understand brand essence, they tend to take a quantum leap in terms of how they think about brand and the associated experiences they build. They realize value lies in intangible assets (brands and experiences) and that these can be scaled, via third-party relationships that are governed, in part, through brand essence. The concept of brand essence can feel rather abstract and hard to grasp, so I provided practical advice on how to define it, as well as making the distinction between brand essence and tagline.

This chapter is accompanied by Toolkit 9.1.

Endnotes

1 For more details on brand essence please see Keller, K L (2007) *Strategic Brand Management: Building, measuring, and managing brand equity*, 3rd edn, Pearson

2 Gutman, J (1980) A means-end chain model based on consumer categorization processes, *Journal of Marketing*, **46** (2) pp 60–72

3 Keller, K L (2007) *Strategic Brand Management: Building, measuring, and managing brand equity*, 3rd edn, Pearson

Brand promise 10

The previous chapter outlined the role brand essence plays in building brand experiences. Brand essence helps you 'sense check' the markets and categories your brand should and shouldn't operate in. It can also help you scale brand experiences through third-party relationships. This chapter clarifies:

- what a brand promise is;
- how you can distinguish features from benefits;
- how to identify the types of benefits you can incorporate into your brand promise.

Reading this chapter will help you articulate and incorporate relevant benefits into the experiences you build. It's likely this will provide you with an advantage over your competitors, who will probably be focusing on brand features that, themselves, deliver limited value. As with brand values and brand essence, I encourage you to think about the development of your brand promise in the context of the Brand Experience Environment. Thinking about the illustrative questions in Table 10.1 will help you do that.

What is a brand promise?

'Making promises and keeping them is a great way to build a brand'.

Seth Godin

Table 10.1   Connecting brand promise and the Brand Experience Environment: questions to ask yourself

Connecting your brand promise with the brand experience environment	
Understanding your stakeholders	
Profiling stakeholders	• Which of the benefits we deliver are relevant to our stakeholders, and which are simply convenient for us to deliver?
Helping stakeholders get 'jobs done'	• Which parts of our brand experience deliver benefits that help stakeholders get relevant jobs done?
Encouraging stakeholder engagement	• In what ways do our experiences deliver benefits that originate from stakeholder engagement?
Managing stakeholder expectations	• Where do we overpromise and under-deliver the brand benefits we communicate?
Fine-tuning your perspective	
Embracing transparency	• To what extent are we honest about the benefits we deliver?
Adopting a holistic mindset	• How do we engage people in departments that we need to contribute to delivering our brand promise?
Competing primarily through value not price	• In what ways are the benefits we deliver primarily based around value rather than price?
Having patience	• Which of our brand experience-related benefits have longevity?
Accepting a loss of control	• Which of the brand experience benefits we deliver give our stakeholders a sense of control?
Considering the mechanics of delivery	
Creating an emotional connection	• Which of the benefits we deliver reinforce the emotional connection we want to create?
Facilitating co-creation	• How do the experiences we build provide our stakeholders with the context, tools and knowledge they need to realize the co-created benefits we can deliver?
Delivering omnichannel experiences	• How do we map the benefits we deliver to their most relevant channel?

(continued)

Table 10.1   (*Continued*)

Connecting your brand promise with the brand experience environment

---

Adopting a data-driven approach

Obtaining robust insights	• How do we obtain data to demonstrate which benefits drive key performance metrics such as revenues, choice, price premiums and word of mouth?
Measuring holistically	• In what ways do we measure the value our benefits deliver to employees, clients or other stakeholder groups?

Brands need to deliver benefits that provide stakeholders with relevant value. These benefits can be wrapped up as your brand promise. Brands have a tendency to focus on features, not benefits; the number of ATMs, data speeds, number of employees, for example. Focusing on features is problematic because:

- **Features are a means to an end.** Value resides in the benefit delivered by the feature, and this ultimately contributes to your brand promise. Customers don't care about anti-locking braking systems or air bags; they care about the safety of their family. The public aren't overly interested in £100m investment in public services but they are interested in what this means in terms of numbers of nurses, doctors and teachers. Clients aren't worried about how many people you employ, but about what those people can do to help their business.

- **Focusing on features commoditizes your offer.** If you create a table showing your brand and competitors against the features you all offer, it's likely you'll find perceived points of differences dissolving into a sea of sameness.

- **A feature-driven mentality adds complexity and cost.** A frequent response to competitive threats and declining performance is to add more features to the goods, services or experiences you offer in the hope this rectifies matters. It seldom, if ever, helps; excessive choice is stressful for customers.[1] More features also means more things can go wrong, whilst customer service becomes more complex and so challenging to deliver. Unnecessary features also add unnecessary cost.

How to distinguish benefits from features

A valued friend of Wavelength, Clive Booth, introduced me to a useful tool that helps tease benefits out of features: '(feature) *which means that* (benefit).' For example, 4G gives ultra-quick data download speeds (feature) *which means that* you deliver more responsive client service (benefit).

You may need to say 'which means that' a few times to tease a core benefit out of a feature. You'll know you're there when you can't say 'which means that' anymore.

For example, a bank could say, 'Our branches open at the weekend, *which means that* you can visit us on a Saturday, *which means that* we'll be able to resolve your account issues in person without delay, *which means that* you'll be able to enjoy greater financial peace of mind at all times.' It's hard to say 'which means that' again, so having 'greater financial peace of mind at all times' is a benefit that could be part of your overall brand promise.

This 'feature which means that' template will also help you establish if one feature delivers multiple benefits – which is frequently the case. For example, 4G data speed means you can:

- deliver more responsive client service;
- stay on top of projects whilst on the move;
- get more out of your day;
- play graphic-heavy games on the train to reduce boredom;
- stream live Birmingham City FC games to cheer you up;
- upload video clips to your YouTube channels to keep your community engaged;
- deliver investor video conferences whilst out of the office.

Once you have identified all the benefits of a feature, you can allocate them to relevant stakeholder groups. But before doing that, it's wise to think about the types of benefits you'll provide, so you can deliver even more value to your stakeholders.

Types of benefits

Professor David Aaker[2] outlines four main types of benefits: functional, emotional, self-expressive and social:

- *Functional benefits* relate to the practical ways in which a brand helps someone. You can identify functional benefits by completing the following sentence: *'(feature) is (adjective).'* For example, 4G is quick or aluminium is light. Competing on functional benefits is problematic because they are relatively easy to copy and do not play the emotive tune the human brain is receptive to.

- *Emotional benefits* relate to the emotion someone feels when they experience your brand. You can identify emotional benefits by completing this sentence: *'When I buy or use this brand, I feel _____.'* Examples include feeling safe (Volvo), valued (AmEx Gold Card), stylish (Armani Collection), reassured (IBM) or secure (Rothschild).

- *Self-expressive benefits* help someone convey part of their personality. You can identify self-expressive benefits by completing this sentence: *'When I buy or use this brand, I show I am _____.'* Examples include successful (Mercedes Benz), creative (Apple), caring (Dove) or informed (Reuters).

- *Social benefits* entail someone using a brand to show membership of a group. You can identify social benefits by completing this sentence: *'When I buy or use this brand, the type of people I relate to are _____.'* Examples include a global football community (FC Barcelona fans), motorbike lovers (Harley Davidson riders) or business leaders (*Financial Times*).

It's best to play down functional benefits because they are easy to compare and so will expose you to price-based competition (see Chapter 4). Emotional, self-expressive or social benefits have the potential to be powerful pieces of your brand promise puzzle. They resonate with people at a deeper level than functional benefits. That doesn't imply you should overlook functional benefits; remember, there's no point buying a Ferrari that won't start.

Research[3] shows three broad benefits underlie human happiness. I find these act as a useful addition to functional, emotional, self-expression and social benefits when I'm helping clients to develop their brand promise. They are:

- *Enablement benefits.* These help customers get jobs done, accomplish tasks, solve problems, alleviate fear or address challenges. For example, Calpol eases infant pain, Just for Men colours over those grey hairs and Credit Suisse's heritage reduces concerns potential merger and acquisition clients may have when selecting an investment bank. When customers experience enablement benefits they feel relieved, empowered, secure, safe or confident.

- *Enticement benefits* stimulate customers' senses (touch, sight, sound, smell and taste) through their thoughts and emotions in ways that are pleasing, fun, interesting, and emotionally involving. Examples include:

sitting in an expensive armchair whilst waiting to see your lawyer; enjoying a sensual spa at a Banyan Tree hotel; feeling the bass booming through your bones in Pacha nightclub. Customers feel comforted, gratified, stimulated, engaged, amused, warm or upbeat when they experience enticement benefits.

- *Enrichment benefits* add value to their sense of who they are (or want to be) as people. Inviting carefully selected customers to a VIP launch event is an example that could enhance feelings of self-worth and pride. Customers feel enriched, inspired, proud, connected, validated, accepted and authentic.

In his Expert Insight, Mohamed Adam Wee Abdullah provides details of CIMB's brand promise and how the company delivers against it.

EXPERT INSIGHT 10.1   How CIMB delivers against its brand promise

Mohamed Adam Wee Abdullah, Group Chief Marketing Officer and Group Chief Customer Experience Officer, CIMB Group – ASEAN

Brands operate at a perceptive level. They create appeal, draw customers in, generate demand and plant expectations in customers' minds that are largely driven through the promises made by the brand. The purpose of customer experience management is to make sure the organization can deliver on that promise. To ensure this happens the key is to have the governance framework in place and apply a customer lens to product creation, process improvement, channel management, service design, communications, etc.

At CIMB we do this through our '**3Es**', ie going the **Extra Mile**, making it **Easy** and **Efficient**. This represents a practical governance framework we apply that helps focus our approach to customer experience. As part of our 3Es framework we apply tools like customer journey mapping to identify the critical pain points to work on. The Lean Six Sigma methodologies and tools are then applied to the business process re-engineering to deliver the customer and financial outcomes.

Capability building is an integral component of driving a continuous improvement culture in CIMB. So that we can continue to deliver against our brand promise, all employees are provided with a custom-designed Lean Six Sigma yellow belt online training tool. Participants of a customer experience project are further provided with more comprehensive Lean Six Sigma yellow and green belt trainings conducted by in-house black belt trainers.

By going beyond the superficial layer of customer experience implementation through using these tools and techniques, CIMB sustains its ability to deliver relevant experiences that win and keep customers, ultimately growing revenue and delivering long-term value for the business.

CIMB is ASEAN's leading universal banking group, providing financial solutions to both retail and institutional customers.

Conclusion

This chapter outlined how you can extract benefits from features by using the 'feature which means that' template. This practical tool will also help you squeeze multiple benefits out of one feature. In turn, this will increase the breadth and depth of stakeholder value you deliver through the experiences you build.

The different kinds of benefits are: functional, emotional, self-expression, social, enabling, enticing and enriching. These benefits combine to comprise your brand promise. Once you've identified the various benefits or facets of your brand promise, you need to map these to your stakeholder groups so you can build experiences that deliver relevant value.

This is why aspects of the Brand Experience Environment such as profiling stakeholders, helping stakeholders get jobs done, and creating an emotional connection are so important. Once you have an in-depth understanding of your stakeholders and have identified the benefits you deliver to them, it'll be clear where your relevant sources of value lie. You can then incorporate these into the brand experiences you build.

This chapter is accompanied by Toolkit 10.1.

Endnotes

1 Schwartz, B (2004) *Paradox of Choice*, Harper Perennial

2 Aaker, D (2009) Beyond functional benefits, *Marketing News*, 30 September, p 23

3 Park, C W et al (2016) *Brand Admiration: Building a business people love*, Wiley

Brand positioning

11

The previous chapter provided guidance on how you can create your brand promise. This chapter focuses on brand positioning with an emphasis on understanding what positioning is, how you should define your competitors and how to write a positioning statement. Reading this chapter will help you broaden your perspective beyond classical 'category-based' positioning approaches which could blind you to new and nimble competitors. Armed with this insight you will be better placed to position your brand experiences with long-term relevance in mind.

By this stage in the brand experience-building process, the Brand Experience Environment can feel like a distant memory. As you read this chapter, you should try to keep the Brand Experience Environment in mind so you position your brand and the associated experiences in relevant ways. Checking back to the illustrative questions in Table 11.1 as you read should help you do this.

Table 11.1 Connecting brand positioning and the Brand Experience Environment: questions to ask yourself

Connecting your brand positioning with the brand experience environment
Understanding your stakeholders

Profiling stakeholders	• How relevant is our positioning to our stakeholders?
Helping stakeholders get 'jobs done'	• In what ways does our positioning help our stakeholders get relevant jobs done?
Encouraging stakeholder engagement	• How does our positioning encourage stakeholders to engage with our brand experiences?

(continued)

Table 11.1 *(Continued)*

Connecting your brand positioning with the brand experience environment	
Managing stakeholder expectations	• In what ways does our positioning accurately represent the experiences we deliver?

Fine-tuning your perspective

Embracing transparency	• Could we defend our positioning if its underlying logic was challenged by our stakeholders?
Adopting a holistic mindset	• Which parts of our organization understand the role they play in delivering our brand positioning? Which parts don't?
Competing primarily through value not price	• To what extent is our positioning focused primarily on value rather than price?
Having patience	• In what ways has our positioning been developed with long-term (however defined) relevance in mind?
Accepting a loss of control	• To what extent do we use social media monitoring to gauge and, if necessary, guide (as best as possible) conversations in a way that aligns with our desired brand positioning?

Considering the mechanics of delivery

Creating an emotional connection	• How does our positioning align with the emotional connection we want to create?
Facilitating co-creation	• What type of role does co-creation play in our positioning?
Delivering omnichannel experiences	• How aligned is the positioning of our brand experiences within and across all channels?

Adopting a data-driven approach

Obtaining robust insights	• To what extent do we make positioning decisions based on data-driven insight not anecdote?
Measuring holistically	• How do we know if perceptions of our brand positioning amongst employee, client and other stakeholder groups are aligned?

What is brand positioning?

Brand positioning concerns the unique associations you want stakeholders to connect with your brand. Coca-Cola is associated with happiness. Audi is associated with German engineering excellence. Nike is associated with winning (note the connection with their essence of authentic athletic performance). McKinsey is associated with high-end, complex management consulting. BlackBerry's initial association with mobile email was very successful but its move into the youth market with BlackBerry Messenger blurred the association in customers' minds. Was it a corporate email brand, a youth brand or both? It could be argued this lack of focus, combined with the technical difficulties it experienced and the advent of powerful brands such as Apple and Samsung, contributed to BlackBerry's decline. The brand now plans on going back to its roots by focusing more heavily on mobile cybersecurity through its Security Technology division; a far better brand fit than a messaging application for the youth market.

When positioning your brand in relation to competitors, you need to consider points of parity and points of difference.[1] **Points of parity** represent parts of your experience also delivered by your competitors. For a bank, this would be loans, ATMs, online banking and credit cards. For an accounting firm, this would be tax, audit and advisory services. If you don't offer points of parity your brand won't be part of your target customers' 'consideration set' when they think about banks or accounting firms. They are the hygiene factors that stakeholders expect you deliver, and represent key points of category or market membership. When Metro Bank opened in 2010 it was the first high street bank to launch in the UK for 100 years. Cash cards, ATMs, current accounts, cheque books and suchlike represented points of parity. These did not comprise new parts of the experience, but were required to make it clear that Metro was a bank and would compete with the likes of Lloyds, HSBC and Barclays. In the luxury yacht market, Sunseeker and Princess compete for high-end customers' cash. Their points of parity primarily relate to the performance of the yachts.

Points of difference represent unique parts of your experience compared to your competitors. Metro Bank's points of difference focused on being open on Sundays, providing water bowls for dogs and being customer service-centric, which converged on positioning around convenience. Points of difference for Sunseeker and Princess focus on the type of yachting experiences they deliver. Sunseeker is confident and bold whilst Princess offers a more understated and refined experience: points that are evident from their respective motorboat show stands.

Whether you are building a new brand or repositioning an existing brand, it's important to sequence points of parity and difference. Lots of brands shout about points of difference before they establish points of parity. This can be problematic, because your target customer may not know what you're different to if the competitive frame of reference is unclear. At the iPod launch, Steve Jobs outlined how it would help people carry their whole CD collection on the move. In a single sentence, he communicated points of parity ('it's kind of like a portable CD player') and difference ('you can carry your whole music collection on the move') which helped customers get a key job done ('have all your music with you when you want it'). This helped potential customers consider the iPod in the context of competitive brands in one swoop.

Dr Sally McKechnie's Expert Insight outlines how Range Rover uses experiences to support its premium positioning, whilst Junman Jia shares her Expert Insight on the type of experiences the British Council delivers to support its 'British' positioning in China.

EXPERT INSIGHT 11.1 How experiences strengthen Land Rover's positioning

Dr Sally McKechnie, Associate Professor in Marketing, Nottingham University Business School, United Kingdom

Land Rover is an iconic British brand which was first produced in 1948 by the Rover Company as an all-terrain vehicle 'for the farmer, the countryman and general industrial use'. 1970 marked a radical departure for the brand when its owner, the British Leyland Motor Corporation, created the 'Sports Utility Vehicle' (SUV) market with the introduction of Range Rover.

In the UK's competitive SUV market, which accounted for one-fifth of 2.7 million new car registrations in 2016,[2] experiences play a pivotal role in strengthening Land Rover's premium positioning. These include:

- enhancing the premium 'feel' of the showroom experience through an augmented reality campaign so customers could explore features of the new Discovery Sport before its launch in 2014;

- opening a Jaguar Land Rover (JLR) retail store in 2016 in a London shopping centre;

- operating 30 Land Rover Experience Centres worldwide, which offer individual and group experience drives;

- launching Land Rover Adventure Travel in 2014, which offers tours and expeditions over challenging terrain;

- running guided factory tours, which give visitors first-hand insights into the state-of-the-art manufacturing process.

With JLR's long-term vision being 'to put our customers first and deliver for them experiences they love, for life', the outlook is promising for the iconic Land Rover brand, which has remained true to its slogan of going 'above and beyond' through the experiences it delivers.

Nottingham University Business School is part of the University of Nottingham, which is ranked in the top 1 per cent of universities worldwide, and has an unrivalled global reach through its campuses in the UK, China and Malaysia.

EXPERT INSIGHT 11.2   How brand experiences support the British Council's positioning in China

Junman Jia, Marketing Officer, British Council, China

In China, the vision of the British Council is for the UK to be China's partner of choice for English language, education, arts and culture. The British Council also aims to create international opportunities and build connectivity for the people of the UK and China. To showcase the UK as a tourist destination, to invite more people to access British culture and to make the intangible British experience tangible, the British Council have launched several culture and education campaigns to create links between the British and Chinese people.

From the art and cultural aspect, the 'Shakespeare Lives' campaign was launched in 2016 to celebrate Shakespeare's work in the 400th anniversary year of his death. A key part of this experience involved inviting Sir Ian McKellen, who is recognized as one of the greatest Shakespearean actors, to Shanghai to meet his fans in China, with his whole journey being broadcast live on social media. Sir Ian McKellen's visit brought Shakespeare-mania to China and this campaign received high acclaim on social media.

From the educational aspect, to inspire the young generation to have some perspective about the innovation and education of Britain, the Red Arrows, officially known as the Royal Air Force Aerobatic Team and the public face of the Royal Air Force, delivered an exclusive 'Smart Talk' in Beijing. Three pilots and two engineers discussed the story behind the Red Arrows – from their day-to-day work to what it takes to join. Their talk shed light on their educational background in the UK and the cutting-edge British technology that supports the team's displays. Their engaging presentation attracted STEM (science, technology, engineering and mathematics) students, trainee pilots, and technology enthusiasts and professionals from across China.

Both campaigns were delivered under the GREAT campaign. This acts as an overarching communication strategy of the British Embassy for the UK and encompasses other campaigns such as 'Education is GREAT', 'Innovation is GREAT', and 'Film is GREAT'. This ensures a diverse range of messages are delivered to support positioning of the British brand in China via a range of experiences in a consistent and coordinated way.

The British Council is the UK's international organization for cultural relations and educational opportunities.

Defining your competitors

To position your brand you need to define your competitors. Competitors should be defined based on the jobs a stakeholder wants to get done rather than just on the category in which you compete.[3] This gives you a broader and more realistic perspective on existing and potential competitors. Years ago, I spoke at a conference and a representative from a famous motorbike brand spoke before me. They outlined how their competitors are not just other motorcycle brands but companies that make conservatories and sell world cruises because these brands compete for the same customers' cash. A deafening silence ensued as the simplicity of this comment sank it.

Kodak is the classic example of a brand that would have benefitted from considering competitors through a 'jobs to be done', not a category lens. Kodak thought they were in the photographic film business, so they focused their competitive efforts on brands like Fuji Film. The company didn't appreciate that the job they helped target customers get done was to capture and share memories. Mobile phones incorporated cameras, and the rest is history. If Kodak had adopted a 'jobs to be done' mentality, they may have seen this change coming and rethought their brand positioning accordingly. Instead they restricted their thinking by focusing on the product category. This was the means to the end, and not the end that people wanted. Kodak is not alone. Xerox, Lucent and Atari were once powerful brands whose category focus hindered their ability to see new competitors coming.

I recall discussing mobile telephony over a game of table football with someone from IT in 2001. They mentioned Skype and the advent of Voice over Internet Protocol (VoIP) technology. From that moment, I knew the days of money pouring into mobile phone brands were numbered. International roaming was no longer required as you could speak for free from anywhere in the world, as long as you had an Internet connection. Fast-forward 17 years, and we now have a tranche of VoIP applications, and brands like WhatsApp, Line and WeChat have put a huge dent in mobile operators' revenues. These are not traditional mobile operators but technology brands that help customers get the same job done – to communicate – via alternative means.

More recently the likes of AliPay, a spin-off of Chinese online marketplace AliBaba, are providing payment solutions in a similar manner to PayPal. Traditionally this would be the preserve of banks. Not anymore. Facebook's Watch will look to challenge established channels like the BBC, CBS or ESPN in addition to Netflix and Amazon Prime Video, whilst also eyeing up a slice of the online video cake from Google-owned YouTube. If you focus on the category or channel, not the job a stakeholder is trying to get done, new and powerful competitors can emerge from adjacent industries and snatch revenues from under your nose.

Wavelength worked with a boutique hotel brand with properties located across Europe. Their target market was the frequent business traveller who could just about cope with corporate life from 9–5 but needed a break after that. These travellers didn't enjoy the stuffy and staid experience most hotels offer. These 'hipsters' craved authentic urban underground experiences where they could connect with like-minded people whilst away from home. A category-based approach to positioning would have focused their competitive frame of reference purely on hotels and sucked the brand into functional and feature-based competition such as pillow choice, free WiFi and gym facilities. Once the client understood the jobs the target customer wanted to get done, a different approach to building and positioning their experience followed. The jobs the target customer wanted to get done included disconnecting from the corporate grind during the evening whilst on business trips, escaping mainstream city experiences, feeling plugged into the local underground community, and demonstrating to friends that they're in the know.

Based on this insight, the hotel brand partnered with local brands that blended with the overall experience and could help customers get these jobs done. Local designers held fashion shows in the bar, and up-and-coming DJs pumped house music through the hotel's sound system. This was a magnet for local hipsters that were in the know. Bringing these experiences to the hotel ensured guests stayed in, and spent their cash at the hotel, rather than elsewhere. Adopting a 'jobs to be done' approach helped this hotel craft highly engaging experiences that delivered relevant points of difference that their discerning, underground, yet affluent target customer craved. These insights fed into their positioning statement.

How to write a positioning statement

Table 11.2 is an example of a positioning statement from the boutique hotel brand Wavelength worked with. It focuses on target market, jobs to be done, key benefits and reasons to believe. Most managers and executives would include a 'category' but my advice would be to trade this for 'jobs to be done' for the reasons outlined above.

The aim is to help your target market get jobs done, via benefits you deliver, as demonstrated through reasons to believe. For example, one key job for this hotel's target customer is to switch off from the corporate grind during the evening when working away from home. This is achieved by being able to chill out, recharge and be yourself during the evening. The fact that 75 per cent of guests said they felt like they could switch off from work in the evening gives us reason to believe the hotel is helping its customers get this job done.

Table 11.2   Brand positioning statement template

Positioning statement component	Template language	Illustrative example from the hotel sector (Wavelength client)
Target market	For...	Young, upwardly mobile, cosmopolitan, corporate business travellers.
Brand name	(brand name)	The Hipster's Hotel (fictitious brand name)
'Job to be done'[a]	Helps you...	1 Disconnect from the corporate grind during the evening whilst on business trips 2 Escape predictable, mainstream city experiences 3 Feel plugged in to a local, underground community 4 Demonstrate you're in the know to friends.
Benefit	Which means that you can...	1 Chill out, recharge and be yourself in the evening 2 Get a 'real' feel for the city's scene and people 3 Connect with like-minded people involved with local scenes 4 Impress your friends when you go back home

(continued)

Table 11.2 (*Continued*)

Positioning statement component	Template language	Illustrative example from the hotel sector (Wavelength client)
Reason to believe	*Because*	1 75 per cent of guests said they felt like they could switch off from work in the evening 2 80 per cent of guests said the experiences delivered felt authentic, eg the local up-and-coming DJs spinning underground house, shows for local designers and displaying local urban art and fashion 3 60 per cent of guests stay in touch with people they met in our hotel due to a common interest 4 75 per cent of guests would bring a friend/partner back to the hotel for a city break

a If you would like to refresh your memory on how to identify jobs to be done, please revisit Chapter 3, Helping stakeholders get 'jobs done'

Conclusion

It's advisable to frame your market, competitors and so positioning around the jobs your stakeholders need to get done – whilst keeping a close eye on your traditional competitors at the same time, for good measure. Doing this will give you a broader, more comprehensive view of your competitive landscape. It will also help you better anticipate and identify potential competitors who may emerge from new or adjacent markets, and to think through how to position your brand experiences in more competitively relevant and resilient ways.

Adopting this 'jobs based' perspective contrasts sharply with the restrictive category-based approach most brands employ. This approach prevents them from seeing what competitive threats or opportunities may lie on, or just beyond, the horizon. As technical innovations disrupt markets and blur the lines between classical category or channel-based competition, adopting a 'jobs based' perspective will become increasingly important.

This chapter is accompanied by Toolkit 11.1.

Endnotes

1 Keller, K L (2012) *Strategic Brand Management: Building, measuring and managing brand equity*, Pearson

2 Mintel (2017) UK Car Review Report; SMMT (2017) UK new car market achieves record 2.69 million registrations in 2016 with fifth year of growth [online] http://bit.ly/wavelength-UK-cars

3 Wunker, S, Wattman, J and Farber, D (2016) *Jobs to Be Done: A roadmap for customer-centred innovation*, AMACOM

Brand personality

12

In Chapter 11, I established the role brand positioning plays in building brand experiences and emphasized the benefits of adopting a 'jobs' rather than category-based approach to positioning your brand experiences. This chapter outlines what brand personality is, why you need to give your brand a personality, and the pros and cons of your brand personality being embodied by a real person. Understanding brand personality will help you appreciate how to make the experiences more emotionally relevant by tapping into peoples' natural tendency to make non-living things living. As with the other Brand Experience Enablers you need to consider your brand personality in the context of the Brand Experience Environment. Thinking about answers to the illustrative questions in Table 12.1 as you read through this chapter will help you connect the two,

What is brand personality?

Brand personality infuses a brand with human characteristics. This could include where they go for dinner, what music they like, interests, shopping habits, social hangouts, their story and values to name a few. A picture will soon emerge of 'who' your brand is via its personality and whether it is sensitive (Dove), daring (Red Bull) or dependable (IBM).

> 'Warby Parker is the person you want to sit next to at a dinner party. They are funny and smart, and they get up to do the dishes.'
>
> Molly Young, Director of Copy, Warby Parker[1]

Table 12.1 Connecting brand personality and the Brand Experience Environment: questions to ask yourself

Connecting your brand personality with the brand experience environment

Understanding your stakeholders

Profiling stakeholders	• How do we use our personality to help our stakeholders identify with our brand in ways that are relevant to them?
Helping stakeholders get 'jobs done'	• In what ways does our personality help our stakeholders get jobs done, eg demonstrate membership of a relevant group?
Encouraging stakeholder engagement	• How do we use our personality to encourage stakeholders to engage with our brand experiences?
Managing stakeholder expectations	• To what extent is our personality a fair reflection of who we really are or are working towards becoming?

Fine-tuning your perspective

Embracing transparency	• If our brand was a person, to what extent would it conduct itself in an open and transparent way, with integrity?
Adopting a holistic mindset	• To what extent does everyone in our organization understand the role they play in bringing our brand personality to life?
Competing primarily through value not price	• Which traits associated with our personality help us compete primarily through value rather than price?
Having patience	• Which of our stakeholders will identify with our personality in the future?
Accepting a loss of control	• What steps do we take to work with 'influencers' who embody our personality?

Considering the mechanics of delivery

Creating an emotional connection	• How do we use our personality to help us create the emotional connection we want to make with our stakeholders?
Facilitating co-creation	• In what ways does our brand personality actively encourage co-creation?
Delivering omnichannel experiences	• How do we express our personality across all channels?

(continued)

Table 12.1 (*Continued*)

Connecting your brand personality with the brand experience environment	
Adopting a data-driven approach	
Obtaining robust insights	• How do we obtain insights that help us understand if our personality is perceived as more or less relevant to certain stakeholder groups?
Measuring holistically	• To what extent is our personality interpreted in the same way by employees, customers and other stakeholders?

To reinvigorate their brand, Direct Line Insurance hired Harvey Keitel and created a fictional gangland 'fixer' called Winston Wolf who would rescue customers in distress – just as Direct Line would do. The campaign returned an estimated £1.22 of net profit for every £1 invested, so highlighting personality clearly resonated with customers.[2]

High-end yoga and fitness brand lululemon engages yoga teachers and fitness trainers who are considered relevant brand ambassadors because they embody the brand's values and lifestyle. These ambassadors deliver classes at shops and share photos of themselves wearing the brand. This provides the brand with advertising exposure that's perceived by the lululemon target audience as aspirational, yet authentic and credible.

As part of a broader brand experiences project, one of Wavelength's education-sector clients wanted to understand its brand personality profile and how relevant it was to three clearly defined stakeholder groups: current students, prospective students and employees.[3] Using a brand personality scale[4] we measured their personality traits across the three groups. Figure 12.1 shows how, broadly speaking, the three groups perceived the brand in a similar way, with the exception of employees who didn't think the brand was 'upper class'. The data implied alignment. Usually, this is good news. The problem was that this is was a youth brand; it needed to be daring, cool, imaginative and contemporary to hold relevance. For the most part, these were not the salient traits associated with the brand. This insight fed into subsequent brand experience strategy work.

Figure 12.1   Brand personality measurement – Wavelength Marketing client example

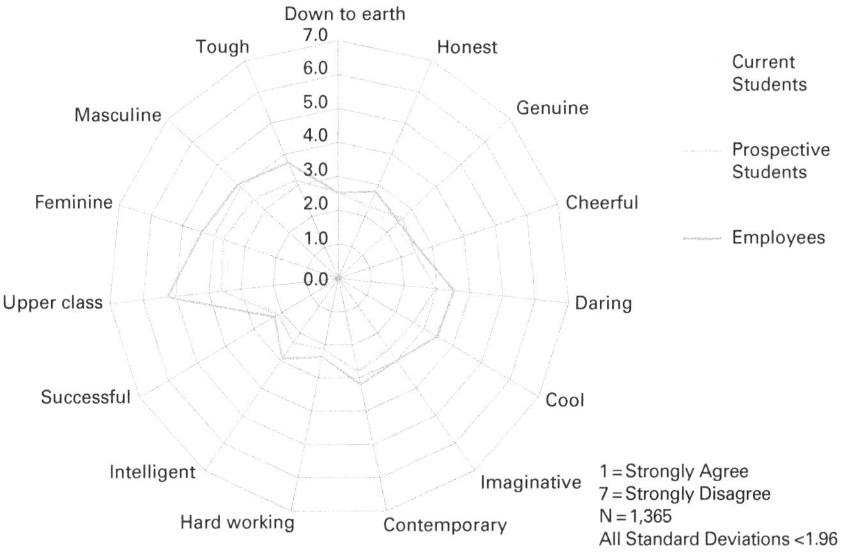

Labels around radar chart: Down to earth, Honest, Genuine, Cheerful, Daring, Cool, Imaginative, Contemporary, Hard working, Intelligent, Successful, Upper class, Feminine, Masculine, Tough

Scale: 0.0, 1.0, 2.0, 3.0, 4.0, 5.0, 6.0, 7.0

Legend:
Current Students
Prospective Students
Employees

1 = Strongly Agree
7 = Strongly Disagree
N = 1,365
All Standard Deviations <1.96

SOURCE Wavelength Marketing project (in partnership with Traffic Marketing & Communications Ltd)

Why give brands a personality?

Giving a brand a personality capitalizes on peoples' natural tendency to ascribe human characteristics to inanimate objects. This process is called 'anthropomorphism' and is important because infusing the brand with personality enables people to relate at an emotional level to organizations, goods, services and experiences associated with the brand. The VW Beetle, Herbie, is a classic brand personality. It wasn't the car that stole hearts around the world; it was Herbie's loyal, cheeky and fun-loving character which created an emotional wrapper around the car and drew people in.

Brand personality delivers self-expressive value. From prehistoric times, people have used symbols to express themselves. Hunters wore the fur of an animal they'd killed to showcase their hunting prowess. Fast-forward a few thousand years and similar principles apply. Eating at the world's finest restaurants says you're discerning, sophisticated and refined. Having a large investment bank manage your stock market floatation implies you're a substantial firm. Drinking beer from your local microbrewery shows you care about local business, your community and are a beer buff.

People are complex and multifaceted. We have, to varying extents, different personalities or 'selves' we express through the brands (or absence of brands) we associate ourselves with in particular contexts.[5] This could be our:

- 'actual self' (a no-frills executive who stays at the Holiday Inn);
- 'ideal self' (sophisticated executive who stays at the Mövenpick);
- 'social self' (an easy-going person who stays at a family-run beachside bungalow);
- 'ideal social self' (sophisticated socialite who stays at the J W Marriott so they can sip cocktails with the city's social set at the rooftop club).

Depending on the situation, we use a brand's personality to make a statement about who we are or who we would like to be perceived as being. This has powerful brand experience-building implications and means you need to think from the stakeholder perspective: 'What does being associated with this brand say about me?'

Research shows brands that help customers express their social and personal identity enjoy stronger brand performance.[6] Such brands have 'social currency' and their customers are, on average, 27 per cent more likely to choose that brand and 19 per cent more willing to pay a price premium because of the social and personal expressive value the brand delivers. Other research lends support to the role played by brands as social currency with respect to how we assess others and vice versa.[7]

A clearly understood and articulated brand personality will also help you manage external agencies more effectively. Let's say you profile your brand and it's George Clooney: mature, sophisticated and stylish. When you brief your agencies and share your brand values, essence, promise and positioning, sometimes the subsequent use of behaviour, communications or design can go wrong because words can be interpreted differently (so please use the Toolkits alongside this book!). If you also state that your brand's personality is like George Clooney, it's another way you can convey your Brand Experience Essentials in a more tangible, concrete and accessible manner that helps minimize the chance of misunderstanding.

Can a brand personality be a real person or mascot?

A brand personality can be based on a person (real or fictional) or a mascot. Irrespective of which you choose, the logic outlined previously underpins their use.

Some brands use real people to personify their brand because they want to benefit from the person's favourable brand associations or 'equity'. For example, Emirates and Etihad enlisted Jennifer Aniston and Nicole Kidman respectively as brand ambassadors. The goal was for these cosmopolitan and sophisticated stars to cast a halo effect on the brands. The Mandarin Oriental has used celebrities like Lucy Liu to reinforce the brand's oriental roots with international undertones, whilst L'Oréal Paris employed Helen Mirren to front their 'The Perfect Age' campaign for their Age Perfect anti-ageing moisturizer. Walkers Crisps has a long-running relationship with ex-England footballer Gary Lineker. He was born in Leicester and played for Leicester City FC, which ties in perfectly with the brand's Leicester-based roots. In her Expert Insight, Ayşegül Yazıcı outlines how Turkish airlines used a social media-driven approach with two international sporting celebrities to raise awareness of the brand's global footprint.

EXPERT INSIGHT 12.1 How Turkish Airlines uses social media and sports stars to build engaging brand experiences

Ayşegül Yazıcı, Online Regional Marketing Specialist, Turkish Airlines

To successfully integrate digital channels into the overall brand experience, marketers need to understand which channels and what type of content perform. According to a McKinsey (2014) report,[8] over the next five years, digital advertising will be the fastest-growing advertising segment, with projected compound annual increases to 2018 of 15.1 per cent, compared with 5 per cent for TV (including advertising, out-of-home advertising and cinema). Turkish Airlines appreciates the importance of understanding which channels perform and deliver business impact when planning integrated digital marketing campaigns.

In 2013, Turkish Airlines launched its 'Widen Your World' campaign. This showcased how Turkish Airlines flies to more countries than any other carrier in the world. The company decided to use the sports stars Kobe Bryant and Lionel Messi as brand ambassadors in the advertising. The TV ads feature Bryant and Messi competing to take the most exotic selfie, using Turkish Airlines as their means of transport (see Figure 12.2). The purpose was to increase brand awareness in Europe, North America, the Middle East and the Far East, and use personalities that have target market appeal. Also, 'selfie' was the most searched word in 2013, so Turkish Airlines wanted to capitalize on that development in an interactive way by using YouTube as a channel.

Figure 12.2 Turkish Airlines used famous personalities (Lionel Messi and Kobe Bryant) to raise awareness of its global footprint

Turkish Airlines wanted to migrate people from TV to digital to deliver a more engaging and relevant experience to the target customers (aged 18–34 years, ie Millennials). This target group is more focused on digital media than TV so Turkish Airlines wanted to build brand experiences using channels that were relevant to them, with YouTube being a priority.

The 'Widen Your World' campaign delivered outstanding performance: 9 per cent increase in global brand recall; 77 million views in the first week; YouTube brand searches for Turkish Airlines tripled; and Google global brand searches increased by 16 per cent. This was a watershed moment for Turkish Airlines and now social media plays a central part in the brand experiences we deliver.

Turkish Airlines is the national flag-carrier airline of Turkey, flying to more countries than any other airline in the world.

Note: Turkish Airlines' agreements with Bryant and Messi were between 2010–14 and 2012–15 respectively.

When selecting celebrities to convey their brand personalities, brands need to think carefully. Barclays' use of Samuel L Jackson in their brand communications was disastrous due to the colourful language Jackson was using in films at that time. Such brand associations did not sit well with Barclays' core customers. The Malaysian Government banned a Toyota advertisement that used Brad Pitt[9] because some members of the Malaysian government felt using a Caucasian and not Asian face could foster a sense of inferiority amongst locals. The use of a celebrity being closely associated with one brand could mean the other brands enjoy the fruits of your work. Alternatively, if the celebrity works with several brands this could dilute brand associations, so more brand spend will be required to obtain the unique associations you require.

An alternative to personifying your brand through a celebrity is to find a person who creates desired brand associations and embodies relevant values. Olay, Capitol Records and Mode partnered on several videos that featured Capitol Records COO Michelle Jubelirer, who was perceived as highly relevant to Olay's target customer. Jubelirer is a powerful music industry executive and a role model for young mothers because she finds time to look and feel great while balancing these two demanding roles. Addressing these challenges through someone like Jubelirer speaks to Olay's target customers, who identify with the challenges of being a mother and career woman. The video series, which featured Olay products, yielded 10 million views in two weeks. The Singapore Airlines flight attendant represents another example. She conveys timeless grace, sophistication and style, which sit perfectly with the broader brand experience. In the UK, Oxo (whose stock cubes are used to make gravy and other sauces) created a fictitious family which it showed enjoying a Sunday roast with lashings of Oxo gravy. The family wasn't real but the situation was. This provided the basis for relevant identification. An increasing number of brands are using social media influencers (who may not be celebrities) with highly engaged communities to reach their audiences, the reason being that people feel closer to an influencer than a celebrity.[10] This approach resonates particularly well with the Millennial generation and Gen Z, who perceive it as being more authentic.

Brands also choose to create fictional characters in the form of brand mascots, where the emotional element of the brand can be conveyed through the personality to provide a meaningful point of difference. This turns these fictitious characters into valuable brand assets. The Michelin Man and Duracell Bunny represent durability. Betty Crocker is homely, nurturing and motherly, signalling a caring and comforting brand. Churchill Insurance's dog isn't just any dog; he's a British bulldog. This breed was favoured by Britain's wartime Prime Minister, Winston Churchill, and the breed is regarded as embodying characteristics of reliability, strength and loyalty. Exactly what you want in an insurance company.

Figure 12.3   Developing Wavey, Wavelength Marketing's brand mascot

Using a fictional personality promotes longevity. The personality can prove a powerful brand asset that lasts years, or even decades. Ronald McDonald, Captain Birdseye and the face of Quaker Oats provide examples of personalities that have taken on almost mythic status and have woven themselves into the fabric of society in ways celebrities cannot. The use of such personalities can also play an important role in delivering tailored yet consistent brand experiences around the globe and for decades. For example, Ronald McDonald greets guests in Thailand with a slight bow and hands joined in prayer to say 'sà wàt dii' (hello). At Wavelength we worked closely with illustrator Claudio Naccari to create 'Wavey' (Figure 12.3). He's a brand man who makes serious brand points, in a slightly light-hearted way (Figure 12.4).

Conclusion

Giving your brand a personality entails infusing it with human characteristics related to lifestyle, interests, values, story and more. Doing this capitalizes on people's tendency to ascribe human characteristics to inanimate objects. Brand personality helps stakeholders connect with the brand at an emotional level, which is critical because emotion is the primary driver of choice (see Chapter 4).

When building brand experiences, you may wish to create a mascot or, budget permitting, work with a celebrity or another individual (real or

Figure 12.4 Wavey delivering brand messages

Millennials are important. Empathise and engage with them.

You're no longer in control of how your brand is perceived, dude.

Give customers the tools they need to co-create brand experiences with you.

Make your brand multisensory so it becomes more memorable.

Never over promise and under deliver. Fatal brand marketing mistake.

Be guided by your brand essence when taking new products to market.

Build transparent brands. Social means there's nowhere to hide now.

Give customers the tools they need to co-create brand experiences with you.

fictitious). Irrespective of the approach you follow, the key is to use or create a personality that embodies your brand and has traits your stakeholders will identify with. That way, your brand will be perceived as relevant and your stakeholders will be keen to be associated with it.

This chapter is accompanied by Toolkit 12.1.

Endnotes

1 Hoflin, S (2017) Building brands: a conversation with Molly Young at Warby Parker, *Percolate*, 25 May [online] http://bit.ly/wavelength-warby-parker

2 IPA Effectiveness Awards Case Study (2016) Direct Line: We solve problems [online] http://bit.ly/wavelength-direct-line

3 This project was delivered in partnership with Birmingham-based agency Traffic Marketing & Communications Ltd, http://www.thisistraffic.co

4 Measurements were primarily based on Aaker, J L (1997) Dimensions of brand personality, *Journal of Market Research*, **34** (August), pp 347–56

5 Belk, R (1988) Possessions and the extended self, *Journal of Consumer Research*, **15**, pp 139–68

6 Vivaldi Partners (2016) Business transformation through greater customer-centricity, the power of social currency [online] http://bit.ly/wavelength-social-currency

7 Santos, J P, Seixas, D, Brandão, S and Moutinho, L (2012) Neuroscience in branding: a functional magnetic resonance imaging study on brands' implicit and explicit impressions, *Journal of Brand* Management, **19** (9), pp 735–578

8 McKinsey & Company (2014) *Global Media Report: Global industry overview*

9 Campaign Live (2002) Brad Pitt spot for Toyota banned in Malaysia, 16 December 16 [online] http://bit.ly/wavelength-toyota-malaysia

10 Dwivedi, A, McDonald, B and Johnson, L W (2014) The impact of a celebrity endorser's credibility on consumer self-brand connection and brand evaluation, *Journal of Brand Management*, **21** (7–8), pp 559–78

Summary: 13
Brand Experience
Environment
and Essentials

The first part of this book introduced the Brand Experience Environment. This is the broader context you need to be mindful of when developing and defining your Brand Experience Essentials. The Brand Experience Environment is made up of four elements:

- **Understanding your stakeholders**: profiling stakeholders; helping stakeholders get 'jobs done'; encouraging stakeholder engagement; managing stakeholder expectations.

- **Fine-tuning your perspective**: embracing transparency; adopting a holistic mindset; competing primarily through value not price; having patience; accepting a loss of control.

- **Considering the mechanics of delivery**: creating an emotional connection; facilitating co-creation; delivering omnichannel experiences.

- **Adopting a data-driven approach**: obtaining robust insights; measuring holistically.

Taking the time to consider how these elements interact with your Brand Experience Essentials is time well spent because it will increase the relevance of those Brand Experience Essentials, introduced in the second part of the book:

- **Brand values**: how would you describe your brand in four or five words?

- **Brand essence**: if you were asked to sum up your brand in two or three words, what would you say it's all about?

- **Brand promise**: what benefits, NOT features, does your brand deliver?

- **Brand positioning:** How are you different from your competitors?
- **Brand personality:** If you were to describe your brand as a person, who would they be?

The Brand Experience Essentials are the foundations upon which your brand experiences will be built. They also:

- focus your mind on the substance and not trappings of building brand experiences;
- help scale and accelerate the pace of your brand experience-building efforts;
- facilitate the more relevant use of Brand Experience Enablers because they are developed and defined within the Brand Experience Environment;
- provide an underlying logic you can call on when you bring your brand to life through Brand Experience Enablers (Part Three).

It's important to embrace a holistic approach to defining and developing your Brand Experience Essentials so your brand experiences are shaped by robust and rounded thinking. There can be some overlap between the Brand Experience Essentials, so you may find the process becomes slightly repetitive.[1]

If this happens, don't worry. Within reason, this is a good sign; it shows your thinking is converging on a common logic. Having multiple prongs of attack decreases the chance of misinterpretation as you move from the intangible world of Brand Experience Essentials to the tangible world of Brand Experience Enablers.

Some managers and executives ask which of the five Brand Experience Essentials they should start with, but there is no set sequence because they are closely related.

You might start with your values, move to your essence and positioning, then refine your values before moving onto your promise then personality. Or you might find it easier to draw the personality then ask key questions relating to that personality. For example: 'How would you describe that person in four or five words?' (values); 'If you were asked to sum up this person in two or three words, what would you say they are all about?' (essence); 'How is that person different to (competitors' personality)?' (positioning); and 'What benefits does that person deliver?' (promise).

The approach I take with clients depends on their organization's sector, culture and comfort zone for creativity. Starting with a brand personality collage works well for creative and liberal thinkers. In a more formal and reserved organization, it's more effective to start with values, as the language may be more familiar. Either way, defining your Brand Experience Essentials is an iterative process; they will emerge as they are developed, refined and defined with the Brand Experience Environment in mind.

Irrespective of the approach adopted to defining your Brand Experience Essentials, the value of taking this iterative and holistic approach will become apparent when you start enabling your brand experiences through behaviour, communications and design.

Endnote

1 'Brand purpose' is growing in popularity in brand circles but I have reservations about the unique benefit it brings to the brand experience-building table. I felt it was important to acknowledge the debate so have shared my thoughts in a cautionary note at the end of the book.

PART THREE
Brand Experience Enablers

Figure P3.1 The Brand Experience Blueprint: time to focus on the Brand Experience Enablers

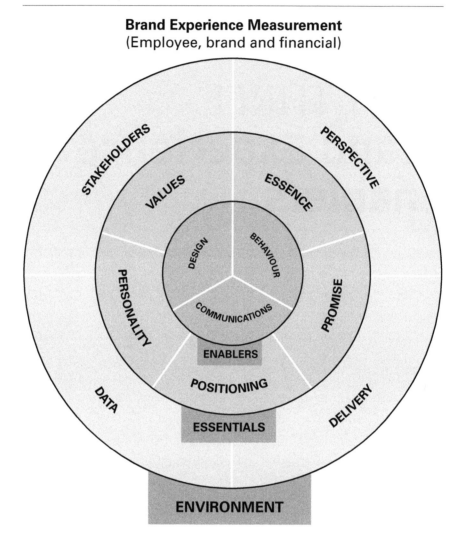

Brand Experience Measurement
(Employee, brand and financial)

Reading Part Three on Brand Experience Enablers will help you bring your Brand Experience Essentials to life through the use of:

- employee behaviour;
- design;
- communications.

As you read through Part Three you need to consider how you'll use Brand Experience Enablers to express your Brand Experience Essentials in practical ways. Table P3.1 details example questions that will help you connect the Brand Experience Environment and Brand Experience Enablers. This is an important table. It encourages you to think about building brand experiences in a deeper (Brand Experience Essentials) and broader (Brand Experience Enablers) way.

In a similar manner to the Brand Experience Environment and Brand Experience Essentials, connecting Brand Experience Essentials and Brand

Table P3.1 Connecting Brand Experience Essentials and Enablers: questions to ask yourself

	Behaviour	Communications	Design
	How can we:	How can we:	How can we:
Values	Recruit employees who will behave in ways that support our values?	Use social media to convey our values in engaging ways?	Use design to bring our values to life?
Essence	Induct/train employees so they understand what behaviour does and doesn't sit within the boundaries of our essence?	Use mobile to help us deliver personalized experiences that sit within the scope of our essence?	Harness design so we can build experiences that sit within the parameters of our essence?
Promise	Train all our employees so they understand the role they play in delivering brand experience-related benefits?	Use gamification to convey some of the benefits our experiences have the potential to deliver in interactive ways?	Use design to help us deliver relevant brand experience-related benefits?
Positioning	Recognize and reward (financially/non-financially) employees whose behaviour aligns with our desired positioning?	Craft internal communications so that they align our employees with our positioning?	Employ design to support our positioning?
Personality	Conduct exit interviews in ways that reflect our personality?	Involve our community in conversations that help us to express our personality?	Express our personality through design?

Experience Enablers is not a tick-box exercise. It may be that you can't think of a way to convey your brand essence through behaviour. Whilst this is unlikely, don't worry. You should be able to compensate for this by using design or communications. Think of the Brand Experience Essentials and Enablers table as a suit that you tailor so it's a good fit for you, rather than vice versa.

Table P3.2 provides an example of how a natural park could connect Brand Experience Essentials and Brand Experience Enablers:

- **Brand values**: intrepid, insightful, family-orientated and conscientious (the example focuses on being intrepid but you should complete the same exercise for the other values).
- **Brand promise**: helping kids get closer to nature, learn how to respect nature, enhance their knowledge of nature, build confidence to explore nature independently, educate those around them about nature and learn how to become more resourceful, eg recycle rainwater (the example focuses on helping kids get closer to nature).
- **Brand essence**: natural educational adventures.
- **Brand positioning**: adventure-loving/eco-friendly community.
- **Brand personality**: an intrepid adventurer with an inquisitive mind who loves the natural world.

Please note how the values are unique, specific, active, deliberate and balanced whilst the Brand Experience Enablers work together in a holistic way.

As you read Table P3.2 you may notice some overlap between Enablers. For example, a GPS-enabled app straddles communications and design, whilst staff encouraging guests to explore the park relates to behaviour and communications. This overlap, within reason, is a good thing. It demonstrates that your thinking is joined up and this will facilitate the delivery of more cohesive and consistent brand experiences.

Table P3.2 Connecting Brand Experience Essentials and Enablers: place brand example

	Employee behaviour	Communications	Design
Value Intrepid	Train employees so they have the skills and confidence to encourage guests to explore and learn about nature for themselves.	Use stories to show how other families have had a real adventure while discovering the natural wonders of the park.	• Branded environments that activate your senses, eg inspiring picture of a vast wilderness, touch certain leaves, smell wild flowers, taste wild food grown at the park. It should feel like an adventure: a voyage of discovery. • Locate discrete multimedia kiosks designed with families in mind that provide information which encourages exploration and discovery in the park.
Essence Natural educational adventures	Recruit knowledgeable employees who can explain complex elements of nature in a simple yet engaging way, eg use metaphors or non-complex language.	Informative and encouraging language/tone of voice.	• Play music at the visitor centre that encourages/inspires people to explore (almost like Indiana Jones). • Map out various customer journeys based on use cases, eg young family, school visits etc, that aim to deliver natural educational adventures.
Promise Get closer to nature	During the induction stress the importance of showing kids how to observe animals so as not to cause distress.	YouTube/Instagram content which shows guests getting up close to animals and plants so they can learn about them.	• Audio/video outlining how to observe animals so you can learn more about how they interact with each other. • Storyboard showing the evolution of various species you are interacting with in their natural habitat to provide context and additional insights.

(continued)

Table P3.2 (*Continued*)

	Employee behaviour	Communications	Design
Positioning Adventure loving/ eco-friendly community	Recruit people who can demonstrate a genuine love of adventure and the natural world.	Connect with guests on social media and invite them to be part of your community and share news and views on adventure/eco topics.	• Simple earth colours (greens, browns). • Wrap food in recyclable/recycled paper. • Open green spaces that encourage visitors to socialize and interact with each other.
Personality An intrepid adventurer with an inquisitive mind who has a love of the natural world	Reward employees who behave in ways that support the brand personality, eg keen to show kids/their parents his/her latest discoveries in the park to inspire them to explore further.	The park mascot walks around the park and encourages kids to explore nature for themselves: 'Why not go and take a look with your Mum and Dad? It's awesome. You'll love it!'	• Dress the brand mascot as an intrepid traveller who loves nature and adventure, eg boots, water flask, back pack over their shoulder etc. • A GPS-based mobile application where a virtual brand mascot escorts you around the park prompting you to discover then answer questions as part of an interactive quiz.

Behaviour 14

This chapter highlights the important but often overlooked role employees play in building brand experiences. In the opening section, I outline the important part your human resources colleagues play in building brand experiences. I then detail how HR processes such as recruitment, induction, training, appraisal, reward and exit interviews can help you to enable your Brand Experience Essentials. Reading this chapter will help you understand why you should work closely with HR colleagues and how, in practical terms, you can do this so employee behaviour can bring your Brand Experience Essentials to life.

While reading this chapter it's important you connect the Brand Experience Essentials with behaviour. Reflecting on possible answers to the illustrative questions in Table 14.1 will help you do that.

Table 14.1 Connecting employee behaviour and the Brand Experience Essentials: questions to ask yourself

	How can we:
Values	Recruit employees who will behave in ways that support our values?
Essence	Induct/train employees so they understand what behaviour does and doesn't sit within the boundaries of our essence?
Promise	Train all our employees so they understand the role they play in delivering brand experience-related benefits?
Positioning	Recognize and reward (financially/non-financially) employees whose behaviour aligns with our desired positioning?
Personality	Conduct exit interviews in ways that reflect our personality?

'You can design and create and build the most wonderful place in the world. But it takes people to make the dream a reality.'

Walt Disney[1]

Employee behaviour and brand experiences

Research shows that companies with a highly engaged workforce outperform their peers by 147 per cent in earnings per share,[2] whilst IBM's Institute for Business Value[3] found that customer experience financial 'outperformers'[4] make the employee experience (EX) a priority (Figure 14.1).

These statistics make sense. Employees have the ability to tailor a brand experience in line with your Brand Experience Essentials. Employees can also satisfy our desire to connect with other people in meaningful relationships and show empathy in ways that even the most advanced artificial intelligence cannot, at present. Bolstering the behavioural side of the brand experience is something big brands are paying more attention to. For example, as part of their omnichannel strategies, Amazon and Microsoft are investing in physical retail spaces to complement the digital side of their brand experiences.

The behavioural challenge associated with building brand experiences is a function of human nature. We are erratic, unpredictable and emotional. We have good days and bad days, and this makes delivering consistent experiences through employees challenging but not impossible. Brand marketers and human resources need to work closely together; this is something an increasing number of brands are starting to do. Beverage and brewing giant InBev actively recruits marketers into its HR function to help with recruitment via its employer brand. Dionne Ligoure's Expert Insight sheds light on the role played by human resources in helping Caribbean Airlines deliver an 'authentically Caribbean' experience.

Figure 14.1 The role of employee experience in brand experience performance (n = 600)

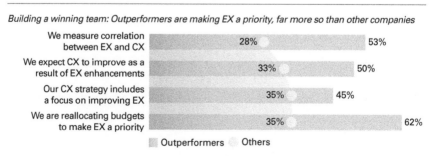

Building a winning team: Outperformers are making EX a priority, far more so than other companies

SOURCE IBM (2016)

EXPERT INSIGHT 14.1 How Caribbean Airlines delivers an
'authentically Caribbean' brand experience

Dionne Ligoure, Head of Corporate Communications, Caribbean Airlines Limited

The airline industry is competitive and dynamic. It is characterized by fierce competition, high costs and low margins, which means our brand experience is a key point of competitive advantage.

Caribbean Airlines is positioned as being 'authentically Caribbean'. The Caribbean theme is reflected in its catering, livery and uniforms, corporate colour scheme and service offerings. Caribbean culture is often associated with being laid back, friendly, warm, diverse and professional. Our brand positioning and Caribbean culture intersect to underpin our company's principles – we care, we connect, we create, we are the Caribbean. Everyone, from senior management to front-line employees, needs to know those principles and understand how they inform their day-to-day behaviour.

The professional conduct of Caribbean Airlines employees plays an important part in reinforcing 'Caribbean' brand associations, because every time they have contact with customers they represent the voice of our brand. Selecting employees who can naturally behave in ways which support this positioning is essential. For example, the airline's warm and friendly atmosphere can only be delivered if the employees are warm and friendly.

During recruitment at Caribbean Airlines all employees are put through an orientation that introduces them to our brand and outlines the role they will play in delivering it. Our Cabin Crew play a particularly important role in delivering our brand experience, so they are exposed to especially rigorous recruitment, orientation and annual refresher training. This training helps our Cabin Crew carry themselves and treat customers in a way that aligns with a brand experience that is intrinsically linked to Caribbean culture. Such human resource practices play an important role in helping Caribbean deliver a consistent brand experience which feels authentically Caribbean, and that lies at the heart of our success.

Caribbean Airlines operates more than 600 weekly flights to 18 destinations in the Caribbean and North and South America. Headquartered in Trinidad and Tobago and with an operational base in Jamaica, Caribbean Airlines employs more than 1,600 people.

Authors such as Kevin Keohane[5] and Denise Lee Yohn[6] outline how human resources departments are responsible for a number of activities that play a crucial role in building the employee experience, which ultimately feeds into the external brand experience. These include recruitment, induction, training, appraisal, reward and exit interviews.

Recruitment

'I think there's Apple values that Steve and Tim carry on and that's a big part of why everyone joins.'

Angela Ahrendts, Senior VP, Apple Retail[7]

Recruitment helps brands identify and assess the suitability of prospective employees based on their skills, experience and ability to behave in ways that will align with their Brand Experience Essentials. It's a critical but often overlooked part of the brand experience-building process.

The recruitment process brings your brand values into sharper focus. The brand values section of the Brand Experience Essentials showed how values are important because they influence beliefs, and beliefs are important because they influence behaviour. If an employee is aligned with your brand at a values level, this will translate into behaviour that supports your overall brand experience. I encourage you to remember that employee and brand alignment relates to the present and the future. It's not static. You need to employ people who are well placed to grow, develop and evolve in ways that support your brand's aspirations – or set the tone for what you want your brand to be.

Let me illustrate how values-based recruiting can work in practice. Wavelength was approached by a luxury resort that was encountering disappointing brand performance. The CMO outlined how they'd worked with a local agency to build a brand shaped by values of being relaxed, cosmopolitan, perceptive and customer-focused. The values sounded good to me, whilst their brand communications, website and, to an extent, social media conveyed these values well. Based on this initial conversation I couldn't understand the problem, so called to investigate further. The person who answered the phone was irritable, spoke poor English, kept interrupting and didn't listen to my questions. The problem became apparent. The person I spoke to was not aligned with the communications, website and social media. Whilst this may sound like an extreme example, it's surprisingly common for employee behaviour to disconnect with communications and design.

To address the problem, we worked closely with the CMO and head of HR on a number of HR initiatives. One workstream focused on the interview process. We advised the client to ask prospective employees some very specific questions during their interview.

For example, 'How would you describe yourself in four or five words?' The goal was to elicit words that were suitable approximations for their values. If the interviewee's response aligned reasonably well with the resort's brand values the interviewers asked a follow-up question. 'You said that you're X. Can you give me some examples of when you feel you've been X, please?' By using this action-based question the resort noticed suitable applicants started to shine through during the interview. They could recall relevant stories in detail that illustrated behaviours that supported the desired brand experience. It also helped the resort sift out candidates who may have conducted some online 'interview research' so they could regurgitate the 'correct' answer.

As a final check during the interview the applicant was asked, 'What would you do if…?' in the context of a practical or recurring issue resort staff often need to address. This could relate to a guest arriving too early for check-in, or a guest not having a credit card to pay at checkout or, for a senior manager, dealing with a sensitive or political matter within their team. This helped the management team understand if the applicant would be able to behave in the desired way in specific circumstances and so revealed whether they held relevant values.

A number of leading brands identify prospective employees' values in a range of ways. Southwest Airlines' recruitment process identifies people that embody three key attributes: a warrior spirit (a desire to excel, act with courage, persevere and innovate); a servant's heart (the ability to put others first, treat everyone with respect and serve customers proactively); and a fun-loving attitude (passion, joy and an aversion to taking oneself too seriously). If two equally qualified applicants make it to final selection, the person that aligns more closely with the company's values will land the job. The CEO of Charles Schwab Corporation, Walt Bettinger, takes prospective employees for breakfast as part of the interview process. What they don't realize is that their order will be intentionally incorrect.

The aim is to test the applicants' ability to deal with adversity. This is a key trait Bettinger looks for in prospective employees. As part of their recruitment process, Zappos asks five or six behavioural questions that indicate how aligned the potential employee is with Zappos' core values. Similarly, W Hotels (note W stands for Wow) expects interviewees to recount the times they have wowed people and outline how they can do that for W as well.

The importance of having values that are unique, specific, active, deliberate and balanced will become apparent during the interview. If you have values that meet these criteria, asking an interviewee, 'How would you describe yourself in four or five words?' will help you select employees who fit, and weed out those that don't. If your values are generic and poorly defined, most interviewees' responses will seem reasonable, as generic values provide greater scope for acceptable responses. Can you now see why having unique, specific, active, deliberate and balanced brand values is so important?

The purpose of recruitment is not restricted to finding employees who embody your brand values. It's important to understand and explore how well prospective employees align with your Brand Experience Essentials. If your brand essence is all about 'adrenaline-fuelled extreme fun', you need employees who naturally embody such characteristics; for example, they like extreme sports. If being dependable is central to your brand promise, you need to find employees you can count on, whilst if your brand positioning is associated with being funky and outgoing, you need to recruit employees whose natural disposition can support this.

One caveat: while it's important to recruit and retain employees who align with your brand's values, and other Brand Experience Essentials, that doesn't imply you should always strive to recruit in your own image. It's important that your workforce is made up of people from diverse backgrounds, who have had varied experiences and think in different ways. Research shows how 'companies with more diverse workforces perform better financially'.[8] Whilst diversity and inclusion don't fall within the scope of this book, they're too important not to warrant a mention.

In her Expert Insight, Kathleen Mullen outlines the role played by recruitment in helping GE attract appropriately skilled talent so it can evolve and develop its positioning as a digital industrial company.

EXPERT INSIGHT 14.2 How recruitment is helping GE retain relevance

Kathleen C Mullen, Commercial Leader, GE Energy Connections

GE's brand is one of the most recognized in the world. A company that has been in existence for 125 years, GE has evolved over the years but has stayed true to delivering state-of-the-art products and services with the principles of unyielding integrity, progress and optimism.

In recent years, GE has become known as the world's leading digital industrial company. All our businesses work together to deliver our brand promise as offerings under the GE brand. We are one GE. Our brand is evolving to express a GE that is transforming industry by connecting machines to data and to people to help our cities run more smoothly, aeroplanes take off and land safely, and hospitals provide integrated care for healthcare communities.

As we evolve to a more contemporary brand (digital industrial company) while respecting our heritage, maintaining our culture of delivering state-of-the-art products and solutions to solve some of the world's most difficult problems (for example, delivering affordable clean power to Third World countries), GE has opened a new location in San Ramon, CA to recruit 'Silicon Valley' talent. This new software division, the start of 'GE Digital', established a shop in Silicon Valley to lure top software talent from titans such as Apple and Cisco. This was the start of GE becoming recognized as a 'digital industrial company' that is doing some really cool things, transforming a historical industrial manufacturing giant into a forward-thinking technology company.

The challenging part is that GE is still a global industrial manufacturing giant that is integrating leading-edge software, cloud and edge offerings, AND connecting large industrial assets into a differentiated offering. To help with this challenge in attracting 'top Silicon talent', GE changed recruiting strategies, including launching a series of commercials to attract new technology talent and offering compensation packages that competed with the likes of Apple, Google, and Cisco. The commercials launched were directed to this new generation of software technology talent who want to know they are 'changing the world'. Today, GE has over 1,700 workers at the San Ramon location, where the offices have some of the design touches common to Silicon Valley workplaces: exposed ceiling mechanicals, table games, and communal kitchens. Other moves GE has made to lure top technology talent include the launch of 'Minds + Machines' and Transform, global events that take place in Silicon Valley and other locations around the world. These premier Industrial Internet events are focused on software, innovation, and helping GE's customers realize the most powerful digital industrial outcomes.

GE recently announced the move of its corporate headquarters from Fairfield, CT to Boston, MA. One of the key reasons for the move was to continue to attract technology talent. Boston is known as the 'Silicon Valley' of the east coast and GE regards attracting and retaining the best digital talent as a cornerstone of our strategy.

General Electric (GE) is a global diversified company that serves the power, oil and gas, industrial, transportation, aviation, and healthcare industries worldwide with locations in over 180 countries.

Finding and attracting the best talent is becoming a more complex task. Brands interact with prospective employees on a growing number of fronts as part of their employer branding work. To deliver a more consistent and co-ordinated recruitment experience, your efforts should be informed by your Brand Experience Essentials. Relevant touchpoints include your website or careers site, websites like Glassdoor, recruitment advertising (on- and offline), employee referral schemes, recruitment agencies, relationships with universities, and even candidate feedback, which can provide you with a steer on where your recruitment may be going wrong.

Social media plays an increasingly important role in recruitment. This could be via recognized recruitment channels like LinkedIn, or by sharing content that will interest and encourage prospective employees to engage with your Brand Experience Essentials. A number of brands are using Instagram to provide an inside view of what it's like to work at their organization. AT&T lets employees showcase for one day #LifeAtATT, whilst the Zappos feed shows how much fun employees have inside and outside the office, encouraging people to sign up for an office tour. Sour Patch Kids (a Mondelez brand) does Snapchat 'takeovers' where employees Snap their day, while Warby Parker create stories around their brand to give people a feel for the company in a fun and practical way.

The advent of artificial intelligence, which uses machine learning and algorithms to make decisions, cannot be ignored as part of the recruitment experience.[9] Advances in artificial intelligence mean brands like Unilever, Goldman Sachs, General Electric, Facebook and IBM are using algorithms to filter online applicants for interview. For initial stages of the recruitment process, AI is definitely one to watch.

Traditional siloed recruitment methods are being superseded by more integrated, sophisticated and subtle approaches. To win in this context, the smartest HR professionals are joining forces with their brand marketing counterparts to enhance recruitment through persuasive messages, relevant brand stories and other experiential activities that contribute to their employer brand.

Once employees have been recruited in line with your Brand Experience Essentials, the next stage is induction.

Induction

Induction helps new employees learn about their employer's policies, procedures, heritage, culture and brand. Luxury brand Hermès runs a three-day induction programme for all new employees called 'Inside the Orange Box'. This shares the company's origins, product development history and story. When employees realize they are a part of something with deep roots it can create a greater sense of organizational identification and pride. The effect can be quite inspiring.

Induction also provides an ideal opportunity to educate employees on the part they will play in enabling your Brand Experience Essentials. Depending on their function and level of seniority, there are a number of activities you could use during induction to engage new employees with your Brand Experience Essentials. You could ask new recruits to:

- **Recall your brand values.** A facilitated discussion could then tease out relevant behaviours associated with these to explore what the values mean in the context of their day-to-day job. It's a good idea to play it safe and let induction attendees know they will be asked this question, so they can come prepared.

- **Explore your brand essence.** Ask employees to brainstorm what type of new experiences could and couldn't sit within the scope of your brand essence, then outline the role they think they could play in bringing those experiences to life.

- **Review your brand promise.** This will help employees understand the key benefits they will contribute to delivering.

- **Play a brand positioning game.** This could entail asking new recruits to identify your main competitors, then locate your brand on a positioning map in relation to them. Subsequent discussion could then highlight the part each employee plays in supporting the brand positioning.

- **Create a brand personality collage.** This is a great icebreaker and could be used in a light-hearted way to outline the types of personality traits you want to associate with the brand.

Using induction as part of your Brand Experience Enablers education is particularly important for customer-facing employees. These employees seldom realize the disproportionate influence they have on your brand experiences. It's not the CMO of a five-star hotel that makes or breaks the experience; it's the receptionist, bellboy, concierge or pool attendant. It's always a good idea to stress the importance of this paradox during the induction as it can instil a sense of pride and responsibility in all employees, irrespective of seniority. I have seen clients do this in very inspiring and empowering ways so employees leave the room feeling 10 feet tall. Saying simple things, sincerely, can mean a lot.

Once employees have been inducted, it's likely they will need to develop skills that will enable them to deliver your Brand Experience Essentials with confidence and consistency. This often requires training.

Training

> Thirty-five per cent of firms that consider their CX initiative 'advanced' are building a training programme and incentives for employees to offer a great experience.[10]

In the context of building brand experiences, training should equip your employees with skills, knowledge and tools so they have the competence and confidence to bring your Brand Experience Essentials to life. If a global courier has a value of being 'supportive', employees should help a distressed customer whose passport has been mislaid in transit by adopting an understanding and empathetic tone, clearly explaining that they will do all they can to help. If an advanced biotech brand is positioned around 'practicality', then all sales representatives need to be able to explain the benefits of complex product features using straightforward language and in 'hands on' ways.

Training should also help employees deal with challenging situations in a natural, autonomous and 'on brand' way. If an airline is positioned around efficiency, pleasantries may come second to solving a specific customer issue when time is tight. The airline's employees need to know this so they can deliver the experience in this way with freedom and not in fear. Ritz Carlton provides a wonderful example of giving employees scope to deliver 'on brand' experiences by providing all members of staff with a discretionary fund of US $2,000 per incident to deal with any customer complaints.

Whilst most brands could not give all employees this kind of budget, I have seen the principle of empowering employees with a more modest amount to resolve issues work well in the leisure, airline and tourism sectors. This means your brand experience training needs to help your employees make judgement calls that reflect your Brand Experience Essentials. They will only be able to do this if they understand Brand Experience Essentials intuitively and contextually. Otherwise there's a danger that at one extreme your experiences could feel inconsistent yet at the other scripted, staged and staid. This is a difficult balance to strike, but effective Brand Experience Essential training will go some way to helping.

Whilst training can represent a significant financial commitment, a growing number of brands have created formal training centres or developed bespoke training programmes because they understand the important part employees play in delivering their brand experiences.

Leading financial institutions in Southeast Asia such as Maybank and CIMB have dedicated training academies, while UK-based challenger brand Metro Bank has a 'university' to train and guide employees on key parts of their service-driven experience.

Pret A Manger's 'Academy' trains employees on how to behave in ways that are consistent with their brand values. High-end boutique retailer Harvey Nichols delivers a two-day training programme at its 'Style Academy'. This enables staff to advise customers so they can become 'fearlessly stylish' – something which lies at the heart of the Harvey Nichols brand. The first day helps employees understand colour, cut, shape and how to style people, whilst the second equips them with the skills they need to help customers find what they're looking for in-store.

William Grant & Sons, which owns brands such as Glenfiddich whisky and Hendrick's gin, has developed a two-year, in-house programme, 'Marketing Fundamentals', which helps employees understand the process and principles of creating a heritage brand and the role this plays in the experiences they deliver.

Belgian luxury chocolate brand Neuhaus also invests heavily in training their retail managers and customer-facing employees so they understand the concept of 'elegance' and the role they play in delivering it. Making sure customers experience a feeling of luxury and being cared for when they enter a Neuhaus shop is an important part of the brand experience.

Disney then has a 'University' for its employees (cast members) where they are trained in how to create happiness and magic as part of the experiences they deliver.

Wavelength delivered a bespoke, one-week Advanced Marketing Programme for one of Southeast Asia's leading banks. Twenty hand-picked high performers from across Southeast Asia were invited to participate in sessions that focused on building experiences in a way that aligns with their Brand Experience Essentials. At Wavelength we also helped reposition a specialist law firm away from lower-value public-funded work to higher-end private work. A key part of this project entailed training non-fee-earning, client-facing staff, including receptionists, to behave in ways that supported the perceptions being created by the broader design and communications work.

When it comes to training, the secret is to keep things interactive. You can use case studies, role-plays, simulations, group activities and games. Adopting these tools helps introduce new content in ways that enable participants to put what they learn into practice.

It sounds obvious, but a lot of training shares knowledge but doesn't help participants apply it in practical and useful ways in their workplace. A few years ago, we were working with an airline client that was encountering brand experience problems. One key issue related to their values; they were too generic and weren't framed actively, and so didn't encourage the desired 'on brand' behaviour. They also overlapped, which made some values redundant. During the early stages of the workshop, all the executive-level participants were happy to almost blindly recite the values. They didn't think their values were problematic. A client–agency role-play aimed to tease out how they could enable their values through behaviour, communications and design. The room slowly ground to a halt and energy levels dropped as it became clear that their values were of limited practical use. A new values definition programme started the following week. Without the client–agency role-play activity, this key insight would not have come to light in a way delegates could relate to.

Appraisal

The likes of Accenture, Deloitte, PwC, Amazon, IBM, Microsoft, Netflix, Adobe and GE no longer depend primarily on annual performance reviews to appraise their employees.[11] The evaluation processes they have adopted unfold continually and incrementally throughout the year based around ongoing conversations or 'check-ins' that provide employees with rolling feedback and guidance. They focus on forward-looking development and mentoring instead of retrospective annual ratings.

Adopting this approach to appraisal brings many benefits:

- It encourages employees to collaborate more and compete less. Annual performance reviews, especially those that use forced distribution ranking, promote competition over collaboration and can undermine teamwork.[12]

- The 'Agile Manifesto'[13] is increasingly moving into the brand marketing mainstream and favours 'responding to change over following a plan'. Relying on annual reviews for employee appraisal inhibits this approach.

- The Millennial generation represents an increasingly important part of the workforce. They tend to want more frequent, on-demand, real-time constructive feedback and coaching.

- An incremental approach means that employees receive support and advice in an iterative, timely and focused fashion, which adds to the human capital of the organization and helps employees feel supported rather than assessed.

- It frees employees and line managers from an annual ritual many come to dread, whilst levelling the playing field against smooth talkers who shine at the performance review but not throughout the year.

- Given evaluation data is collected and reviewed in real time, this solves the problem of managers having to recall and evaluate events which happened several months ago.

Interesting examples of real-time or 'on the fly' performance evaluation are starting to emerge. European retailer Zalando uses an online real-time app that obtains performance feedback data from meetings, problem-solving sessions, projects and product launches. It also provides a platform for employees to request feedback from line managers or other colleagues in a more immediate and engaging way. GE's approach to ongoing review is shaped around an app called 'PD@GE' ('performance development at GE') which sets each employee a series of near-term 'priorities'. Managers frequently discuss progress with their teams. Notes on what was discussed, agreed and resolved are then uploaded onto the app. The focus isn't on grading employees' performance; it's about facilitating constant improvement and progression via timely insights, combined with a coaching-oriented approach. Employees can give or request feedback at any point through a feature which isn't limited to their immediate manager, or even their division. Using technology in this way gives the employee more timely, continual and focused performance development in the moment, which feeds into a summary document discussed by a line manager and their reports at the end of the year.

Adopting a real-time, forward-thinking, mentoring approach does not come without challenges in a brand experience-building context. Managers will require a deep understanding of the Brand Experience Essentials so they can coach and evaluate their team's performance in line with the desired brand experience on a day-to-day basis. This will be a challenge but a positive one, as it will encourage them to deepen their understanding of the brand. Real-time mentoring also means managers have to get closer to projects because more frequent feedback, advice and guidance is required to deliver the coaching that forms part of this approach. If their team needs a lot of support, this can start to eat into managers' productive time. I have seen this fester into frustration and even resentment. Finally, peer-based feedback can be 'gamed' by employees to help or hurt colleagues. This adds an unwanted layer of subjectivity and politics to the appraisal process which can cloud management opinion.

If you use, or plan to use, similar appraisal methods it's important to keep your Brand Experience Essentials in mind. If your brand is positioned as ambitious yet unassuming, then the tasks set and the mentoring approach should support this. For example, objectives should stretch employees but when they are successful this should be celebrated in a low-key, understated way.

Reward

Most organizations that award bonuses, do so on the basis of company, departmental and individual performance. It's rare for an organization to allocate at least a percentage of an employee's bonus depending on how well their behaviour supports the desired brand experience, but doing this is important. It encourages employees to behave in ways that reinforce the desired brand experience and helps encourage the delivery of consistent experiences.

Let's assume a brand has a value of being 'bold'. During a performance review session, a line manager could ask their team member to share some examples of when they've been bold. The employee should be able to describe occasions when their behaviour has brought this brand value to life. Their line manager would then ask about the remaining values and their other Brand Experience Essentials. For example, the employee may be asked when they have demonstrated behaviours that are all about authentic athletic performance, to show how they have helped to enact the brand essence, behaved in ways that aligned with the personality, or reinforced the desired positioning. They should then allocate a proportion of the individual's bonus for demonstrating 'on-brand behaviour'.

During Southwest Airlines' performance appraisals and 360-degree reviews, employees are measured not just on results but on how well they have lived by core attributes of a warrior spirit, servant's heart and fun-loving attitude.[14] Pret A Manager uses weekly mystery shopper visits to evaluate employee behaviour.[15] If the mystery shopper receives a good experience, everyone in that location receives an extra £1 an hour for the hours they work that week. If the mystery shopper received a poor experience, no one receives the bonus. Whilst the reward is financial, the mechanism for the reward is behavioural, which itself gravitates to the enabling of the brand's values.

At Wavelength, we have worked with a handful of organizations that are particularly committed to building brand experiences. They realize the central role played by employees in achieving this goal, so take a more focused approach to reward. As part of this, the percentage of bonus awarded for on-brand behaviour increases with seniority. This may seem counterintuitive, given most C-suite executives focus on stock performance and other financial metrics, but it makes sense. CEOs and other executives are responsible for demonstrating leadership. If they behave in ways that align with the desired brand experience, employees will follow. If they don't, employees will think it's acceptable to behave in other ways. Multiply this by the number of employees and touchpoints they deliver, and the brand experience soon unravels.

This way of allocating bonuses may not be popular with some employees. Being asked to demonstrate brand-aligned behaviour during a coaching session or performance review can feel controlling. It may result in some employees choosing to leave. This can be difficult in the short term but in the long run tends to be a good step for all concerned; building brand experiences requires an authentic employee commitment to enabling your Brand Experience Essentials. And once your recruitment, induction and training align with your Brand Experience Essentials, this problem shouldn't persist.

Exit interviews

Current employees may feel too inhibited to give you frank and open feedback on the brand experiences you deliver. Exit interviews provide a wonderful opportunity for you to discover what employees really think. It may be that the brand has drifted from its initial values, personality and positioning whilst falling short on key parts of its brand promise. Or it could be that your induction, training or rewards don't align employees with the Brand Experience Essentials that were outlined during their initial interview, and so their expectations weren't met. These types of brutally honest insights are invaluable, as they may be indicative of deeper brand experience issues.

The exit interview also offers your brand an opportunity to stay true to its Brand Experience Essentials in a potentially difficult situation. For example, if your brand personality is 'dignified and respectable', the exit interview is a good time to showcase these credentials (although the outgoing employee may not). This can also save you the trouble of a potentially unfavourable and unjust negative review on a website like Glassdoor.

Conclusion

Employees play a crucial but often overlooked role in enabling your Brand Experience Essentials. They are crucial because they can personalize and 'humanize' the brand experiences you deliver. However, people are emotional and erratic. We make irrational decisions and have good days and bad days. This makes delivering consistent experiences through people difficult but not impossible. To address this problem, brand and human resource executives need to forge close working relationships. At the heart of this relationship is a common understanding of how key HR processes such as recruitment, induction, training, appraisal and reward can dovetail with your Brand Experience Essentials.

This chapter is accompanied by Toolkit 14.1.

Endnotes

1   Britton, V (2015) 5 success tips for startups, *Medium*, 19 May [Online] bit.ly/wavelength-walt-disney

2   Gallup (2016) The engaged workplace [online] http://bit.ly/wavelenth-gallup

3   IBM Institute for Business Value (2016) The experience revolution: new teams, new rules, *IBM*, November, Study reference # GBE03786USEN [online] http://bit.ly/wavelength-ibm-gameon

4   Financial outperformers are those respondents who report outperforming their competition, based on profit and revenue, over the last three years

5   Keohane, K (2014) *Brand and Talent,* 1st edn, Kogan Page

6   Yohn, D L (2015) Design your employee experience as thoughtfully as you design your customer experience, *Harvard Business Review*, 8 December [online] http://bit.ly/wavelength-yohn

7   Ahrendts, A (2017) Why Apple's new in-store experience aims to fuel creativity in everyone, LinkedIn, 16 May [online] http://bit.ly/wavelength-apple-recruitment

8   Hunt, V, Layton, D and Prince, S (2015) Why diversity matters, McKinsey Quarterly, January [online] http://bit.ly/wavelength-diversity

9   Chalfin, A et al (2016) Productivity and selection of human capital with machine learning, *American Economic Review*, **106** (5), pp 124–27

10 Oracle (2016) Global insights on succeeding in the customer experience era [online] http://bit.ly/wavelength-oracle

11 Ewenstein, B, Hancock, B and Komm, A (2016) Ahead of the curve: the future of performance management, *McKinsey Quarterly* (May) [online] http://bit.ly/wavelength-mckinsey-appraisal

12 Deloitte (2014) It's official: forced ranking is dead, *Wall Street Journal*, 10 June [online] http://bit.ly/wavelength-appraisals

13 See http://agilemanifesto.org

14 Weber, J (2015). How Southwest Airlines hires such dedicated people, *Harvard Business Review*, 2 November [online] http://bit.ly/wavelength-southwest

15 Preston, R (2015) Smiley culture: Pret A Manger's secret ingredients, *Telegraph*, 9 March [online] http://bit.ly/wavelength-pret

Communications 15

In the last chapter I emphasized the role of employee behaviour when enabling your Brand Experience Essentials. It outlined the importance of brand teams developing closer working relationships with their human resource colleagues, so HR processes align with, and help to enable your Brand Experience Essentials.

This chapter will give you a practical understanding of how communications[1] can be used to enable your Brand Experience Essentials in aligned, personalized, engaging and interactive ways, so I will be focusing on:

- internal communications;
- social media;
- content/conversations;
- communities;
- brand language;
- mobile;
- stories;
- gamification.

As you read, you'll find it useful to think through the illustrative questions presented in Table 15.1. They will help you connect brand experience-related communications and your Brand Experience Essentials.

Forty-seven per cent of brands say they have a strong capacity for providing relevant communication while only **35 per cent** of consumers say communications from their favourite brands are 'usually relevant'.[2]

Table 15.1 Connecting communications and the Brand Experience Essentials: questions to ask yourself

	How can we:
Values	Use social media to convey our values in engaging ways?
Essence	Use mobile to help us deliver personalized experiences that sit within the scope of our essence?
Promise	Use gamification to convey some of the benefits our experiences have the potential to deliver in interactive ways?
Positioning	Craft internal communications so that they align our employees with our positioning?
Personality	Involve our community in conversations that help us to express our personality?

Communications and brand experiences

Powerful brands have clearly defined Brand Experience Essentials and communicate these, with impressive consistency, across and through a variety of channels. Audi conveys German engineering and intelligence through its use of digital and traditional media. Four Seasons Hotels' communications support the positioning of its serene and exclusive residences. Irrespective of how their communications touch you, brands like Audi and Four Seasons have a consistent feel that is the envy of many brands. They can do this because they have thought through their Brand Experience Essentials, which act as guiding principles to shape subsequent brand experience-related communications.

Internal brand communications

When building brand experiences you need to craft internal brand communications that:

- educate employees about brand experiences so they appreciate their strategic importance;
- involve your employees in the brand experience-building process, so they feel a greater sense of ownership for the experiences they deliver;
- clarify the role employees play in building and delivering brand experiences so they realize their contribution counts;

- occur *before* external communications so employees feel informed and an integral part of the brand experience-building process. This may slow short-term progress but in the long term it will be time well spent. In the name of speed, executives can have a tendency to dive head first into external brand communications, then 'update' employees. How would you feel if you were treated this way? Less than motivated to deliver a great brand experience, I suspect.

A convenience retailer asked Wavelength to assess how well their 'rebrand' was received by its employees. In reality, this was a visual refresh, not a rebrand, but this was only part of the problem. The mystery shopper prompt we used was, 'I see (brand name) has freshened up its look recently. What do you think of it?' One employee responded, 'I don't know and to be honest I don't care.' Another said, 'It's just another excuse to keep the senior management busy. What a waste of time, effort and money.'

This was difficult insight to deliver to the chief marketing officer, who suggested we remedy the problem using internal brand communications and a 'retrofitted' internal brand engagement programme. My father often says to me, 'Sometimes in business you've got to walk away from a bad dinner, son.' So that's what we did. A communications agency agreed with this approach. The employees considered the initiative an insincere afterthought.

When shaping your internal communications don't lose sight of your Brand Experience Essentials. A brand shaped around values of being transparent and caring could create an internal social media platform to show how big decisions are made in open and transparent ways, delivered with a sensitive tone of voice.

Don't be seduced by social media

The volume of social media channels and the speed they come and go at is overwhelming. This makes it difficult to identify the right channels to invest your time and money in when building brand experiences.

To tackle this problem, you need to focus on the message and then the medium so you can ensure your brand, content and channel align. First, your message should focus on enabling your Brand Experience Essentials. Next, you can select the most relevant social media through which to convey your message. The key is to use channels that are relevant to your stakeholders and fit with your Brand Experience Essentials.

It is simple to spot a brand that has clearly defined and understood Brand Experience Essentials. Just go to one social channel and scan their stream; if it feels consistent this is a good sign. Next, review their other social media channels; if that consistency endures across different channels, this is another sign they have clearly defined their Brand Experience Essentials.

> 'You've got to start with the customer experience and work back toward the technology – not the other way around.'
>
> Steve Jobs[3]

In November 2015, extreme outdoor gear brand REI decided to close its doors on Black Friday, give all employees a paid day off work and encourage everyone to head outside away from the hustle and bustle of the sales. It used #OptOutside to guide communications and the broader conversation. This refreshingly unique and inspiring message showed how the brand placed a priority on quality time with family and friends over bagging a bargain to save a few bucks. If REI did not have such a clear understanding of, and belief in, their Brand Experience Essentials they would not have had the self-confidence and conviction to initiate and engage with this type of brand communication. #OptOutside is still going strong today.

Vikram Krishna's Expert Insight outlines how Emirates NBD used a range of digital technologies in focused ways to develop a relevant connection with their customers.

EXPERT INSIGHT 15.1 How digital experiences helped Emirates NBD build a $3.4 billion financial services brand

Vikram Krishna, Executive Vice President, Head of Group Marketing and Customer Experience, Emirates NBD

While we spend our days at Emirates NBD trying to make our customers' lives easier, marketing is becoming anything but. Caught between revenues that are hard to find, elusive budgets and ever more demanding customer expectations, the rules of the game refuse to sit still. Furthermore, brands are competing harder than ever to be heard, understood and loved by their audiences.

This is perhaps no truer than for financial services brands, for whom a good day of building brand affinity is nothing short of an uphill struggle. Imagine then, the challenge that Emirates NBD faced when it entered the market amidst the industry turbulence of 2009. Where the marketing norm would call for a brand that speaks to the heart at launch, we took a different tack and still hold to the decision eight years later.

We believe the best approach to building sustainable emotional connections with customers is achieved via the transactions they have with us. It's this thinking that continues to drive Emirates NBD's approach to building brand experiences. Rather than rely on contentious ads that tell people what we want them to think or feel about us, we focus on showing people what we offer, and ultimately let them make up their own minds. From channelling our efforts into initiatives like creating the largest network of partner brands, or developing the most intuitive mobile banking app, it challenges us to make sure the business delivers the most innovative experiences possible.

Adopting this approach also makes listening to customers more important, and that's why digital and social channels play a major role in the experiences we deliver. We use them to actively encourage feedback, listen to it, and constantly work on new ways of making things better, such as introducing mini-statements through Twitter, or providing educational videos to help people get the most out of their online services.

While brands spend millions on ads that hope to build a perception of size or status, in such a connected and transparent digital world, we believe that there's never been a more relevant time to ensure that the experiences we deliver do the talking over anything else.

Emirates NBD was launched in 2009 and is one of the top banks in the UAE. It has seen its brand value grow from US $940 million to US $3.4 billion and now ranks 75th amongst the world's financial brands.

Understand content and the conversation

Stakeholders increasingly look for brands to share useful, educational or even entertaining content – this is especially the case for the Millennial generation and the trend looks set to continue as Gen Z move into the marketing mainstream.

To identify relevant content, you need to go back to your Brand Experience Environment. This will help you understand your stakeholders' broader interests, the jobs they need to get done, the emotional connection you want to create etc, so you can start conversations that engage stakeholders with your Brand Experience Essentials in subtle yet relevant ways.

Standard Chartered shares content that stimulates debate around corporate citizenship, which ties in with its 'Here for Good' brand ethos. IBM shares artificial intelligence research, white papers and thought leadership pieces that demonstrate its AI competence. Carling's 'Be the Coach' invited football fans to select and substitute players for the Carling Black Label Cup between Kaizer Chiefs FC and the Orlando Pirates, which created conversations that centred on a love of football. In his Expert Insight, Alin Dobrea outlines how Marks and Spencer creates engaging content at key touchpoints in the customer journey to build brand experiences for their homeware and furniture business unit.

EXPERT INSIGHT 15.2 How Marks and Spencer combines content and the customer journey to build brand experiences

Alin Dobrea, Brand Marketer, Marks and Spencer, UK

In 2015, Marks and Spencer was looking to drive sales in its homeware and furniture business unit. While M&S is well known for its clothing and food businesses, there was significantly lower awareness of its homeware and furniture offer. Research revealed that 50 per cent of regular M&S customers were not aware of the breadth of the offer, and 25 per cent assumed it was too expensive for them.

The first stage of M&S's strategy entailed establishing a clear brand positioning for the category. Next, we conducted an end-to-end analysis of the customer journey. This allowed us to identify any pain points and opportunities to deliver the right content, to the right customer, at the right time. This led to the development of guidelines for content creation at each stage of the journey, as well as the right strategy for distributing this through earned, owned and paid channels.

The analysis gave us a thorough understanding of our customer journey and the key stages where our customers were interacting with our brand. The next step was to plan how to leverage our existing photographic and video assets to deliver an integrated content strategy with relevant, bite-sized content across all customer touchpoints. To do this we revisited all the content that we were creating in-house and with our agencies across all channels including in-store, digital, social, print, catalogues, packaging etc, and developed an integrated content strategy.

The content review also prompted the launch of a Home Hub on the M&S.com website which features educational and inspirational content based on search terms and trends in the category. M&S also created native content partnerships which helped further enhance our brand expertise through inspirational photography and videos which were seeded across various websites and social media.

The project was a great success. Awareness of M&S Home increased by 25 per cent (as measured through a weekly panel survey), traffic to the home and furniture section of the M&S website grew 30 per cent year on year, and homeware and furniture sales for the 2015/16 financial year had year-on-year growth exceeding the business plan and the market for both stores and online.

Marks and Spencer plc is a major British multinational retailer headquartered in the City of Westminster, London.

Having clearly defined Brand Experience Essentials gives brands like Standard Chartered, IBM and Carling guiding principles that help them consistently create, curate and share relevant content. Clearly defined Brand Experience Essentials also help these brands to engage in consistently relevant conversations, at scale, because they have a framework that guides brand-aligned responses.

Some would argue that customers don't want to have conversations with brands but research shows customers are willing to engage with branded content when brands are transparent about who authored it.[4]

Emirates NBD's 'Hey Future Me...' campaign invited kids to speak to their future selves, outlining their hopes, dreams and aspirations. When parents watched these videos, the need for financial planning so they could enable their kids to realize their dreams became apparent. The campaign prompted a 20 per cent increase in savings plans applications by families during 2013.[5]

During the 2014 World Cup, Canadian bank CIBC created and shared real-time, country-specific content to drive conversations around #CIBCSoccerNation. Their campaign led to CIBC being ranked third in brands most associated with the FIFA World Cup on Twitter (following Adidas and Nike) and resulted in 1,200 people signing up for Aventura credit cards.[6]

Dutch bank ING has long been supportive of Dutch arts and culture. To connect this goal with its positioning as a forward-thinking bank in a way that resonated with 20–34-year-olds, it set out to create 'The Next Rembrandt' using facial recognition and machine learning software. The project sparked an online conversation about how classical art and modern technology intersect, and produced the equivalent of €12.5 million total earned media; in the weeks following the launch, Google reported a 61.29 per cent increase in searches for ING.[7]

To raise awareness around kids' increasingly sedentary lifestyles in the Middle East, the detergent brand OMO launched a 23-hour Facebook Live campaign to highlight how most kids are idle and inactive for 23 hours per day. The campaign showed how kids spend their time indoors – which reduces the chance of kids getting their clothes dirty and so potential demand for OMO's products. As online conversations developed, a team of child psychologists were on hand to respond to parents' concerns and to suggest activities they could do with their kids. The campaign stimulated conversation around active lifestyles for kids, with 3.4 million hashtag mentions (#KidsToday), 3.3 million Twitter mentions, 1.97 million Facebook mentions and 40,000 comments on YouTube.

For the launch of Goosebumps (children's horror fiction books), Sony Pictures Entertainment used Facebook's artificial intelligence platform, Messenger for Business, to facilitate real-time personalized conversations at scale between Slappy (the evil puppet) and Goosebump fans using Facebook Messenger. Thirty-five per cent of conversations lasted more than 10 minutes and 35 per cent of consumers returned to the Facebook page to engage with Slappy.[8]

In the B2B space, HCL technologies created Straight Talk. This peer-to-peer content platform showcased thought leadership insights from IT professionals and deepened the company's relationship with current and potential clients by building a community and engaging in specialist conversations. Straight Talk engaged over 3,000 IT decision makers, created sales opportunities worth US $700 million and had a direct impact on sales of US $122 million.[9]

The power of communities

Edelman's Trust Barometer shows trust in senior executives, business, NGOs, government and the media is in a sorry state.[10] Corruption, globalization and the erosion of social values are cited as contributory factors. The same report highlights how the most credible people are technical or academic experts and 'people like you' who we can relate to. This is why influencer marketing and communities are becoming increasingly important brand experience-building tools.

Brands' growing interest in building communities has also been fuelled by the increasing significance of the Millennial generation, who love to engage with like-minded people around a common interest. They also tend to seek help, advice and guidance before making decisions so they don't make a mistake. Community-driven experiences provide a perfect platform for the objective and peer-supported decision making sought by the Millennial generation. Communities also appeal to Gen Z, who were born into a connected world and so want to connect and share their experiences and accomplishments with others.

> 'We involve communities of people and influencers to participate in the creative; that helps us have an edge.'
>
> Gary Milner, Director of Global Digital Marketing, Lenovo[11]

The need for belonging is deeply rooted in human behaviour[12] and a number of brands capitalize on this through their communities. Vans transformed London's Old Vic Tunnels into 'House of Vans London', housing an indoor skate park, a music venue, a cinema, an art gallery, two bars and a café. This created a communal space for the Vans community to congregate and 'be seen' whilst supporting the brand's urban positioning perfectly. Building these kinds of shared experiences capitalizes on communities' self-referencing and reinforcing qualities. When people see and interact with like-minded people at such experiences it strengthens their community bond and identification with the brand. The subliminal message is, 'They're wearing Vans shoes. That means they must be cool.' Similarly, by purchasing the product, the consumer confirms their membership of this community in symbolic terms. The next iteration of the Vans community is 'Living off the Wall'.[13] This is a lifestyle portal that shares the stories of people who follow their own path in life and have a commitment to originality; an aspirational and highly relevant message that resonates with the core Vans customer and wider community.

In 2017, a number of brands are using communities to great effect. GoPro encourages customers to use the #GoPro hashtag to share images taken with its products. The result is a community of brand advocates who share an interest in video and photography but, at a deeper level, values of being creative, adventurous, dedicated and expressive. With over

5.3 million YouTube subscribers they must be doing something right. The Dollar Shave Club encourages members to share photos on social media and reposts their favourite content. In return, that member receives a t-shirt to reward them for contributing to the community. Adidas's Glitch app is built around an invite-only community. Once you have obtained the access code you can talk to other Glitch owners and build and buy your own pair of personalized Glitch boots. Wavelength recently worked with an Italian brand of hair products aimed squarely at hipster – or, more precisely, 'wannabe' hipster – hairdressers (according to the client!) who were aspiring fashionistas. Our client quickly realized the value didn't reside in the products that turned an average hairdresser into a style supremo, but in the involvement and association with the community built around the product.

At one level, the benefit delivered by these communities resides in their perceived objectivity concerning brand- or product-related advice and opinion. At another, deeper level these shared experiences help like-minded people connect via Brand Experience Essentials that are subliminally relevant to them. Powerful brands understand this and use communications to enable Brand Experience Essentials that their communities will naturally gravitate towards.

The value of building communities is not restricted to 'commercial' organizations. In her Expert Insight, Caron Thompson provides detail about The Waiting Room. This is a user-generated online directory that connects local communities with local support services in areas such as abuse, suicide prevention and mental health.

EXPERT INSIGHT 15.3 How an ambitious charity uses technology to connect communities

Caron Thompson, Founder and Director, Common Unity Social Enterprise

URBRUM is a website that engages and educates local communities about health and well-being. The Waiting Room is an important part of the URBRUM platform. It is a user-generated directory that connects local communities with local support services in areas including abuse, suicide prevention and mental health. Access to The Waiting Room and its resources can be gained through the web (desktop/mobile) or through The Waiting Room Resource Key, which utilizes the QR code located on the key fob to load The Waiting Room home page (see Figure 15.1).

Figure 15.1   UK-based charity Common Unity using QR codes to build communities

The beauty of the QR code is that it can be presented across communities in many forms – on beer mats in pubs, on clothing, bus shelters, billboards, in accident and emergency departments, in staff canteens, GP practices, the courts, prisons, police stations, cinemas, on taxis, buses, email signatures or pharmacy bags – the list goes on. Wherever there is a physical space there is an opportunity to help communities help themselves through The Waiting Room.

Common Unity is a Health and Social Care organization specializing in working on mental health and well-being with 'invisible' communities.

Given that communities are so powerful and represent such a good way for brands to engage with stakeholders, how can you build one? Social media marketing expert Luke Brynley-Jones provides more details in his Expert Insight.

EXPERT INSIGHT 15.4   How to build a social media community

Luke Brynley-Jones, Founder and Managing Director of OST Marketing

Building and maintaining a social media community can drive customer loyalty[14] and increase levels of spending.[15] For brands wishing to build a social media community there are four key steps to achieving success:

1 **Focus on an existing community.** Many brands fail by trying to create communities around themselves. Identify an existing community and devise a strategy that aligns the brand with the community. In 2016, Sun-Pat, the UK's leading peanut butter brand, partnered with sports celebrities and networks, leading to a significant increase in social media engagement.[16]

2 **Create opportunities for conversations.** Post relevant, topical or fun posts. Insightful ideas or requests for assistance also attract engagement. Supermalt, the popular malt drink, has a knack for publishing fun posts on its Facebook Page that fans share with their friends, consistently delivering reach and positive sentiment.

3 **Actively court advocates.** Actively involving 'power users' helps brands share the burden of community management and drive engagement. Sony Europe has a created a community of volunteer forum moderators from among their super fans[17] who are empowered to answer queries across social media.

4   **Mix always-on with campaigns.** To build a sustainable community, most
    brands integrate day-to-day content to keep the brand front of mind with one-
    off campaigns to boost reach, attract new fans and drive existing fans to take
    actions. Cats Protection's #blackcatday provides an example and attracted
    over 5,000 competition entries in 2016.

*OST is an award-winning social media agency which provides social media
and digital marketing services for brands such as VISA, Thomson Reuters, Gala
Bingo and Marriott Hotels.*

Mind your brand language

The brand-related language used as part of your 'verbal identity' plays an
important role in enabling your Brand Experience Essentials. The contrast-
ing Twitter feeds of British Airways and Virgin Atlantic provide clues to
the type of Brand Experience Essentials their experiences deliver. British
Airways' Twitter bio reads: 'Official British Airways Twitter account. We
love reading your Tweets & are here 24 hours a day, 7 days a week to help.'
Virgin Atlantic's bio reads: 'Hello Gorgeous! Follow us for news, banter
& assistance. Visit our blog at virg.in/rubyblog or for official concerns
visit virg.in/CR' (see Figure 15.2).

Virgin Atlantic's tone is fun, playful, gregarious and mildly mischievous.
British Airways' 'voice' has more conservative, formal and corporate undertones. If you've flown with both airlines you'll appreciate how these words
signal the type of experience you'll have. Virgin's tone of voice extends to
other experiences they deliver. When booking a Virgin train ticket you'll
be asked the reason for your journey. Responses include 'Hanging with my
friends', 'On my hols' and 'Retail therapy', along with more conventional
responses such as 'On business'. The consistency is impressive and is clearly
informed by well-articulated and understood Brand Experience Essentials.

Warby Parker, the eyeglasses and sunglasses retailer, used its brand
personality to develop the tone of voice it uses in product descriptions, the
CEO's speeches and so forth. This also extends to retail signage. For example, in stores with photo booths the sign above the slot where your photos
come out reads, 'Your photo will magically appear here.' A perfect fit with
their fun and quirky brand personality.

Figure 15.2   Virgin Atlantic's tone of voice on Twitter

Getting your brand voice right is even more important in mobile, where communications real estate is tight and people don't have time to scroll through irrelevant content. This means mobile-based brand communications need to be particularly short, salient and carefully considered – having clearly defined Brand Experience Essentials will help you do this.

Making the most of mobile

The importance of mobile as means of communication and building brand experiences has grown exponentially in recent years. I have been in and around mobile brand experiences for over 20 years. This experience not only makes me feel horrifically old but has taught me a lot, so I encourage you to consider the following points when using mobile to build brand experiences:[18]

> Seventy-four per cent of Gen Z respondents claim to spend an hour or more a day on their mobile device compared to 55 per cent for Gen X.[19]

Enabler

Mobile is a means to an end, not an end in itself because it facilitates the building of brand experiences. Strictly speaking most customers or other stakeholders aren't interested in mobile capabilities but how mobile can help them get jobs done.

Location

Pioneering mobile marketers depended on a device's 'cell ID' to identify a phone's location. This provided location accuracy ranging from tens of meters in urban areas to tens of miles in the countryside. Around 2002, I showed the chief marketing officer at Orange our first map on a Nokia 6210 and he said to me, 'Darren, please tell me I haven't just invested €12 million in a dead spider.' Limited accuracy and phone specifications made the delivery of engaging and commercially viable location-based experiences problematic. Nowadays GPS and advanced mapping are the mainstay of new smartphones, and have created a number of location-based brand experience opportunities.

When Nike launched its Hyper Warm and Hyper Shield products in China, it delivered a location-based experience on Sina Weibo. Users were encouraged to add and follow the four elements (rain, dark, snow and cold) as Weibo friends who then sent daily messages to taunt and so motivate them into going for a run. People could log their runs using #WinAgainstTheElements and were awarded points if their route brought them into contact with any of the four elements. Scores were then added to a leaderboard, which gave the experience a competitive dimension; a perfect fit for Nike's 'authentic athletic performance' brand essence.

Privacy

A mobile device is unique when compared with other technology because it is seldom, if ever, shared. This makes it incredibly personal and means you would be wise to respect peoples' privacy by obtaining 'informed consent' through an active opt-in before using mobile as a marketing channel. In 2000 I was working at the Wireless Marketing Association (now part of the Mobile Marketing Association); opt-in was a core requirement.

Ford got this right when they launched their new Escape and Taurus models. People who wanted more information were encouraged to send a text with the word 'FORD' to 63611. A member of the Ford team then contacted the potential customer and asked which car they were interested in along with their name and postcode. This information was sent to local Ford dealerships who made follow-up calls. This approach respected potential customers' privacy and was highly personalized.

Personalized

Mobile feeds people's increasing appetite for, and expectation of, personalized experiences. Snapchat filters allow people to add individual overlays to their images while their Geofilters tie filters into a specific location. IKEA's catalogue app allows customers to virtually place certain products in their room by overlaying the product on the device's camera to see if the furniture suits their style tastes.

Timely

Mobile provides a powerful means of delivering experiences at highly relevant times because most people keep their device with them at all times. Marks and Spencer's 'Dine in for two for £10' entailed the brand sending multimedia messages to customers late in the afternoon. At this time people were either just about to leave work or were on their way home. Either way, it's likely their stomachs were rumbling and they were thinking about what to cook. M&S solved that problem in a timely manner.

Direct

Mobile provides a powerful way of communicating directly with an end customer. This means brands can cut through the clutter in ways other direct response tools such as email, which may not get past spam filters, cannot. Messaging apps have taken over the mantle of SMS and allow brands to communicate directly with the device owner. Customers at Saks Fifth Avenue can use iMessage to inquire about and purchase products. ABN AMRO has started to use WhatsApp to answer customer queries, whilst in South Africa, Hellmann's uses it to connect consumers with chefs who provide personalized recipe recommendations based on the food they have at home.

Always connected (generally)

Unlike a TV or other digital media it's uncommon for a mobile device to be switched off. This provides opportunities for delivering timely experiences. The challenge is to identify when and how to engage with your target customer. Understanding the Brand Experience Environment and being guided by your Brand Experience Enablers will help you do that.

Commerce

Mobile devices increasingly permit payment. The Starbucks Card Mobile App helps customers pay for their daily dose of caffeine whilst Apple Pay, Android Pay and AliPay are being integrated into devices and retail experiences to facilitate ease of payment.

Visual

The inclusion of good-quality cameras and the advent of emojis have changed the way we communicate. This creates new styles of communication and brings new brand experience-building opportunities. Mobile phone cameras have fuelled Instagram's astronomical growth. As part of their employer brand experience, L'Oréal accepts job applications written using emojis. The goal is to increase its relevance with the Millennial generation, make a clear statement about its commitment to digital, and position the brand in ways that chime with its target employees.

In a similar manner to social media, mobile is seductive. It's new, emerging and provides a sea of brand experience opportunities. To avoid seduction, revisit the Brand Experience Essentials you've created in the context of the Brand Experience Environment. You will then be well placed to decide if and how mobile can be used to enable your Brand Experience Essentials in relevant ways. If your coffee brand is positioned as being open and ethical, being able to scan a product's QR code to demonstrate provenance would go down well. The point is to consider mobile as a means, not an end, to building brand experiences.

Crafting brand stories

'Marketing is no longer about the stuff that you make, but about the stories you tell.'

Seth Godin

Stories are powerful. For thousands of years, stories have been woven into the fabric of our daily lives. Ancient civilizations like the Mayans, Incas and Egyptians told their history through vivid and often visual stories. We recount monumental events – wars, celebrations or disasters – through stories, so they can be understood in more tangible terms. Parents and carers read children bedtime stories. When we sleep we create stories in the form of dreams. Some people gossip and embellish situations through stories. Our brains naturally orientate to stories, so they can be used to add depth, meaning and context to the brand experiences you build. Research also shows how stories can drive brand performance.[20]

Stories help us converge on common thoughts, acting as a source of shared understanding and meaning. Research conducted by Uri Hasson and colleagues at Princeton University[21] outlines how stories bring people together via 'neural coupling', which entails the brain of the person receiving the story synchronizing with the brain of the storyteller. This allows the recipient of the story to feel what you feel, to empathize with you and your story at a deeper level because, in effect, they experience events for themselves.

The key is to craft stories that are relevant and so resonate with your stakeholders. This takes us back to profiling stakeholders in the Brand Experience Environment, with Bank of Singapore's 'Building on your Values' campaign providing a relevant example.

> 'They [people] don't buy, actually, products anymore, they buy experiences that are meaningful to them, they buy solutions that are real, that transcend the product, that go beyond the product, and mostly they buy stories that need to be authentic.'
>
> Mauro Porcin, Chief Design Officer, PepsiCo [22]

Mini is built around stories that intimate a fun-loving and adventurous brand. J W Marriott created three short films around 'Two Bellmen' who work at one of their hotels. The goal was to create entertaining and informative content that appeals to the Millennial generation while communicating that Marriott is a luxurious hospitality provider. 'Two Bellmen' has 5.2 million YouTube views, while the sequel has 7.9 million and the third instalment 9 million (as of January 2018). More recently, Marriott created a Snapchat series, 'Six Days, Seven Nights', where social influencers shared their experience at a Marriott via their Snapchat stories, using Snap's Spectacles to give their content a more authentic and realistic feel. Guinness created films such as 'Wheelchair Basketball' and 'Sapeurs' to share stories of individuals who display strength of character. This generates a powerful and inspirational feeling that dovetails with the brand's gritty 'Made of More' tagline. Mitsubishi UFJ Financial Group take a more nostalgic approach to their brand story by tracing their roots back to 17th-century samurai origins. They draw parallels with the samurai, who were characterized by prudence, caution and adherence to an ethical code – elements which form the cornerstones of Mitsubishi's business practices today.

The use of stories is not restricted to global blue-chip brands. In their Expert Insight, David and Mark Coleman[23] illustrate this point by outlining how their medium-sized business used the Coleman story to great effect as part of their 50th anniversary celebrations.

EXPERT INSIGHT 15.5 How an SME family business uses stories to build their brand

David Coleman (Chairman, Coleman Group) and Mark Coleman (Managing Director, Coleman Group)

The Coleman Group (formerly Coleman & Company Ltd) was founded by John and Nora Coleman just after World War II. During its formative years, the business traded from the back room of John and Nora's home and was formally incorporated on 16 October 1962. Fast-forward five decades and the business is still run as a family concern, employs hundreds of people, generates millions in revenues and delivers technically complex projects for blue-chip clients across the globe.

We're proud of our story and heritage, so when The Coleman Group reached its 50th anniversary we wanted to celebrate this fact. Our story was shared in a number of ways. A coffee table book charted the Coleman story via a treasure trove of photos, company correspondence and project case studies. These painted the picture of a progressive, resilient and socially responsible firm that was, and still is, shaped by family values. Key decision makers could relate to pictures of vintage trucks, machinery they had grown up with or projects they were familiar with. Collectively, these acted as an emotional hook in an otherwise hard-nosed industry. The Coleman Group Chairman also wrote a blog, 'Dave's Demolition Diaries', which shared the Coleman story via weekly posts. This generated considerable interest in the UK and abroad from people who identified with the family story. The blog also served as a powerful tool to show employees they were part of something that had deep roots; this had an emotive and inspiring effect.

Telling the Coleman story dovetailed with a broader 50th Anniversary campaign, but our story acted as the cornerstone of our efforts and proved to be a valuable brand asset we still use today.

Coleman Group is a multi-discipline award-winning specialist contractor providing a range of globally recognized services in the field of demolition, remediation, specialist cutting and engineering.

So where do you start when it comes to creating or telling a story? It's a good idea to create some type of tension or imbalance that your brand set out to address, and still works to do so. This positions your brand as a helper or hero for the reader to align with and support. Virgin has used this strategy to great effect, positioning itself as the underdog pitting its wits against powerful established brands. Figure 15.3 shares a practical framework that will help you start thinking about your brand story in a more structured way.

Figure 15.3 A template for crafting brand stories

When we started, <insert person here> *believed...*
We were so <insert feeling here> *by this, we decided to...*
At first we...
Suddenly <insert person here> *found they could...*
So we...
Today, our customers...
And we continue to...

For example, this could work as:

When we started, <chief marketing officers> *believed* <brand experiences could not be built in a scientific way>.

We were so <surprised> *by this, we decided to* <start Wavelength so we could help CMOs build brand experiences in a more scientific way>.

At first we <shared our knowledge through brand insight and education programmes>.

Suddenly <CMOs> *found they could* <adopt a more scientific approach to brand experiences, which enhanced their credibility in the boardroom>.

So we <continue to demonstrate to existing and potential clients how we can help them by adopting a more scientific approach to building brand experiences>.

Today, our customers <build brand experiences with greater confidence and conviction because they are built on scientific insight, advice and education – not anecdote>.

And we continue to <help other CMOs do this through our suite of brand experience related services which we offer to clients located around the globe>.

If you would like to take a more sophisticated approach to your brand story you may want to initiate and direct 'communal' stories where stakeholders actively participate in and shape the story. When Mercedes Benz launched the A-Class in the UK they anchored the campaign around #YouDrive and allowed the public to vote on how the story would develop during the course of three primetime TV adverts. The goal was to engage 25–45-year-old drivers, and the campaign delivered impressive results: more than 40,000 people engaged with #YouDrive during the Saturday evening launch event, and #YouDrive appeared in Twitter users' timelines 16 million times in the first week of the campaign. Google reported a 360 per cent increase in organic A-Class-related searches and 3.8 million people visited the YouDrive YouTube channel in the first three weeks of the campaign.

Carefully crafted stories help brands express their Brand Experience Essentials in ways that are more meaningful and emotionally relevant than a product- or price-based strategy. They also provide an opportunity for stakeholders to relate to and identify with the story, which is important because our brains naturally orientate to stories. The key point is to ensure you retain focus and use stories to communicate your Brand Experience Essentials in consistent ways.

Explore gamification

Gamification entails the use of game mechanics and thinking to engage stakeholders with a core idea. The underpinning logic is informed by social psychology and social sciences. When it comes to brand experiences, gamification can be used to enhance brand awareness, increase stakeholder engagement, facilitate internal brand education, encourage behavioural change or help employees acquire new skills.

> 'Gamification is an incredible way to generate engagement while keeping the authentic look and feel of our luxury brand. In China, we created a WeChat game to open a vault to win a luxury handbag. We saw over 300,000 people involved within a few days.'
>
> Anne-Marie Gaultier, Vice President, Global
> Marketing and Communications, Bally[25]

A growing number of brands realize that gamification can be a powerful tool for building engaging brand experiences. In 2014, 5 Gum, a youth chewing gum brand, turned its packaging into a game of Truth or Dare, which produced a 17 per cent sales lift over the previous year.[26] To address childhood inactivity and obesity in the Philippines, Milo, the milk-based drink, created a gamified nutrition and activity tracker through the Milo Champions Band and app. This wearable tech helped parents monitor their kids' calorie intake versus activity, made nutritional suggestions, and incentivized increased activity through games. The campaign saw a 41 per cent increase in the number of steps children took (within four weeks of using the app) and product consideration increased by 9 per cent.[27]

Gamification has also been used in B2B markets. In 2011, Hewlett Packard introduced 'Project Everest', which generated over US $1 billion of revenue by gamifying their resellers' approach to selling HP's Industry Standard Servers and Enterprise Software Solution products. 'Project Everest' incorporated e-learning and Pac-Man-style gaming which was visualized through avatars who 'climbed' the sales mountain in return for prizes as sales were achieved. AstraZeneca uses a web-based game, 'Go to Jupiter', to improve agents' product-related knowledge to support the roll-out of new medicines. Agents earn points by answering quizzes and playing different mini-games focused on the features of a new product.

As with social media and mobile, it's important you're not seduced by the novelty of gamification. A game should be a means to an end, not the end in itself. This is yet another reason why clearly defining your Brand Experience Essentials is so important. Your Brand Experience Essentials provide focus and direction for the gamification approach you employ – on the assumption it's relevant to your brand. If your brand is characterized by a fun-loving personality, then incorporating the odd joke or prank into your game won't go amiss.

Conclusions

Stakeholders increasingly expect your communications to be aligned, personalized, engaging and interactive. Focusing on internal communications, social media, mobile, content/conversations, communities, brand language identity, stories and gamification, this chapter has outlined a number of ways you can achieve these goals.

One caveat: the innovative nature of social media, mobile and gamification can be seductive. If you're using these means of communication, I would encourage you to keep checking back so they are used in ways that enable your Brand Experience Essentials. If you don't they could cloud the clarity of your brand experience, doing more damage than good.

This chapter is accompanied by Toolkit 15.1.

Endnotes

1   If you would like to read more around the fundamentals of marketing communications, I recommend: Zook, Z and Smith, P R (2006) *Marketing Communications: Offline and online integration, engagement and analytics,* Kogan Page.

2   IBM (2015a) The great customer experience divide, April [online] http://bit.ly/wavelegth-IBM

3   Solomon , M (2014) How to think like Apple about the customer service experience, *Forbes*, 21 November [online] bit.ly/wavelength-steve-jobs

4   BBC (2016) The science of engagement [online] http://bit.ly/wavelength-bbc

5   Rais, T (2015) Emirates NBD, 'Hey Future Me...': a social experiment to start a conversation between parents and children, WARC Prize for Social Strategy, Shortlisted [online] www.warc.com

6   Frances, K (2015) FIFA World Cup CIBC Soccer Nation, WARC Prize for Social Strategy, Entrant [online] www.warc.com

7   Warc (2017) ING: The Next Rembrandt, WARC Innovation Awards, Entrant, 2017 [online] www.warc.com

8   Yoong, J and Gaudette, D (2016) Sony Pictures Entertainment: Goosebumps – movie magic comes to life, Warc Prize for Social Strategy, Shortlisted

9   Anand, N (2016) Straight Talk: A new approach to thought leadership marketing, WARC Innovation Awards, Entrant, 2016 [online] www.warc.com

10 Edelman Trust Barometer (2017) [online] http://bit.ly/wavelength-edelman-2017

11 Gee, R (2017) Lenovo: Millennials want interactive ads, not just a 30-second spot, *Marketing Week*, 29 March [online] http://bit.ly/wavelength-lenovo

12 Baumeister, R F and Leary, M R (1995) The need to belong: desire for interpersonal attachments as a fundamental human motivation, *Psychology Bulletin*, **117**, pp 497–529

13 See http://bit.ly/wavelength-vans

14 Erdoğmuş, I E and Çiçek, M (2012) The impact of social media marketing on brand loyalty, *Procedia – Social and Behavioral Sciences*, **58** (12) October, pp 1353–60

15 Kumar, A et al (2016) From social to sale: the effects of firm-generated content in social media on customer behavior, *Journal of Marketing*, **80** (1), pp 7–25

16 See http://bit.ly/ost-sun-pat for details

17 Taylor, J (nd) Social CRM case study: Sony Europe creates a community of super-fans, *Our Social Times* [online] http://bit.ly/OurSocialTimes_Sony

18 Mobile is a fast-moving area. To keep abreast of the times I would encourage you to review online sources such as warc.com, Mashable or Mobile Marketing Magazine

19 Hollis, N (2017) What marketers must do to appeal to Gen Z, Kantar Millward Brown, 16 January [online] http://bit.ly/wavelength-genz

20 Lundqvist, A et al (2013) The impact of storytelling on the consumer brand experience: the case of a firm-originated story, *Journal of Brand Management*, 20, pp 283–97

21 Zadbood A et al (2017) How we transmit memories to other brains: constructing shared neural representations via communication, *Cerebral Cortex*, 27 (10), 1 October

22 Toh, M (2017) PepsiCo's first chief design officer: people don't just buy products anymore, *Fortune*, 20 March [online] http://bit.ly/wavelength-pepsi

23 Full disclosure: David is my father and Mark is my brother.

24 If you would like to read more about gamification, Gabe Zichermann's book is a good place to start: Zichermann, G (2013) *The Gamification Revolution: How leaders leverage game mechanics to crush the competition*, McGraw-Hill Education.

25 IBM (2015b) Marketing is a (buyer) journey, not a destination

26 Arling-Giorgi, A et al (2016) 5 Gum: Truth or Dare Challenge, Institute of Practitioners in Advertising, Entrant, IPA Effectiveness Awards 2016 [online] www.warc.com

27 Warc (2016) MILO: MILO Champions Band and App, Direct Marketing Association (US), Bronze, DMA International ECHO Awards 2016 [online] www.warc.com

Design

16

The previous chapter highlighted how you can use communication to enable your Brand Experience Essentials in aligned, personalized, engaging and interactive ways. To complement classical communication tools such as TV, radio or print, this entails using mobile, social media and gamification to name a few.

This chapter details how 'design', in the form of multisensory design and service design, can be used to enable your Brand Experience Essentials. Multisensory design refers to the use of sight, smell, sound, taste and touch. Service design uses practical tools like customer journey mapping, prototyping and storyboards to facilitate the design of services that are part of the brand experiences you build.

Reading this chapter will help you understand how to embrace a more holistic approach to enabling your Brand Experience Essentials through design.

As with behaviour and communications, design will help you enable your Brand Experience Essentials. Whilst reading this chapter you'll find it helpful to reflect on the illustrative questions in Table 16.1.

Table 16.1 Connecting design and the Brand Experience Essentials: questions to ask yourself

	How can we:
Values	Use design to bring our values to life?
Essence	Harness design so we can build experiences that sit within the parameters of our essence?
Promise	Use design to help us deliver relevant brand experience-related benefits?
Positioning	Employ design to support our positioning?
Personality	Express our personality through design?

Design and brand experiences

From a branding perspective, design historically tends to be associated with visual brand assets such as brand name, logo, font, website, apps or brochures. But design encompasses much more than this.

Purists from specific design disciplines might contest my point of view but I find it useful to consider design from multisensory and service design perspectives, primarily because it breaks the topic into digestible chunks, which facilitates a deeper and more complete understanding. It also stretches clients' thinking beyond visual identity so it gives them the potential to enable their Brand Experience Essentials in more rounded, interesting, and ultimately, relevant ways. Finally, considering design in this way compels clients to embrace a 'human-centred design' mentality and challenges them to think about experiences from the stakeholders' perspective.

Scientific research shows how our senses work together[1] to help us better understand our surroundings and give us a more 'accurate' impression of the world. Consequently, the smartest brands take a holistic, multisensory approach when enabling their Brand Experience Essentials, so they appeal to more of our senses. Designing with more than one sense in mind also means that your brand experiences will be more accessible to people with sensory disabilities.

The business case for design is emerging[2] (see Figure 16.1) and world-class brands increasingly think beyond visual design when using design

Figure 16.1 Design-centric organizations vs S&P 500: 2005–15 Comparison

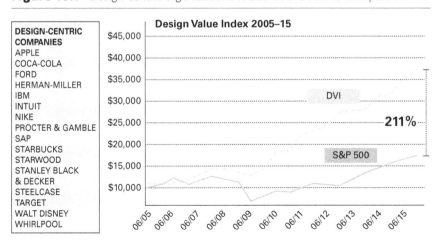

SOURCE Used with permission of the Design Management Institute and Motiv Strategies. For more go to dmi.org/value

to build brand experience. Organizations like GE, 3M, IBM, PepsiCo and SAP lead the way with their design centres. These brands understand and embrace design in a broader sense that encompasses service design.

The remaining sections explore the role played by multisensory and service design in enabling Brand Experience Essentials.

Multisensory design

Forty-seven per cent of 18–34-year-olds (versus 25 per cent of over-55s) say that engaging with them in innovative and creative ways to provide a multisensory experience influences their overall feeling of loyalty toward a brand or company (Accenture).[3]

Visual

You can use a variety of visual cues to enable your Brand Experience Essentials.

Logos

Virgin's slanted logo indicates a nonconforming corporation. This contrasts with the more structured and corporate undertones of IBM's logo.

Colour

Healthcare brands such as BUPA embody their caring and sincere values through the gentle blue and green tones they use on a white background. Conversely, Versace use bright and bold colours to convey their confident and extrovert brand personality.

Colour carries cultural meaning. Red implies good luck and happiness in the East and danger in the West. White is used to celebrate weddings in the West, but funerals in the East. Brands need to be careful of these idiosyncrasies when going global. In her Expert Insight, Kirsi Mantua-Kommonen shares five points you should consider if you plan on taking your brand to one of the world's great opportunities – China.

EXPERT INSIGHT 16.1 Taking your brand to China: five top tips

Dr Kirsi Mantua-Kommonen, Founder, CEO, CMO/AuroraXplorer 极行客

1 **Semantics of the name.** In China, your Western brand's original alphabetic name is often translated into Chinese. Angry Birds was translated into 'Angry little bird', 'Fènnù de xiǎo niǎo' (愤怒的小鸟).

2 **Phonetics of the name**. Chinese characters have multiple meanings. Coca-Cola's 'Kěkǒukělè' (可口可乐) sounds like the original name and consists of characters with fitting connotations: literally 'can mouth, can fun', where (可口可) also means 'delicious', adding up to 'delicious fun'.

3 **Colour of your logo**. Red is the most important colour in China: it represents happiness and has the power to expel evil spirits. Green carries the biggest risk in one situation: a green hat connotes betrayal in a marriage. Consequently, the staff of a Shanghai Starbucks wear black-brimmed hats.

4 **Shape of your logo.** In Chinese culture the circle is the shape of heaven while the earth was believed to be square, so the square has come to represent worldly laws and regulations. Ancient Chinese coins were round with a square hole in the centre. The Bank of China uses the shape of those coins as their symbol to represent prosperity and wealth.

5 **Symbolism of numbers.** Number eight is the luckiest number in Chinese culture. The character for eight, '八', is pronounced 'bā', which rhymes with 'fa' (发), prosperity. Number four suggests bad luck and even phone numbers containing the digit four are avoided.

AuroraXplorer 极行客 sells once-in-a-lifetime experiences for the Chinese travelling to Europe.

Imagery

Harrods' imagery is quite different to that of Costco and sends a clear Brand Experience Essential message in terms of its premium brand promise, personality and positioning.

Typography

Coca-Cola creatively shaped its invitation to 'open happiness' in the form of its iconic bottles. They were so confident this would be successful they did not use the Coca Cola name or logo outside the bottle design.

Typeface

Toy brands like Hasbro and Lego use rounded fonts to give their brands a playful, fun, friendly and youthful feel, whilst Ralph Lauren's Purple Label font is sophisticated, intricate and well crafted, just like the clothes.

Video

Airbnb is experimenting with 360-degree applications such as Periscope to create immersive tours, which ties in perfectly with the brand's positioning: 'living like a local'. John Lewis's Christmas adverts are filmed in detached suburban houses, located in leafy suburbs, with nice gardens. This sends the relevant message to its middle-class target market,[4] which is quite different to the playful and mildly sarcastic approach Aldi adopts with its 'Like Brands'[5] campaign.

Packaging

Your first shipment from the Dollar Shave Club arrives in an attractively branded box with a fun welcome note that supports its playful and slapstick positioning. To support their quintessentially English positioning, Fortnum and Mason redesigned their tea packaging, which increased like-for-like volume sales by 103 per cent.[6]

Branded environments

Global law firms like Baker McKenzie locate their offices in locations such as Fifth Avenue, New York City to reinforce premium positioning. The industrial design used in Diesel stores contrasts sharply with the clean lines that adorn Prada stores to convey a minimal and timeless essence.

Although many brands and banks in particular are focused on digital transformation, classic bricks-and-mortar retail still has a part to play in delivering brand experiences. In their Expert Insight, Charlotte Barry and Charlie Green outline how Lloyds Banking Group's brand and segment-specific requirements intersect and are expressed through retail experience design.

EXPERT INSIGHT 16.2 How Lloyds Banking Group uses retail experiences to support its positioning

Charlotte Barry (Strategy Manager) and Charlie Green (Senior Portfolio Brand Manager)

At Lloyds Banking Group we hold a portfolio of brands that provide products and services for distinct customer segments, brought alive by the different brand values, visual identities and brand experiences associated with each one. These values and experiences thread through propositions, marketing, and branch colleague interactions with customers.

For Lloyds Bank, the current brand positioning is, 'Whatever your next step, Lloyds Bank will be by your side.' This is demonstrated in a variety of ways with the brand positioned to provide the support and guidance for customers to face their next steps with confidence. Brand experience toolkits, internal support and training enable colleagues in branches to bring this to life. By helping colleagues to take the time to understand our customers and listen to what they need, they are able to give our customers financial confidence – a key tenet of our brand values.

We are bringing this to life with our new-style concept branch in Clapham, as it has been specially designed to address the changing ways our customers

Figure 16.2 Lloyds Bank, Clapham Junction Branch

choose to bank on the high street and focus on the needs of the customer base in that area. When launching the new branch, research showed that getting on the property ladder, saving for holidays, and setting up a new company were particularly relevant themes to customers in the Clapham area. As a result, branch colleagues have been upskilled to hold deep expertise in these areas and the in-branch material has been weighted to reflect this.

New concepts in the branch help support these service requirements and include an interactive digital map on a large screen to help customers thinking of moving home to 'map their move'. There's free WiFi and phone charging available, as well as colleagues equipped with iPads who can now have more in-depth conversations with customers in the banking hall.

The branch opens seven days a week and has extended opening hours on some days to make it easier for local residents – many of whom commute to central London each day for work – to visit the branch when it's convenient to them.

Note: this case and the associated images were provided by Lloyds Bank in August 2017 and were current at that time.

Lloyds Banking Group operates the UK's largest retail and commercial bank and has a footprint that touches nearly every community and household in the UK.

Vehicles

Your fleet of hybrid vans or bicycle subsidy policy suggests you are a brand shaped by socially responsible values. Five-star hotels in Dubai have fleets of Rolls-Royces to reinforce their premium positioning, whilst a new fleet of courier vans helps deliver a key benefit – peace of mind.

Clothing

The minimalist and timeless clothes your employees wear to meetings reflect your premium brand personality, whilst the funky shirt, immaculately groomed beard, trendy shoes and carefully-chosen vintage accessories highlight your brand's hipster roots.

Smell

Smell is the only sense that has a direct line to your brain's limbic system. This is important because the limbic system deals with long-term memory and emotion, so plays a crucial role in how you make decisions (see Chapter 5).

Have you ever walked into a shop to buy salad but smelled some fried food sizzling? Before you know it, you're tucking into the fried food. This happens because scent connects directly to the emotional receptors in your brain before logic or reason can have their say.

Our 'odour' memory is also resistant to forgetting. Images fade days or even hours after viewing but recall of smells can remain for much longer periods of time. Think back to your childhood where you may have used Crayola crayons at school or enjoyed the smell of your favourite homemade food. It's likely that your associated emotions will flood back.

A number of brands use scent to enable their Brand Experience Essentials. Singapore Airlines uses 'Stefan Floridian Waters' in its aircraft, as a cabin crew fragrance, and on hot towels. The patented scent is based on a mixture of rose, lavender and citrus to convey the premium oriental feel the brand embodies. Ritz-Carlton Doha uses ultra-expensive oud to reinforce its prestige with a Middle Eastern twist, whilst its Kyoto property blends locally grown matcha with lemon, cardamom, cider wood and jasmine to reinforce the brand's premium positioning with Japanese undertones.

Sound

When brands use music that fits with their brand, people are:

- 96 per cent more likely to recall them than those with non-fit music or no music at all;
- 24 per cent more likely to buy a product with music that they recall or like.[7]

- 73 per cent of music fans believe a brand improves its image by associating itself with music.
- 62 per cent felt that aligned music encourages them to test a brand's products and services.
- 70 per cent think it makes a brand stand out from its competitors.[8]

Research shows that music influences our memory, emotion and movement. One study found that music activates parts of the brain associated with intensely personal and emotional memories referred to as 'autobiographical memories'.[9] Another identified how the 'pulse and tonality' of music activates wide networks in the brain including the limbic system, which is associated with emotion.[10] So, now you know why that bass feels so good.

> 'What seems to happen is that a piece of familiar music serves as a soundtrack for a mental movie that starts playing in our head. It calls back memories of a particular person or place, and you might all of a sudden see that person's face in your mind's eye... Now we can see the association between those two things – the music and the memories.'
>
> Professor P Janata, University of California, Davis[11]

'Sound of Porsche' was created for the launch of the 911 GTS in New York, London and Shanghai so people could learn more about Porsche's values and the 911 GTS through sound and light visualization. Burberry Acoustic gives up-and-coming British bands an opportunity to share their music online or in Burberry stores. This supports Burberry's positioning, which is increasingly aimed at the more well-heeled members of the Millennial generation. Wrangler jeans teamed up with Universal Music Group Nashville to bring unique music videos to fans. The goal was to associate the brand with the positive feeling country music generates amongst its core target customers. The Champions League uses an anthem developed by the composer Tony Britten from a musical phrase in Handel's *Zadok the Priest* to give the tournament a premium feel.

When enabling brand experiences through sound you need to consider the growing area of voice. Amazon's voice-activated Echo enables customers to order from the store, play music and search the Web. The integration of Alexa, Amazon's virtual assistant, into the Ford Fusion dashboard allows drivers to use a variety of voice control commands. Starbucks is rolling out 'My Starbucks Barista', which lets you order your coffee via voice on their app.

This type of 'conversational commerce' offers great customer convenience. It also caters for notable, yet underserved customers such as those who are visually impaired or have other disabilities.

Considering how your brand interacts with customers via voice provides another opportunity for your brand to enable its Brand Experience Essentials in a relevant way. If your brand personality is supportive then a caring tone should be adopted. A more playful or mischievous brand may adopt a more sarcastic tone from time to time to keep customers on their toes.

Online music platforms such as Spotify and Pandora are pioneering an alternative approach to building brand experiences through sound. Spotify has developed segments around six different 'moments' of the day: chill time, workout, party, dinner, focus and sleep. Brands like Wendy's, for instance, sponsor 'dinner'. Pandora has segmented around lifestyle: their 'fitness enthusiast' acts as a draw for Gatorade's Propel Water electrolyte replacement brand. Here, music acts as a means of enabling their Brand Experience Essentials at timely moments relevant to a given customer's lifestyle.

Taste

Passengers on Swiss Airlines flights can look forward to a complimentary piece of Swiss chocolate; this reinforces the Swiss element of the airline's brand. DoubleTree hotels are famed for their delicious, warm, chocolate-chip cookies which are baked fresh daily and given to guests when they check in. These help guests feel cared for whilst the smell helps evoke homely emotions, complimenting the brand's positioning perfectly. Some Wavelength clients send locally produced organic hampers at Christmas to reinforce their commitment to sustainability, whilst others have retro, playful sweets at reception to show they're an outgoing, fun and young brand.

Touch

A number of Jean Paul Gaultier's perfumes are presented in evocative body-shaped bottles; a perfect fit for this sensual and sexual brand. Fedrigoni, a paper manufacturer, partnered with the camera brand Leica to replace the leather casing on 25 of its cameras with fine and tough Fedrigoni Constellation Jade paper. The 'Paper Skin' campaign produced a 36 per cent and 57.2 per cent year-on-year revenue uplift across the business and in the Constellation Jade product lines respectively, and delivered a media value equivalent of €477,549.[12]

An increasing number of brands are incorporating haptics into their brand experiences. Stolichnaya Vodka's 'spin' advert was specially designed for mobile to simulate the feel of a cocktail being made in a person's hand. Cadillac's sensor-linked Safety Alert Seat sends vibrations through the driver's seat if they are in danger of collision. Foxtel created the Alert Shirt for Aussie rules soccer. When spectators wear the Alert Shirt they feel every tackle and even flutters in players' heartbeats if they're nervous before taking an important kick. A great fit for a brand that is all about bringing its customers closer to the game.

Service design

Service design spans a number of disciplines including product design, interaction design, operations management, ethnography and more. In her Expert Insight, Ksenija Kuzmina sheds some light on what service design is and how it dovetails with broader design thinking.

EXPERT INSIGHT 16.3 Understanding design thinking and service design

Dr Ksenija Kuzmina, Programme Director of Design Innovation Programme, Institute for Design Innovation, Loughborough University London

Design thinking is an approach to problem solving that designers use based on knowing by doing. There are four stages of design thinking:

1 discovery (understanding user needs);
2 definition (defining insights);
3 development (developing prototypes);
4 delivery (delivering the result).

Service design is a design field that creates new or improves existing private and public services to make them more usable, useful, effective and efficient. To bring stakeholders into the design thinking process, service design adopts and adapts a series of practical design thinking tools during the four stages of design:

- In the Discovery stage, empathic tools and methods (eg cultural probes) are used to explore the problem space as it is understood by stakeholders.
- In the Definition stage, a set of generative tools (eg storytelling) helps stakeholders to visualize, react to and discuss the findings in order to construct a shared meaning and vision for the new service.

- Finally, in the Development and Delivery stages, the vision is developed and explored using prototyping tools (eg living labs). These tools help stakeholders model the change and evaluate it prior to implementation by the designer and other stakeholders.

Design thinking in service design, therefore, is a process facilitated by the designer to engage all in order to develop the most effective service solutions.

Loughborough University London is an inspiring postgraduate campus located on the Queen Elizabeth Olympic Park.

Service designers use a use a range of practical and visually oriented tools that can help enable your Brand Experience Essentials, which I will introduce now.[13]

Customer personas

Customer personas are imaginary (or sometimes real) characters that represent a given segment and were introduced in Chapter 6. Personas bring the customer to the forefront of the organization's minds and can deliver powerful service design insights. Although they are referred to as 'customer personas' they can be used to help you understand other stakeholder groups.

Based on quantitative data analysis, Wavelength developed customer personas with names such as Abdul, Amr and Fatima for a healthcare brand in the Middle East. We created life-size mannequins representing each segment and these were located around the client's office, providing employees with a constant reminder of their customer-centric brand promise. The mannequins also provided a timely visual reminder to customer services representatives who could then tailor the language and tone they used based on the segment they were speaking to. We have also trained retail assistants to ask customers a handful of carefully scripted questions so they can identify which segment a person belongs to before escorting them to a relevant part of the store.

Customer empathy maps

Customer empathy maps help you obtain deeper customer insights if customer personas do not suffice. They encourage you to explore what customers think feel, see, say, do and hear, in addition to understanding what they want to gain and where they feel pain in life.[14] The result is a deep appreciation of their psyche, context and worldview which you can take into account when building brand experiences. Walt Disney used to join customers in lines to understand the experience better, whilst Michele Ferrero, owner of the Nutella, Kinder Surprise, Ferrero Rocher and Tic Tac brands would crawl around retail stores on his hands and knees to see if children could reach the chocolates on display.

Customer journey maps

These identify the key touchpoints a stakeholder will experience when engaging with your brand. These touchpoints could bring stakeholders into contact with technology, people, spaces or products.

At Virgin Holidays, within seven days of purchase a customer is introduced to a Virgin Holidays expert who will help them personalize their holiday. Fifteen days before departure a member of staff based at their destination calls to introduce themselves and ask if they need any help or have any questions. A few days before they travel, Virgin Holidays will send the customer an SMS detailing where they should meet their Virgin Holiday Rep at the airport. When customers return from their holiday, they receive a 'welcome back' call.

Porsche's Vehicle Delivery app is a thoughtful pre-delivery touchpoint that allows customers to learn about their car before it arrives. When they get their Porsche, customers want to drive it, not waste time figuring out how to use the cruise control or electric seats.

The role of post-purchase experience should not be overlooked. Once you have a customer, you have opportunities to cross-sell, up-sell, or simply thank them for their business to deepen your commercial relationship. Research with B2B executives supports this point. Sixty-one per cent of 'CX Leaders' regard aftersales service and support as 'very important' in comparison to 20 per cent of 'CX Laggards'.[15]

When Audi wanted to increase sales of services and genuine Audi parts in Germany, their 'Don't let your Audi fall into the wrong hands' campaign aimed to show customers that going for a cheaper option may not always be the right choice. Comparing March/May 2014 with March/May 2015, Audi saw a 7.4 per cent increase in service hours, 10.1 per cent increase in genuine spare parts sold, 30.51 per cent uplift in perceptions as a 'top-level service partner' and a 16.53 per cent uplift in perceptions as an 'exclusive partner for service issues'.[16]

Matthew Wong's Expert Insight outlines how Audi Singapore uses a Customer Delight programme as part of the post-sales customer experience.

EXPERT INSIGHT 16.4 How service design helps Audi
Singapore delight customers

Matthew Wong, Aftersales Operations Executive, Audi Singapore Pte Ltd

The Audi Customer Delight programme is an important part of service design at Audi
Singapore Aftersales. This programme is in place at the dealership and empowers
employees to delight random customers on special occasions throughout the year.
This could include gifting mooncakes to customers during the mid-autumn festival,
providing Audi toys for children who visit the service centre with their parents
during the school holidays, or using our Audi A8 Top Service Shuttle to drop off
customers who have left their car for service at their preferred location.

It is important to note that delighting customers does not always necessarily
refer to monetary gifts; it also refers to how employees carry out the service and
the task at hand as Audi representatives. The aim of the Audi Customer Delight
programme is to make customers' experience at the service centre positive and
memorable. By doing so, our aim is to thank customers and encourage them to
become Audi brand advocates.

To continuously ensure that the service design is kept up to date and remains
relevant, customers' experiences toward the service centre are measured and
recorded through phone interviews and feedback via the Audi Top Service app
after they have left the centre. A fixed number of customers are contacted every
day. Through these interviews and feedback from all frontline staff, gaps and
shortcomings will be constantly identified and amended. With that, all staff can
always deliver the positive brand experiences based on the service design of
Audi Aftersales.

*The Audi Group, with its brands Audi, Ducati and Lamborghini, is one of the
most successful manufacturers of automobiles and motorcycles in the premium
segment. It is present in more than 100 markets worldwide and produces at 16
locations in 12 countries.*

There are lots of ways to illustrate customer journey maps. Some great,
some good, but many are simply confusing. It's better to keep it simple and
build from there. Figure 16.3 provides an example Wavelength used with a
place brand client located in the Middle East.

Figure 16.3 Simplified customer journey map: Wavelength Marketing client example (tourist destination in the Middle East)

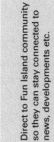

wavelength
marketing®

DELIVERING EMOTIONALLY CHARGED BRAND EXPERIENCES AT FUN ISLAND

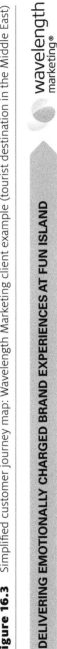 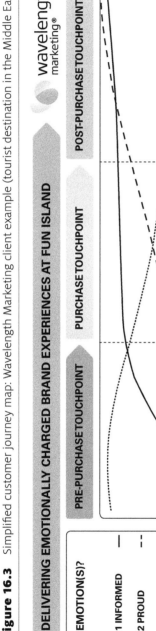 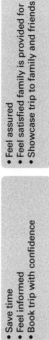 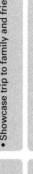 

	PRE-PURCHASE TOUCHPOINT	PURCHASE TOUCHPOINT	POST-PURCHASE TOUCHPOINT
EMOTION(S)? 1 INFORMED — 2 PROUD - - 3 APPREHENSIVE ····			
JOB(S) TO BE DONE?	• Show the family you love them • Reward yourself/satisfy ego • Identify and understand all relevant options	• Save time • Feel informed • Book trip with confidence	• Feel assured • Feel satisfied family is provided for • Showcase trip to family and friends
PROPOSITION? BOOKING A FAMILY HOLIDAY ON FUN ISLAND	Engage with Fun Island-related content (infographic)	Mobile portal/micro site with optimized user experience	Personalized follow-up email
DELIVERY? BEHAVIOUR	Not pushy. Be available on relevant channels (on/offline)	Support if required eg 'click for call back'/Chat pop up providing support	Direct to Fun Island community so they can stay connected to news, developments etc.
COMMUNICATIONS	Informative and engaging content using an upbeat tone of voice	Concise, practical and goal-oriented content/direct to community for opinion and advice	Use sincere and personable language to show gratitude
DESIGN	Branded multimedia infographic with embedded video, that sells key benefits and direct to www	Simple user experience, family visuals, video aligned with target market interests eg musical	Ability to redeem special coupon that lets you use fun filters on your favorite family pictures
METRICS?	Number of views/shares/clicks to www	Sales/dwell time/video views/shares	Mail opens/clicks/voucher redemption

NOTE 'Fun Island' is a fictitious name. Also, this illustration is an abbreviated version so not every emotion or job is connected at every stage to behaviour communications and design. This was required to [illustrate] [fit the].

When working with clients to create a customer journey map similar to Figure 16.3 I find it useful to follow these six steps:

1 **Identify the proposition.** Booking a family holiday on Fun Island.

2 **Pinpoint the most important touchpoints for before, during and after purchase.** These could be interacting with an infographic (pre-purchase), visiting an optimized mobile/micro site (during) and a personalized follow-up email (post-purchase).

3 **Understand the 'jobs' your stakeholder needs to get done at each touchpoint.** When booking a family holiday, the 'jobs' Dad may need to get done include: show the family he loves them (pre-purchase), save time (during purchase) and feel assured (post-purchase). Please note in this example Dad was considered the key decision maker in the family, but in other markets and contexts it may well be someone else.

4 **Define the emotions you want customers to feel at each touchpoint.** Dad may want to feel increasingly informed and proud but less apprehensive as he progresses through the customer journey. You can then draw a line to profile these emotions during the customer journey.

5 **Use behaviour, communications and design to help customers get those jobs done and feel the desired emotion at each touchpoint.** At the pre-purchase touchpoint, Dad may want to show the family he loves them (the job) whilst feeling less apprehensive and more informed before he speaks to them about the trip (the desired emotion). To achieve these goals the brand could use:

   a *Behaviour*: non-pushy sales approach so he knows help is there if required. This aims to ease his apprehensions.

   b *Communications*: informative and engaging tone of voice used in copy to help him feel increasingly informed.

   c *Design*: A branded infographic with embedded clips of relevant video he can share with the family. If the content is great, he will feel increasingly proud (and his ego will be satisfied) whilst showing the family he loves them by taking them to a fantastic place.

6 **Identify key metrics for each stage of the journey.** At the pre-purchase stage this could be infographic views, shares or clicks through to the microsite.

An alternative approach to customer journey mapping would change the 'emotions' element in Figure 16.3 to the 'relative importance of brand values'. Figure 16.4 illustrates how The Edgbaston Priory Club, a premium racquets and lifestyle members' club located in the UK, worked with Wavelength using this approach. The example focuses on reception but other parts of the

Figure 16.4 Customer journey map: Wavelength Marketing client example (Edgbaston Priory Club, UK)

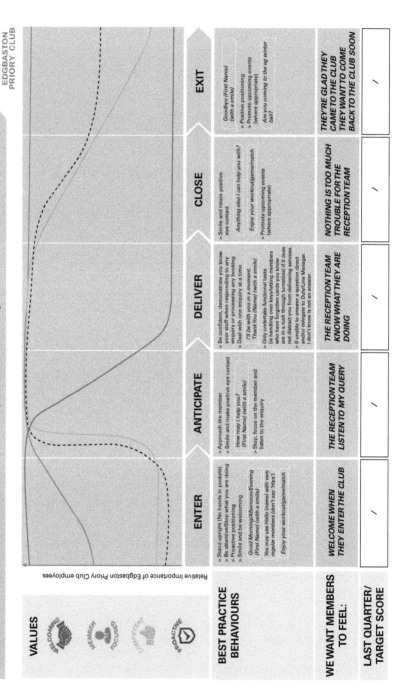

SERVICE DELIVERY BLUEPRINT (RECEPTION)

EDGBASTON PRIORY CLUB

Relative importance of Edgbaston Priory Club employees

	ENTER	ANTICIPATE	DELIVER	CLOSE	EXIT
BEST PRACTICE BEHAVIOURS	> Stand upright (No hands in pockets) > Be attentive/Stop what you are doing > Proactive positioning > Smile and be welcoming *Good Morning/Afternoon/Evening (First Name) (with a smile)* *You may use Hello (name) with very regular members (don't say 'Hiya')* *Enjoy your workout/game/match*	> Approach the member > Smile and make positive eye contact *How may I help you? (First Name) (with a smile)* > Stop, focus on the member and listen to the enquiry	> Be confident, demonstrate you know your stuff when responding to any enquiry or processing any booking > Deal with one enquiry at a time *I'll be with you in a moment. Thank You (Name) (with a smile)* > Only undertake functional tasks (ie handling over keys/letting members who have forgotten cards you know are in a rush through turnstiles) if it does not distract you from delivering services. > If unable to answer a question direct and/or delegate to DutyLine Manager. I don't know is not an answer.	> Smile and retain positive eye contact *Anything else I can help you with?* *Enjoy your workout/game/match* > Promote upcoming events (where appropriate)	*Goodbye (First Name) (with a smile)* > Positive positioning > Promote upcoming events (where appropriate) *Are you coming to the eg winter ball?*
WE WANT MEMBERS TO FEEL:	*WELCOME WHEN THEY ENTER THE CLUB*	*THE RECEPTION TEAM LISTEN TO MY QUERY*	*THE RECEPTION TEAM KNOW WHAT THEY ARE DOING*	*NOTHING IS TOO MUCH TROUBLE FOR THE RECEPTION TEAM*	*THEY'RE GLAD THEY CAME TO THE CLUB THEY WANT TO COME BACK TO THE CLUB SOON*
LAST QUARTER/ TARGET SCORE	/	/	/	/	/

VALUES

WELCOMING

MEMBER FOCUSED

COMPETENT

PROACTIVE

club followed a similar process to facilitate the delivery of a more consistent member experience.[17] Initially, we ran ideation workshops with the senior management team, club employees and members which:

- Identified stages of the member experience as 'enter', 'anticipate', 'deliver', 'close' and 'exit'.

- Highlighted the relative importance of certain values at specific stages as part of the member experience or 'service delivery blueprint'. During the 'enter' stage, Best Practice Behaviours encourage staff to be more welcoming, member-focused with relatively less emphasis on being competent and proactive at that stage in the experience.

- Developed 'Best Practice Behaviours' that brought the values to life, relative to their importance at a given stage. These were expressed through employees' posture, language and tone of voice, with indicative, baseline phrases being provided to facilitate the delivery of more consistent experiences.

- Selected performance metrics that dovetail with a range of human resource processes including recruitment, induction and training.

Annual brand experience measurement at the club showed membership satisfaction with the reception team enjoyed a year-on-year increase of 10 per cent. Given no other reception-focused initiatives occurred during that time, it's reasonable to attribute that to the service delivery blueprints.

Adopting this end-to-end view of the whole experience reduces the chances of organizational silos and introspective thinking taking root whilst encouraging collective responsibility. Research supports the adoption of a holistic approach to building brand experiences because it's the overall experience (not individual touchpoints) that drives metrics like customer satisfaction, willingness to recommend and revenue.[18] I agree the sum is more important than the parts, but I also think it's wise to obtain both Big Picture *and* Touchpoint metrics. If Big Picture metrics are sliding, you will then be able to dig deeper to identify the heart of the problem. I cover this in chapter 18.

When thinking about customer journey maps it's worth considering 'Peak End Theory'.[19] This outlines how two things really matter when building experiences: the peaks or troughs (the best or worst moments), but more importantly, how we felt at the end of the experience. Think back to the last time you went for a meal; even if the experience was characterized by wonderful moments this all went to waste if the waiter was rude as you left.

Use case scenarios

Use case scenarios are examples of situations in which a customer or stakeholder will interact with your brand. An airport check-in counter, online chat support, or dealing with a demanding client are examples. The objective is to enhance the user experience delivered by understanding a use case scenario from a stakeholder's perspective.

To maximize the benefit delivered by the scenarios, you should locate use cases in the context of the overall experience. This will shed light on the various flows, outline who is involved, their emotional state and enhance your appreciation of the surrounding environment. Framing the use case within this context will also help you understand how the customer may feel when they enter that scenario. These insights can then feed into service design, which should be underpinned by your Brand Experience Essentials.

Wavelength worked with a bank that had operations across Southeast Asia and wanted to align its brand experience with its brand promise built around three tenets: simplicity, solutions and speed. A key customer persona was an established business executive who didn't like technology but valued personal service and respect. The bank's reputation was built on this type of customer, so they were important. This customer preferred to draw cash from the cashier but when they were confronted with a long queue, became frustrated and the perceived complexity of an ATM made them nervous. The bank wanted to encourage this customer to 'self-serve' more. Working closely with the bank, we sought to understand the ATM use case scenarios for this customer. This required an understanding of:

- the overall experience: wanting to withdraw cash but usually in a rush as they've parked their expensive car illegally;
- various flows: cashier, ATM, wait, walk out;
- people involved: staff, other customers, security;
- stakeholder's emotional state: 'hot 'n' bothered';
- environment: signage, ATM interface, aesthetics and functionality, lighting, music, furnishings.

Service/experience prototyping

Service/experience prototyping helps brands understand how customers interact with a service delivered as part of the overall experience and provides a useful basis for iterative service development. Developing the previous retail banking client example, we created ATM prototypes with the bank's brand promise in mind. Because the brand promise majored on simplicity, solutions and speed we developed and fine-tuned ATM prototypes until the user experience struck a balance of all three. This didn't require advanced prototyping tools. We used pens, paper, cardboard and tape and only built the final few iterations out of more robust and expensive materials.

When Emirates designed the upstairs bar for its A380 aeroplane, they built a wooden mock-up to assess appeal. This temporary bar could be removed within a few days and replaced with eight business-class seats. The bar proved to be enormously popular and is now a permanent and important part of the Emirates experience for business- and first-class travellers.

Mood boards

Mood boards combine images, words or even materials to capture the feeling associated with your brand. They are useful in focus groups when you want to understand how certain stakeholders feel about your brand, but they find it difficult to articulate themselves. A mood board can also help reduce the ambiguity concerning the 'atmosphere' you want your brand to convey in the context of the experiences you build – particularly useful when briefing agencies.

Wavelength worked with a pharmaceutical brand that wanted to shape its brand experience around values of being diligent, informed, commercial and inquisitive. Initial mood board insight from focus groups revealed their brand was not perceived that way. They were regarded as cold, unapproachable and sometimes even condescending. This brand audit insight fed into specific plans around employee behaviour, communications and design that aimed to change stakeholders' perceptions. Subsequent mood board-centred focus groups highlighted in very clear and visual ways how the various initiatives delivered the desired effect.

Storyboards

Storyboards visualize the use cases scenarios that represent part of or all of the brand experience. These sequential images will provide you with unique insights because they'll immerse you in the 'character's' journey from their perspective. By exploring real or imaginary stories and their associated scenarios it is possible to refine or identify where you need to change current services or design new ones.

Inspired by Disney's Snow White story, Airbnb's CEO, Brian Chesky, storyboarded the process of people who host and rent properties. These storyboards delivered nuanced insights that helped Airbnb create travel experiences supporting their positioning of 'living like a local'.

The storyboard doesn't need to be a work of art; it's the ideas and engagement that count. Figure 16.5 provides an example of how Wavelength, in partnership with illustrator Claudio Naccari, created a storyboard for a fictional character, Wavey. Some of the final illustrations are included so you

Figure 16.5 Using Wavey to tell brand stories at Wavelength Marketing

Use employee, brand and financial metrics to measure brand performance.

Craft an authentic brand story your market can relate to.

can see how the finished product looked. Wavey is used in a variety of ways such as in a calendar we send to clients or to storyboard brand messages and at keynote talks so we can convey serious points in a more light-hearted and visual way.

We looked at stories earlier (Chapter 15) but I wanted to share some 'lighter touch' tools you can use as the basis for creating use cases. You can unearth stories from customers or other stakeholders by asking them to complete one of the story templates provided in Figure 16.6.

Figure 16.6 Story creation template

- 'There was a time I felt so _____ that I really wanted to _____ but couldn't _____ so I _____.'

  For example: 'There was a time I felt so disappointed with the speed of the check-in that I really wanted to leave the hotel and stay somewhere else but couldn't get a refund at such short notice so I decided against staying at that hotel again.'

- 'I thought I was going to be able to _____ but couldn't _____ this meant I _____.'

  For example: 'I thought I was going to be able to withdraw $500 from the ATM when I was overseas but couldn't withdraw any money as I hadn't informed the bank of my travel plans and this meant I had to call the bank and wait on the line whilst they updated my account so I could withdraw the money.'

Once you have the stories you can then use other tools to design services that resolve customer issues or help them get jobs done. For the above scenarios this could entail ensuring a member of management staff is always on hand to help customers check in via a kiosk to expedite the process, and sending customers a roaming SMS when they arrive overseas informing them that they need to notify the bank, via a dedicated Freephone number, before they can withdraw money overseas.

At the start of an ideation workshop for an airline, Wavelength brought into the room four customers who represented segment personas. Using the above template to structure their stories, each person shared a series of frustrating experiences they had encountered with the airline. Check-in and food service were particularly problematic. These stories provided rich insights that inspired service design improvements at these key touchpoints, guided by their Brand Experience Essentials.

Conclusion

This chapter outlined how you can use multisensory and service design to enable your Brand Experience Essentials.

Multisensory design incorporates all the senses. Service design comprises a suite of stakeholder-centric, practical and visually oriented tools that will enable you to see the world through your stakeholders' eyes. This encourages empathy and so facilitates the delivery of more relevant brand experiences.

The use of multisensory and service design requires you to take a holistic approach to enabling your Brand Experience Essentials. The use of sight, sound, smell, taste and touch, where applicable, needs to be co-ordinated so your brand experiences feel cohesive and consistent. Service design tools should be used in ways that complement each other. For example, customer empathy mapping should feed into customer journey maps that benefit from use case scenarios, prototyping, and mood boards. Multisensory design and service design are not mutually exclusive. For example, your customer journey maps should appeal to as many of the senses as possible to make the most of the way our brains work.

When enabling your Brand Experience Essentials through multisensory design and service design, focus is key. You need to ensure multisensory design is used to enable your Brand Experience Essentials; the same applies with service design. If this isn't the case, don't use them as they will cloud your thinking and the experiences you build.

This chapter is accompanied by Toolkit 16.1.

Endnotes

1 Carvalhoa, F R et al (2017) 'Smooth operator': music modulates the perceived creaminess, sweetness, and bitterness of chocolate, *Appetite*, **108** (1), pp 383–90

2 Rae, J (2015) Design Value Index results and commentary: the power and value of design continues to grow across the S&P 500, *DMI*, December [online] http://bit.ly/wavelength-dmi

3 Accenture (2016) Seeing beyond the loyalty illusion: it's time you invest more wisely [online] http://bit.ly/wavelength-loyalty-1

4 Butler, S (2016) John Lewis Christmas ads: watch all the previous ones here, *Guardian* [online] http://bit.ly/wavelength-john-lewis-adverts

5 IPA Effectiveness Awards Case Study 2012, Aldi: The Like Brands campaign, viewed at bit.ly/wavelength-aldi

6 Warc (2015) Fortnum & Mason Teas packaging, Design Business Association, Gold, Design Effectiveness Awards, 2015 [online] www.warc.com

7 North, A C, Hargreaves, D J and McKendrick, J (1999) The influence of in-store music on wine selections, *Journal of Applied Psychology*, **84** (2), pp 271–76

8 Havas Media (2016) Music partnerships improve brand image, finds new research, Press Release [online] bit.ly/wavelength-sonicbranding-havas

9 Janata, P (2009) The neural architecture of music-evoked autobiographical memories, *Cerebral Cortex*, **19** (11), 24 February

10 Toiviainen, P A V et al (2012) Large-scale brain networks emerge from dynamic processing of musical timbre, key and rhythm, *Neuroimage*, **59**, pp 3677–89

11 Janata, P (2009) The neural architecture of music-evoked autobiographical memories, *Cerebral Cortex*, **19** (11), 24 February

12 Warc (2016) Fedrigoni: The Paper Skin, Cannes Creative Lions, Shortlisted, Creative Effectiveness Lions, 2016 [online] www.warc.com

13 To learn more about design thinking, service design and the associated tools, a good place to start is Stickdorn, S and Schneider, J (2012) *This is Service Design Thinking: Basics, tools, cases*, BIS Publishers, Amsterdam

14 Osterwalder, A, Pigneur, Y and Smith, A (2010) *Business Model Generation*, Wiley

15 Accenture Strategy (2015) Managing B2B customer experience [online] https://bit.ly/wavelength-B2Baccenture

16 Warc (2017) Audi: Mechanics, Cannes Creative Lions, Entrant, Creative Effectiveness Lions, 2017 [online] www.warc.com

17 Strictly speaking the project delivered customer journey maps but they were called 'Service Delivery Blueprints' for a variety of internal reasons.

18 McKinsey (2016) *Customer Experience: Creating value through transforming customer journeys* (No 1, Winter 2016) [online] http://bit.ly/wavelength-cx-mckinsey

19 Do, A M, Rupert, A V and Wolford, G (2008) Evaluations of pleasurable experiences: the peak-end rule, *Psychonomic Bulletin & Review*, **15** (1), pp 96–98

Summary: Brand 17 Experience Environment, Essentials and Enablers

The first part of this book introduced the Brand Experience Environment. This represents the context you need to keep in mind when developing and defining your Brand Experience Essentials. The Brand Experience Environment comprises four elements:

- **Understanding your stakeholders:** profiling stakeholders; helping stakeholders get 'jobs done'; encouraging stakeholder engagement; managing stakeholder expectations.

- **Fine-tuning your perspective:** embracing transparency; adopting a holistic mindset; competing primarily through value not price; having patience; accepting a loss of control.

- **Appreciating the mechanics of delivery:** creating an emotional connection; facilitating co-creation; delivering omnichannel experiences.

- **Adopting a data-driven approach:** obtaining robust insights; measuring holistically.

The second part of the book introduced the Brand Experience Essentials:

- **Brand values:** how would you describe your brand in four or five words?

- **Brand essence:** if you were asked to sum up your brand in two or three words, what would you say it's all about?

- **Brand promise:** what benefits NOT features does your brand deliver?

- **Brand positioning**: how are you different from your competitors?
- **Brand personality**: if you were to describe your brand as a person who would they be?

The Brand Experience Essentials are important. They are the foundations your brand experiences will be built on, will help focus your mind on the substance and not trappings of building brand experiences, whilst providing you with a scalable, underlying logic you can call on when you bring your brand to life through Brand Experience Enablers.

The third part of the book introduced the Brand Experience Enablers, which comprise:

- employee behaviour;
- communications;
- design.

The importance of well-defined Brand Experience Essentials becomes apparent at this stage of the brand experience-building process. If you have well-defined and understood Brand Experience Essentials, you will have clear principles guiding your use of Brand Experience Enablers.

The Brand Experience Blueprint provides you with a simple, comprehensive and robust framework you can use to build brand experiences. At its heart lies the three-staged 'Environment–Essential–Enablers' approach, which provides a practical guide on how to build brand experiences.

This chapter is accompanied by Toolkit 17.1.

PART FOUR
Measuring Brand Experiences

Figure P4.1   The Brand Experience Blueprint: couched in a brand experience measurement context

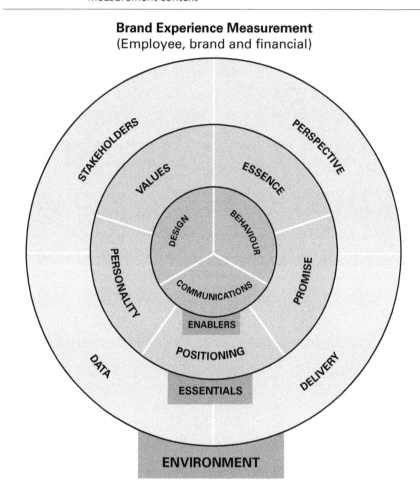

This part of the book provides practical advice on how you can measure brand experiences.

Although measurement is not a direct brand experience-building activity, being able to demonstrate the value delivered to your business by the brand experiences you build is a critical skill.

Reading Part Four will help you:

- get started with brand experience measurement;
- appreciate the benefits of adopting a holistic approach to measuring brand experiences;
- measure brand experience performance in a robust, objective and scientific way.

Getting started with measuring brand experiences 18

This chapter provides an overview of how you can get started with brand experience measurement by obtaining Big Picture and Touchpoint metrics. Understanding these metrics will provide you with a pragmatic framework to guide more detailed brand experience performance measurement and analytics.

Obtaining Big Picture and Touchpoint metrics

Measuring brand experience performance should operate at two levels.

Level 1: Big Picture metrics

These help senior leaders, managers and executives assess brand experience performance from a high level. They should include: *financial metrics*, eg sales, profit, contribution margin and EBITDA (earnings before interest, tax, depreciation and amortization); *employee metrics*, eg employee engagement, advocacy, relative satisfaction, brand knowledge, well-being (mental and emotional) and emotional intelligence; *brand metrics*, eg relevance, advocacy, awareness, associations, price premiums, reputation, relative satisfaction, purchase intent and value for money.

Whilst Net Effort Score is closely associated with experiences, it's another useful 'brand' metric because it provides clues about the amount of friction within the brand experiences you build.

Obtaining social media sentiment metrics is also advisable because it will help you measure the associations and feelings connected with your brand. It's advisable to obtain 'active' social media metrics such as shares, comments, mentions, retweets or average engagement per follower. They are indicative of brand relevance due to the fact someone has taken the time to engage and possibly associate with the content. This contrasts with commonly collected 'vanity' metrics such as numbers of followers, fans or likes which require, at best, limited effort. A small number of our clients have also started to include metrics around the brand doing social good and having a positive impact on the quality of life in society. Such decisions are based on their desire to measure how their belief system impacts business performance but also to bolster their employer branding efforts aimed at the Millennial generation and Gen Z, who are particularly cause-driven.

Figure 18.1 provides an anonymized example from a Wavelength client in the educational sector detailing some Big Picture metrics.

In the context of brand experience analytics, Big Picture metrics tend to be useful dependent variables; that is, they are variables whose value is the outcome of a change in another variable or variables.

Level 2: Touchpoint metrics

These are associated with specific moments in the brand experience. They could include the first impression of your social media channels, client debriefs or a post-purchase service call. When thinking about Touchpoint metrics it's advisable to break the brand experience into digestible chunks such as 'before', 'during' or 'after' a sale, so the data collection and analysis does not become overwhelming. Figure 18.2 shares part of a monthly dashboard Wavelength collates for a chain of boutique hotels. It focuses on the 'during the stay' stage of the experience.

Working closely with our client, we identified key or 'signature' touchpoints within each stage. For example, during their stay: the reception (check in), lobby, their room (facilities/service), restaurant, spa, bar, gym, concierge and reception (check out). Across these touchpoints the client was keen to increase relative satisfaction vs comparable hotels, make it very easy for guests to get things done, and help guests feel like individuals. These goals translated into the following, equally weighted, questions:[1]

- In comparison to other hotels I have stayed at I was extremely satisfied with the <reception/in the lobby etc>.
- <At reception/in the lobby etc> it was very easy to get things done.
- <At reception/in the lobby etc> I feel like I'm treated like an individual, not a number.

Given the service nature of this brand we also obtained employee metrics that were related to the customer metrics. For the 'during' phase some of the metrics obtained were:

Figure 18.1 Big Picture Dashboard: Wavelength Marketing client example (UK Educational Sector)

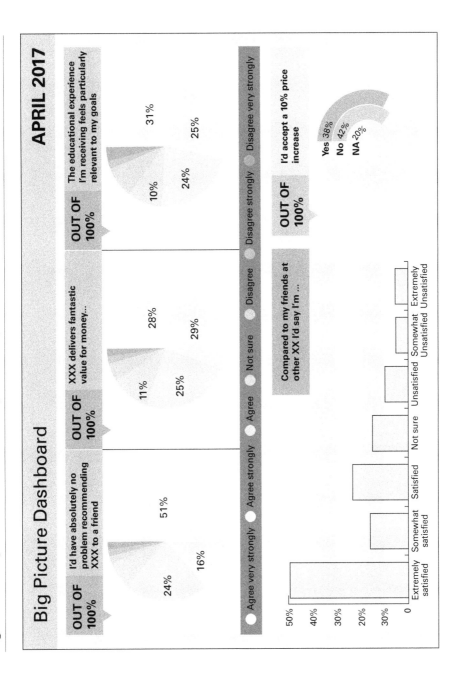

Figure 18.2 Touchpoint Metrics dashboard: Wavelength Marketing client (boutique hotel chain)

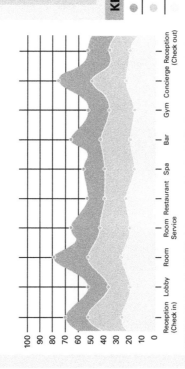

Touchpoint Metrics (During Stay)   APRIL 2017

Brand-Related Touchpoint Metrics (During Stay) April 2017

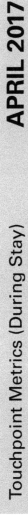

Brand Touchpoint Metrics

► **up 5%**
(vs Q1 2017 average)

► **up 2%**
(vs 2016 average)

KEY

● Relative satisfaction

● Very easy to get things done

— Treated like an individual not a number

Employee-Related Metrics (During Stay) April 2017

OUT OF 10

6
Feel empowered to serve the guest as an individual

7
I have the necessary skills to help guests get things done

9
If I can't help a guest get things done I know who I should ask for help

6
If I was a guest, I'd feel satisfied with the level of service received

- I feel empowered to serve the guest as an individual.
- I have the necessary skills to help guests get things done.
- If I can't help a guest get things done I know who I should ask for help.
- If I was a guest, I would feel satisfied with the level of service received.

These metrics feed into monthly, quarterly and annual dashboards that take data feeds from online customer surveys sent to guests when they check out. This data is used by the organization to: create key performance indicators (monthly, quarterly and annual); celebrate success; focus employee training and attention on areas that require more effort; and help managers evaluate employee performance as part of annual performance reviews which tie in with demonstrating values-based behaviour.

The Touchpoint metrics data is analysed in conjunction with the Big Picture metrics using statistical models to help the executive team understand which touchpoints drive overall brand experience performance. For instance, is it satisfaction with the spa, gym or restaurant that drives overall guest satisfaction? To do this, methods such as regression and structural equation modelling are used (see Chapter 6).

Equipped with these insights the management team can measure cause and effect in the context of building brand experiences in a more scientific and robust way. This helps them focus their efforts, and budgets, on the brand experience metrics that matter.

Conclusion

This chapter has outlined how you can get started with brand experience performance measurement. This entails obtaining two sets of data in parallel: Big Picture data and Touchpoint data. Big Picture data allows you to obtain a high-level snapshot of brand experience performance, whilst Touchpoint data provides more detail when you need a deeper dive into specific parts of the brand experience. It is advisable to analyse the two data sets in conjunction with each other, so you can understand which touchpoints help or hinder brand experience performance.

This chapter is accompanied by Toolkit 18.1.

Endnote

1 Questions are measured on a seven-point scale (agree very strongly to disagree very strongly) then translated into a percentage.

Adopting a holistic approach to measuring brand experiences

19

The previous chapter aimed to help you get started with measuring brand experiences by obtaining Big Picture and Touchpoint data.

This chapter outlines why it's advisable to adopt a holistic approach to measuring brand experiences. This entails obtaining a suite of baseline measures that span employee, brand and financial metrics, building experiences, then continuing to measure again at predetermined intervals. Doing this will give your measurement efforts more balance because you'll be collecting short-/long-term, internal/external and hard/soft measures. Adopting a holistic approach to measuring brand experiences will also help you demonstrate, in no uncertain terms, the value delivered to your organization by brand experiences, whilst obtaining employee and brand measures means you'll be well placed to take any necessary pre-emptive action before financial performance suffers.

The dangers of focusing on purely financial metrics

Chief marketing officers are under pressure to deliver against short-term financial targets such as sales, profit margins, and earnings before tax depreciation and amortization. This is understandable because CEOs need to deliver financial returns to satisfy investors and other stakeholders with a financial interest in the company. But financial metrics are only one piece of the brand experience measurement puzzle.

'Very successful companies need to be extremely focused on forward-looking indicators. I often jokingly say that in business we all drive cars where the whole windshield is a rearview mirror. And we have only a small opening somewhere in that mirror surface through which we can look forward. That's because, in general, we are so focused on the historical numbers that we have little ability to look forward. None of our neighbours, in their right mind, would want to drive such a car, but we run huge businesses with exactly that approach. It doesn't make any sense!'

Risto Siilasmaa, Chairman, Nokia[1]

Financial metrics are retrospective

Whilst we all need to learn from the past, those responsible for brand experiences cannot be guided by history alone. If last quarter's sales are down you can't do anything about that now. This contrasts with employee and brand metrics, which are forward-looking or 'leading' metrics. If, during the last quarter, the number of customers willing to pay a 5 per cent price premium decreased, this will translate into revenue decline during subsequent sales cycles (all other things being equal). Similarly, if employee engagement drops, it's likely this will adversely affect financial metrics later down the line (all other things being equal). This 'lag effect' means brand and employee measures can act as a brand experience crystal ball that can prompt pre-emptive action before financial performance suffers. For example, if a customer's willingness to pay a 5 per cent price premium slides there may be time to change that attitude before they buy again. Or if employees become less engaged you have a window of opportunity to do something before that translates into an action that has financial repercussions, such as being disinterested in a customer enquiry.

'Typically, brand equity scores take 12 [to]18 months to really show improvement, sustained improvement… We are beginning to see improvement across most of the brand portfolio. And I think as the quarters go on, you'll see even more benefit and that will then translate to higher value share… We're watching this virtuous circle very, very carefully, and making adjustments as we go along.'

Indra Nooyi, CEO, PepsiCo[2]

Financial metrics are short-term

Even with advanced econometric models it is hard to predict performance beyond a few quarters (at best). This perspective is diametrically opposed to the strategic mentality that needs to underpin brand experience building.

Financial measures tend to have a return on investment (ROI) focus

With a longer-term initiative such as building brand experiences it is difficult to directly attribute return to investment in the way you can with short-term activities such as sales promotion or an email marketing campaign. The longer time horizons involved in building brand experiences blur the line of sight.

Obtaining employee, brand and financial metrics

Instead of concentrating purely on financial metrics, a more informed approach to measuring brand experiences entails obtaining a holistic suite of baseline measures, building experiences then continuing to measure again at predetermined intervals which have been agreed to by key members of your team. Doing this will help you establish, in no uncertain terms, the benefits your brand experience endeavours deliver. The measurements should span employee, brand and financial metrics.

Employee metrics could include employee engagement, advocacy, relative satisfaction or well-being. Brand metrics could encompass data on brand salience, relevance or your ability to charge price premiums. Financial metrics include data such as sales or profit margins.

A holistic approach can be considered balanced because it includes:

- hard (financial) and soft (brand/employee) metrics;
- internal (employee) and external (brand and financial) metrics;
- short-term (financial) and long-term (brand/employee) metrics.

Taking a more holistic and balanced approach to brand performance measurement is advocated by leading academics,[3] and I would encourage you to follow this approach because:

- Employee metrics drive brand metrics[4] and vice versa via brand equity[5] and your employer brand.[6]

'Clients do not come first. Employees come first. If you take care of your employees they will take care of your clients.'

Sir Richard Branson, Founder, Virgin Group

'If the employee comes first, then they're happy... A motivated employee treats the customer well. The customer is happy so they keep coming back, which pleases the shareholders.'

Herb Kelleher, Founder, Southwest Airlines

- Employee metrics drive financial metrics.[7]

Figure 19.1 Employee engagement and financial performance, Towers Perrins (now Willis Towers Watson) (2009)

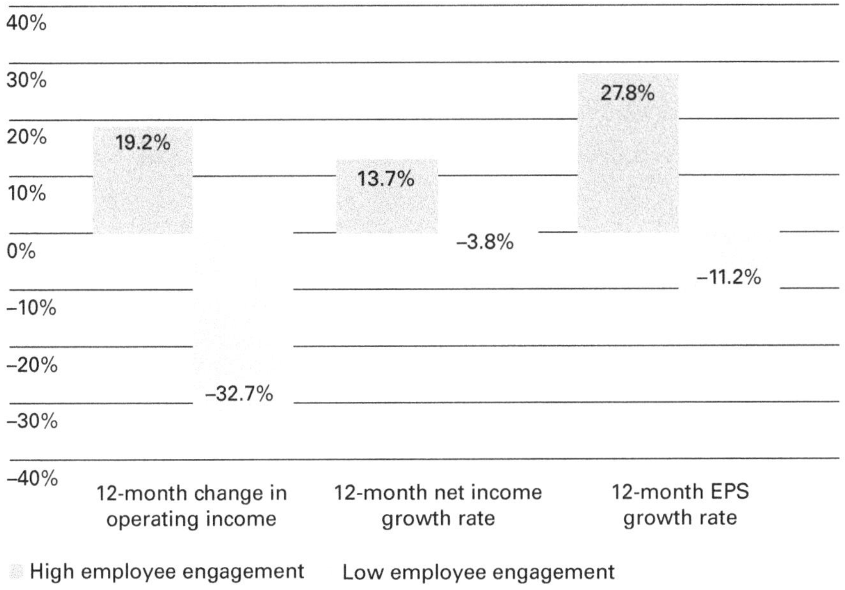

- Brand metrics drive financial metrics.[8]

The relationships between employee, brand and financial metrics are nuanced and complex. Because the nature of the industry, organization size and other factors drive financial performance, when it comes to non-financial metrics one size doesn't fit all. Research supports this.[9] So, you need to identify a small number of key metrics relevant to your organization, explore their relationship with key financial metrics, monitor, learn and iterate where necessary.

However, the underlying principle is clear. If you want to understand how to drive financial performance you need to start with carefully selected employee and brand measures and focus your efforts there. If these improve, your financial metrics will also improve. Conversely, if employee and/ or brand metrics drop, you have time to rectify the situation before they adversely affect financial performance due to the 'lag effect' associated with these metrics. The challenge is to identify the key employee and brand levers for your market, and this is where senior executive experience and external advice comes in.

Conclusion

This chapter recommends adopting a holistic approach to measuring brand experiences. This entails taking employee, brand and financial performance metrics. Employee and brand metrics drive financial performance and give you a window of opportunity to take corrective action, if necessary, before financial performance suffers. Obtaining a suite of balanced baseline measurements before you start building brand experiences and then at predetermined intervals was also advocated as part of a holistic approach to measuring brand experiences. Doing this will help you demonstrate, in no uncertain terms, the value delivered by your brand experiences.

This chapter is accompanied by Toolkit 19.1.

Endnotes

1 McKinsey Quarterly (2016), Nokia's next chapter, December [online] http://bit.ly/wavelength-nokia

2 Warc (2012) New ad strategy paying off for PepsiCo, 19 October [online] www.warc.com

3 Ambler, T (2003) *Marketing and the Bottom Line: Marketing metrics to pump up cash flow*, Prentice Hall; de Chernatony, L (2006) *From Brand Vision*

to Evaluation: The strategic process of growing and strengthening brands, Butterworth-Heinemann, Oxford

4 Gelb, B D and Rangarajan, D (2014) Employee contributions to brand equity, *California Management Review*, **56** (2)

5 Kimpakorn, N and Tocquer, G (2010) Service brand equity and employee brand commitment, *Journal of Services Marketing* **24** (5), pp 378–88

6 Schlager, T et al (2011) The influence of the employer brand on employee attitudes relevant for service branding: an empirical investigation, *Journal of Services Marketing*, **25** (7), pp 497–508

7 Cascio, W and Boudreau, J (2010) *Investing in People: Financial impact of human resource initiatives*, FT Press

8 Mizik, N (2014) Assessing the total financial performance impact of brand equity with limited time-series data, *Journal of Marketing Research*, **51** (6)

9 O'Connell, V and O'Sullivan, D (2016) Are nonfinancial metrics good leading indicators of future financial performance? *Sloan Management Review*, Summer

How to measure 20 brand experiences scientifically

Chapter 19 outlined how you can take a holistic approach to measuring brand experience performance through employee, brand and financial metrics. The importance of taking baseline measures, then again at predetermined intervals was also advised so you can demonstrate the value delivered by your brand experiences.

This chapter provides practical pointers for how you can adopt a more scientific approach to measuring brand experience performance through:

- constructs;
- dimensions;
- measures;
- indices.

Adopting a scientific approach to measuring brand experiences tends to be well received in the boardroom. It inspires confidence and trust in your approach and the subsequent brand experience-building decisions you make.

Understanding constructs, dimensions, measures and indices

A construct is a mental abstraction that you want to make more tangible and accessible; brand equity is an example of a construct. Each construct consists of dimensions. One dimension of brand equity, for example, could be relative satisfaction. Measures are the questions related to each dimension. One measure of relative satisfaction would be, 'In comparison to other hospitality firms you've used, how satisfied are you with our service?' To quantify the response you could ask your stakeholder to answer on a rating scale, eg 1 = extremely satisfied and 7 = extremely unsatisfied. An index (plural: indices) is the score created when you add or take an average of measures (dimension index) or dimension scores (construct index). For instance, if you ask stakeholders three questions about their relative satisfaction with different aspects of your brand experience, your dimension index would be either the sum of all the ratings on your rating scale, or the average (usually the mean, although if there's a lot of divergence in responses as indicated by the standard deviation, the median is a better metric).

Figure 20.1 visualizes the relationship between constructs, dimensions and measures.

Let me illustrate 'constructs', 'dimensions', 'measures' and 'indices' in practical terms by way of a hospitality industry client example:

- Our client wanted to measure brand equity and employee equity (the *constructs*).
- The *dimensions* of brand equity our client wanted to measure included relative satisfaction, perceived quality, advocacy, and relevance.

Figure 20.1 Visualizing constructs, dimensions and measures: a practical example

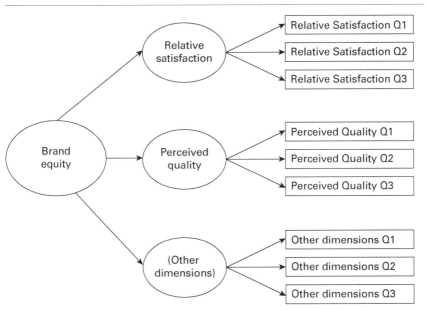

Brand equity is a construct
Relative satisfaction and perceived quality are dimensions (of brand equity)
The questions are the measures used for each dimension

- To measure dimensions of brand equity such as relative satisfaction we asked a number of questions (*measures*) via an online survey. Figure 20.2 provides some examples of the relative satisfaction (*dimension*) questions (*measures*) we asked about food/drink and staff.

- To create an *index* for relative satisfaction we took an average (the mean) of all the relative satisfaction measures. We did the same for perceived quality, advocacy and relevance to give us *dimension indices*. An average (the mean) of the dimension indices was then taken to provide a brand equity index (*construct index*). This meant we had a 'number' for the dimensions and a construct that could be used in subsequent data analysis.

- The same process was followed for employee equity using dimensions of employee advocacy, employee engagement and well-being to provide a construct and dimension 'numbers' respectively.

Understanding constructs, dimensions, measures and indices will help you measure abstract concepts in more concrete ways. It will also help you analyse two sides of the brand experience equation: inputs and outputs. Adopting this approach helped our hospitality client answer questions including:

- Does brand equity or employee equity have a greater influence on sales?
- Does relative satisfaction, perceived quality, advocacy or relevance have more influence on sales?
- Does relative satisfaction, perceived quality, advocacy or relevance have a greater influence on brand equity?
- Does employee advocacy, engagement or well-being have a greater influence on profit?
- Does employee advocacy, employee engagement or well-being drive employee equity?

At a more detailed level, adopting a scientific approach to measurement also helped our client understand more sophisticated causal relationships. This helped focus their efforts on activities that trigger a desired sequence of events. For example, we helped them answer questions including:

- If both employee equity and brand equity drive gross profit, which one should we focus on first?
- If relative satisfaction and perceived quality both drive gross profit, which comes first?

Figure 20.2 Relative satisfaction measures: Wavelength Marketing client example (hospitality sector)

Customer Feedback

We would like to obtain your views on the food and drink

1. In comparison to other hospitality firms I have dealt with I was extremely satisfied with (please answer every question):

	Agree very strongly	Agree strongly	Agree	Neither agree /disagree	Disagree	Disagree strongly	Disagree very strongly	Don't know/ not applicable
Taste of food	○	○	○	○	○	○	○	○
Freshness of food	○	○	○	○	○	○	○	○
Variety of food	○	○	○	○	○	○	○	○
Quality of drinks	○	○	○	○	○	○	○	○
Taste of drinks	○	○	○	○	○	○	○	○
Cleanliness of plates	○	○	○	○	○	○	○	○
Cleanliness of glasses	○	○	○	○	○	○	○	○
Cleanliness of cutlery	○	○	○	○	○	○	○	○
Quality of serviettes	○	○	○	○	○	○	○	○

Customer Feedback

We would like to obtain your views on our members of staff

2. In comparison to other hospitality firms I have dealt with I was extremely satisfied with (please answer every question):

	Agree very strongly	Agree strongly	Agree	Neither agree /disagree	Disagree	Disagree strongly	Disagree very strongly	Don't know/ not applicable
Courteousness of staff	○	○	○	○	○	○	○	○
Responsiveness of staff	○	○	○	○	○	○	○	○
Staff presentation	○	○	○	○	○	○	○	○
Knowledge of staff (concerning food/drink)	○	○	○	○	○	○	○	○

We then incorporated this data into statistical models that helped our client predict what an increase in the score for a dimension or construct meant in terms of financial metrics such as revenues and profit.

The practicalities of measuring scientifically

I recommend using *The Handbook of Brand Management Scales*[1] when you are getting started with measuring brand experiences in a more scientific way. It contains published scales that have been tested for their 'psychometric properties'. This means they measure what they intend to measure (they are valid), are consistent (reliable) and are short enough to be of practical use (parsimonious). You may also want to look at *The Handbook of Marketing Scales*[2] or search peer-reviewed academic papers on Google Scholar. The brand experiences scale published by Brakus and colleagues[3] will give you a feel for how to measure brand experiences.

Although academic work is sometimes criticized in practitioner circles for inaccessible writing and limited relevance, don't let this deter you. The statistical methods and peer review processes used to enhance scientific rigour and robustness are valuable. If you have any questions about a scale, contact the authors; they tend to be responsive to people who express an interest in their work.

It's likely you'll need to modify the wording of some measures to suit your industry. For example, you may work at an accounting firm but can only find a scale that was developed in the hotel industry. This means a loyalty-related measure could change from 'I'd recommend this hotel' to 'I'd recommend this accounting firm'. Scale measurement purists will argue for the need to develop a new scale and to establish its psychometric properties, but in the name of commercial practicality this approach will suffice.

As with all measurement start small, evaluate then develop a more sophisticated approach. This will entail collecting data on a handful of employee, brand and financial measures then analysing the relationships that develop over a period of time. It's better to adopt a more focused approach than to spend your time obtaining measures that overwhelm you and deliver limited practical insight. Professor Tim Ambler's research with the Marketing Leadership Research Council[4] suggests between 8 and 10 measures. This is good advice but ultimately the measures you take should be informed by budgets, practicalities and broader strategic priorities.

In line with the view that great brands are built from within (see Chapter 3) it's advisable to invite a key colleague from each of Finance, Human Resources or other departments that play an important brand experience-building role to discuss the brand experience metrics you would like to obtain and the relationships you would like to analyse. Securing colleagues' buy-in will be as, if not more important than the measures you obtain.

Conclusion

This chapter has provided practical guidance on how you can start measuring brand experiences scientifically. Whilst the ideas and techniques introduced are quite academic and abstract, they have the potential to offer real practical value through the insights they generate. Understanding how to incorporate 'indices', 'constructs' and 'dimensions' into your brand experience analytics via the 'measures' you obtain will elevate the sophistication of your analysis to a level seldom seen but appreciated in the boardroom. This will inspire confidence and trust in those around you.

This chapter is accompanied by Toolkit 20.1.

Endnotes

1 Zarantonello, L and Pauwels-Delassus, V (2015) *The Handbook of Brand Management Scales*, Routledge, London

2 Bearden, W O, Netemeyer, R G and Haws, K L (2010) *Handbook of Marketing Scales: Multi-item measures for marketing and consumer behaviour research*, Sage Publications

3 Brakus, J J, Schmitt, B H and Zarantonello, L (2009) Brand experience: What is it? How is it measured? Does it affect loyalty? *Journal of Marketing*, 73 (3), pp 52–68

4 Ambler, T (2003) *Marketing and the Bottom Line: Marketing metrics to pump up cash flow*, Prentice Hall

Closing thoughts: Building brand experiences as a route to retaining brand relevance

The world's most astute leaders, managers and executives appreciate that building brand experiences provides an attractive route to retaining brand relevance. But knowing where to start and how to structure brand experience-building endeavours is a problem I see many struggle to address.

To recap, the Brand Experience Blueprint solves this problem via a three-stage process.

1 **The Brand Experiences Environment** (Part One) comprises the context you need to be mindful of whilst developing and defining your Brand Experience Essentials. It encompasses four elements: understanding stakeholders; fine-tuning your perspective; considering the mechanics of delivery; and adopting a data-driven approach to building brand experiences.

2 **The Brand Experience Essentials** (Part Two) are the intangible brand assets that inform the brand experiences you build: brand values, brand essence, brand promise, brand positioning and brand personality.

3 **The Brand Experience Enablers** (Part Three) are the tools you can use to bring your Brand Experience Essentials to life in three practical and tangible ways: employee behaviour, communications and design.

Figure 21.1 The Brand Experience Blueprint: a practical management tool

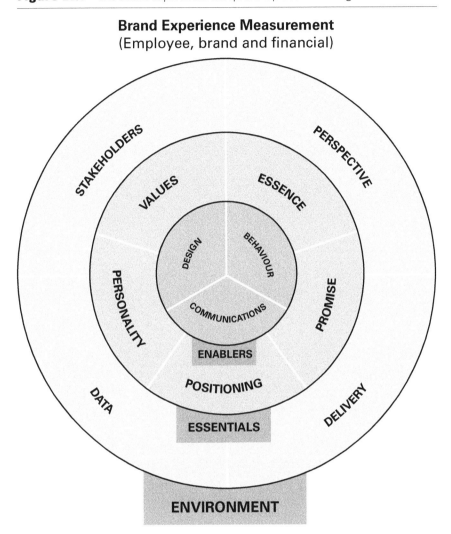

So you can demonstrate the value delivered by your brand experiences to your organization, I advise you to measure holistically and scientifically (Part Four). This entails taking baseline employee, brand experience and financial measurements *before* you implement the tools and techniques offered in this book. Then repeat the exercise at predetermined intervals so you can see what is working. Adopting this approach will add rigour and robustness to your brand experience-measurement endeavours whilst giving your brand experience business case greater credibility and clout in the boardroom: always a good thing.

Guided by the Brand Experience Blueprint I have provided a practical guide on how your brand can retain relevance through brand experiences. I have used this Blueprint with clients all round the world. I hope you find it as useful as they did, and wish you every success.

I would love to hear how you get on, and if you have any questions, do get in touch.

'BRAND PURPOSE': A CAUTIONARY NOTE

The idea of a brand having a purpose is gaining popularity in many branding circles. Brand purpose concerns *why* a brand exists.

Patagonia and Toms Shoes are frequently cited as brands with a purpose grounded in social responsibility and ethical norms. Dutch bank Triodos has a strong purpose; it only invests in activities that have positive social and environmental impact. Purpose is not restricted to social good. Premier Inn's purpose is 'Making guests feel brilliant through a good night's sleep'; for KPMG it is to 'turn knowledge into value', and at Barclays it's 'helping people achieve their ambition – in the right way'.

For these, and other 'purpose-driven' brands, the goods, services and experiences they deliver are a means to an end, because they express the brand purpose, in theory.

The benefits of brand purpose have been highlighted[1,2] but my concern is that it can introduce unnecessary jargon and is already accounted for by other Brand Experience Essentials.

Some brand commentators and executives outline how brand purpose should guide recruitment, strategy and a broad spectrum of operational and strategic business decisions. If you've defined your brand values and they're properly embedded within your organization, won't they do the same thing? Next time you see the word 'purpose' in a brand context, try changing it to 'values' and I think you'll find this will suffice. For example, 'We're guided by our brand purpose' becomes 'We're guided by our brand values'; 'We recruit people who align with our brand purpose' becomes 'We recruit people who align with our brand values'.

Purpose is often considered as a reference point when you need to take tough decisions or recover from difficult situations. Shouldn't you be able to call on your values when you need to do this? And won't your personality shape how you respond in the face of adversity?

Brand essence concerns what your brand represents.[3] To make brand essence more concrete it's useful to consider brand essence as 'what your brand is all about' (see Chapter 9). If KPMG's purpose is to 'turn knowledge into value', isn't this what the brand represents or is all about? The same applies to the other brand essence examples outlined above. It's also interesting to see how some marketing commentators feel brand purpose will morph into brand positioning, which itself is closely connected to brand essence.[4]

When considering brand purpose in this way, it doesn't feel like there is enough daylight to help its unique contribution shine through. I have read around this topic – a lot – and have questioned my own views, but I come back to the points I have made. An alternative could be to bundle your Brand Experience Essentials into one purpose statement that informs your Brand Experience Enablers. But I encourage you not to confuse simplicity with simplification. If you distil your Brand Experience Essentials into a brand purpose statement, you'll struggle to give your brand thinking the breadth and depth required to help your brand retain relevance.

And, if I broaden the debate to include strategic topics such as mission and vision, which are frequently confused or worse still used interchangeably, the benefit that brand purpose brings to the brand experience-building table becomes increasingly unclear.

Brands have had a purpose beyond profit for decades. For example, Johnson & Johnson's famed 'Credo' is an example of a brand purpose. It was written in 1943. Cadbury's roots were grounded in a strong moral commitment to the local community in Bourneville, Birmingham, UK, where the company was founded in 1824. Joseph Rowntree (1836–1925), the philanthropist and businessman who founded the Rowntree confectionary brand, was famed for his social reform and charitable work. This indicates that the notion of an organization being guided by a purpose is not new. It feels like corporate social responsibility has been rebranded as brand purpose by branding professionals. These points beg the question, why reinvent the wheel?

However, if you feel that brand purpose is important, you need to weave it into the fabric of your brand experience alongside the other Brand Experience Essentials introduced here.[5] But I suspect that when it comes to bringing your Brand Experience Essentials to life through employee behaviour, communications and design you are likely to see any unique contribution made by brand purpose melting into other Brand Experience Essentials.

Endnotes

1 Sisodia, R, Sheth, J N and Wolfe, D (2014) *Firms of Endearment: How world-class companies profit from passion and purpose*, 2nd edn, Pearson FT Press

2 Deloitte (2015). Mind the gaps: the 2015 Deloitte Millennial survey (2015) [online] http://bit.ly/2sxdmuz

3 Keller, K L (2007) *Strategic Brand Management: Building, measuring, and managing brand equity*, 3rd edn, Pearson

4 Tesseras, L (2017) Trends for 2018: purpose will morph back into positioning, 11 December, *Marketing Week* [online] http://bit.ly/wavelength-brand-purpose

5 If you would like to read more about brand purpose: Smith, S and Milligan, A (2015) *On Purpose: Delivering a branded customer experience people love*, Kogan Page

FURTHER READING

Prelims

Holbrook, M B and Hirschman, E C (1982) The experiential aspects of consumption: consumer fantasies, feelings, and fun, *Journal of Consumer Research*, **9** (September), pp 132–40

Pine, B J II and Gilmore, J (1988) Welcome to the experience economy, *Harvard Business Review*, 1 July

Pine, J and Gilmore, J (1999) *The Experience Economy*, Harvard Business School Press, Boston, MA

Schulze, G (1995) *The Experience Society*, Sage, London

Toffler, A (1970) *Future Shock*, Random House

Chapter 1

Biedenbach, G and Marell, A (2010) The impact of customer experience on brand equity in a business-to-business service setting, *Journal of Brand Management*, **17** (6), pp 446–58

Boston Consulting Group (2015) What really shapes the customer experience, September, [online] http://bit.ly/wavelength-BCG

Gilovich, T, Kumar, A and Jampol, L (2015) A wonderful life: experiential consumption and the pursuit of happiness, *Journal of Consumer Psychology*, **25**, pp 152–65

Iglesias, O, Singh, J J and Batista-Foguet, J M (2010) The role of brand experience and affective commitment in determining brand loyalty, *Brand Management*, **18** (8), pp 570–82

Nysveen H, Pedersen, P E and Skard, S (2013) Brand experiences in service organizations: exploring the individual effects of brand experience dimensions, *Journal of Brand Management*, **20**, pp 404–23

Van Boven, L and Gilovich, T (2003) To do or to have? That is the question, *Journal of Personality and Social Psychology*, **85** (6), pp 1193–202

Chapter 3

Rayton, B, Dodge, T and D'Analeze, G (2012) The evidence: employee engagement task force 'nailing the evidence' workgroup [online] http://bit.ly/wavelength_employee_engagement2

Winkler, S, Konig, K J and Kleinmann, M (2012) New insights into an old debate: investigating the temporal sequence of commitment and performance at the business unit level, *Journal of Occupational and Organizational Psychology*, **85**, pp 503–22

Chapter 5

Lynch, J and de Chernatony, L J (2004), The power of emotion: brand communication in business-to-business markets, *Journal of Brand Management*, **11** (5), pp 403–19

Watzlawick, P, Bavelas, J B and Jackson, D D (1967) *Pragmatics of Human Communication*, Norton & Co Inc, New York

Watzlawick, P J et al (1967) Some formal aspects of communication, *American Behavioral Scientist*, **10** (8), pp 4–8

Chapter 8

de Chernatony, L, McDonald, M and Wallace, E (2017) *Creating Powerful Brands*, 4th edn, Routledge

Kapferer, J N (2012) *The New Strategic Brand Management: Advanced insights and strategic thinking*, 5th edn, Kogan Page

Keller, K L (2012) *Strategic Brand Management: Building, Measuring and Managing Brand Equity*, Pearson

Chapter 15

Fiske, S T (2010) *Social beings: core motives in social psychology*, 2nd edn, Wiley, New York, NY

Schacter S (1959) *The Psychology of Affiliation: Experimental studies of the sources of gregariousness*, Stanford University Press, Stanford, CA

Silbert, L et al (2014) Coupled neural systems underlie the production and comprehension of natural narrative speech, *Proceedings of the National Academy of Science USA*, 28 Oct **111** (43)

Yeshurun Y et al (2017) Same story, different story, *Psychological Science*, **28** (3)

Chapter 16

Alpert, J I and Alpert, M I (1990) Music influences on mood and purchase intentions, *Psychology and Marketing*, 7 (2), pp 109–34

Bartholmé, R H and Melewar, T C (2016) The end of silence? Qualitative findings on corporate auditory identity from the UK, *Journal of Marketing Communications*, **22** (4), pp 419–36

Bruner, G C (1990) Music, mood, and marketing, *Journal of Marketing Management*, **54** (4), pp 94–104

Fredrickson, B L and Kahneman, D (1993) Duration neglect in retrospective evaluations of affective episodes, *Journal of Personality and Social Psychology*, **65** (1), pp 45–55

Kahneman, D (2000) Evaluation by moments, past and future (PDF), in *Choices, Values and Frames*, ed D Kahneman and A Tversky, Cambridge University Press

Herrington, J D and Capella, L M (1994) Practical applications of music in service settings, *Journal of Services Marketing*, **8** (3), pp 50–65

Herrington, J D and Capella, L M (1996) Effects of music in service environments: a field study, *Journal of Services Marketing*, **10** (2), pp 26–41

Milliman, R E (1982) Using background music to affect the behaviour of super-market shoppers, *Journal of Marketing*, **46** (3), pp 86–91

Milliman, R E (1986) The influence of background music on the behavior of restaurant patrons, *Journal of Consumer Research*, **13** (2), pp 286–89

Mirabitoa, A et al (2017) Glass shape influences the flavour of beer, *Food Quality and Preference*, **62**, December, pp 257–61

North, A C et al (2004) The effects of musical and voice 'fit' on responses to adver-tisements, *Journal of Applied Social Psychology*, **34** (8), pp 1675–708

Rosenblum, L D (2010) *See What I'm Saying: The extraordinary powers of our five senses*, W W Norton & Company

Spence, C and Wang, Q (J) (2015) Wine & music (II): Can you taste the music? Modulating the experience of wine through music and sound, *Flavour*, **4**, p 33

Van Doorna, G et al (2017) Does the shape of a cup influence coffee taste expectations? A cross-cultural, online study, *Food Quality and Preference*, **56**, Part A, March 2017, pp 201–11

Velasco, C et al (2016) Colour-taste correspondences: designing food experiences to meet expectations or to surprise, *International Journal of Food Design*, June

Wang Q (J) and Spence, C (2017) Assessing the role of emotional associations in mediating crossmodal correspondences between classical music and wine, *Beverages*, **3** (1)

Wang, Q, Keller, S and Spence,C (2017) Sounds spicy: enhancing the evaluation of piquancy by means of a customised crossmodally congruent soundtrack, *Food and Quality*, **58**, June, pp 1–9

Wedin, L (1972) Multidimensional study of perceptual-emotional qualities in music, *Scandinavian Journal of Psychology*, **13** (4), pp 241–57

Yalch, R F and Spangenberg, E R (1990) Effects of store music on shopping behavior, *Journal of Consumer Marketing*, **7** (2), pp 55–63

Chapter 19

Baumgarth, C and Schmidt, M (2010) How strong is the business-to-business brand in the workforce? An empirically-tested model of 'internal brand equity' in a business-to-business setting, *Industrial Marketing Management*, **39** (8), pp 1250–60

Coco, C T, Jamison, F and Black, H (2011), Connecting people investments and business outcomes at Lowe's: using value linkage analytics to link employee engagement to business performance, *People & Strategy*, **20** (1), pp 28–33

Fleming, J H and Asplund, J (2007) *Human Sigma: Managing the employee-customer encounter*, Gallup Press

Heskett, J L, Sasser, W E and Schlesinger, L A (1997) The Service Profit Chain, Free Press

Heskett, J L et al (2008) Putting the service-profit chain to work, *Harvard Business Review*, July–August

Ittner, C and Larcker, D F (2003) Coming up short on nonfinancial performance measurement, *Harvard Business Review*, **81** (11), pp 89–95

Jones, D C, Kalmi, P and Kauhanen, A (2010) How does employee involvement stack up? The effects of human resource management policies on performance in a retail firm, *Industrial Relations*, **49** (1), pp 1–21

Towers Perrin (now Willis Towers Watson) (2009) *Employee Engagement Underpins Business Transformation*

Vomberg, A, Homburg, C and Bornemann, T (2015) Talented people and strong brands: the contribution of human capital and brand equity to firm value, *Strategic Management Journal*, **36** (13), pp 2122–31

INDEX

Page numbers in italic indicate figures or tables.

3M 218
4G 140
5 Gum 213
20th Century Fox 101

AA 132–33
Aaker, David 140
ABN AMRO 207
Abu Snaineh, Wafa 43
Accenture 186, 218
Adidas 47, 76, 198
    Glitch 201
    influencer marketing 66
    Snapchat 76
Adobe 186
Ahrendts, Angela 178
Airbnb 36, 41, 220, 235
Aldi 61, 220
AliBaba 150
AliPay 150, 208
Amazon 1
    Alexa 224
    Amazon Affiliates 66
    Echo 224
    employee appraisals 186
    growth rate 61
    Leadership Principles 55–56
    Prime 83
        Prime Video 150
    retail space 176
Ambler, Tim 260
American Express 141
Android Pay 208
Angry Birds 219
Aniston, Jennifer 159
Apple 1, 146, 181
    Apple Pay 208
    Apple Store 67
    benefits 141
    iMessage 207
    iPad 82
    iPhone 52
    iPod 36, 41, 147
    price vs value 60
    recruitment 178
Ariely, Dan 71

Armani 75, 117, 141
artificial intelligence (AI) 8
AstraZeneca 213
AT&T 61, 182
Atari 149
Audi 193
    brand positioning 146
    co-creation 77
    'Drive Back in Time, A' 84
    post-purchase experience 228, 229
augmented reality (AR) 84
Axe 123

Baidu 83
Baker McKenzie 220
Ballmer, Steve 178
Bank of China 219
Bank of Singapore 32, 209
Banyan Tree 142
Barbour, Hilton 52–53
Barclays 146, 160, 265
Barranquilla Zoo 93–95, *94*
Barry, Charlotte and Green, Charlie 220, 221
Beats by Dre 83
Beautiful Bung, The: Corruption and the World Cup 52
benefits, types of 140–42
    emotional 141
    enablement 141
    enrichment 142
    enticement 141–42
    functional 140–41
    self-expressive 141
    social 141
Bentley 126
Berry, Halle 82
Bettinger, Walt 179–80
Betty Crocker 161
Biles, Simon 66
Billabong 120
biometrics 101
BlackBerry 146
Blockbuster 1
Blockchain 53–54
Bloomberg.com 52
BMW 66, 84

Index 273

Body Shop, The 126
Booth, Clive 140
brain physiology 74–75
    limbic system 74, 74–75
    pre-frontal cortex 74
Brakus, J J, Schmitt, B H and
        Zarantonello, L 260
brand essence 129–36, 265, 266
    and the Brand Experience
        Environment 129–30
    defining 130–31
    formulating your 134–35
    purposes of 131–33
    vs tagline 135
    value of 133, 133
Brand Experience Blueprint 14–22, 15, 24,
        108, 170, 244, 262, 263
    benefits of 14–15
    Brand Experience Enablers 19, 19, 170,
        170–72, 241
        see also communications; design;
            employee behaviour
    Brand Experience Environment 16,
        17–18, 24, 24, 104–05, 165, 240
        see also data, using; delivering brand
            experiences; stakeholders, your;
            perspective, your
    Brand Experience Essentials 16, 18–19,
        18–19, 108, 108–09, 165–67,
        240–41
        see also brand essence; brand
            personality; brand positioning;
            brand promise; brand values
    flexibility of 20
    iterative nature of 21
    measurement, of brand experience 16,
        244–61
brand experience, defining 3
    vs customer experience 4
    vs user experience 21
Brand Experience Enablers 19, 19, 170,
        170–72, 241
    see also communications; design;
        employee behaviour
Brand Experience Environment 16, 17–18,
        24, 24, 104–05, 165, 240
    and brand essence 129–30
    and the Brand Experience
        Essentials 110–14
    and brand personality 155–56
    and brand positioning 144–45
    and brand promise 138–39
    and brand values 116
    see also data, using; delivering brand
        experiences; stakeholders, your;
        perspective, your

Brand Experience Essentials 16, 18–19,
        18–19, 108, 108–09, 165–67,
        240–41
    and the Brand Experience Enablers 171,
        173–74
    and the Brand Experience
        Environment 110–14
    and communications 193
    and design 216
    and employee behaviour 175
    see also brand essence; brand personality;
        brand positioning; brand promise;
        brand values
brand language 204–05, 205
brand metrics 245, 252, 253
brand mission 266
brand personality 154–64
    brand ambassadors 159, 160–61
    and the Brand Experience
        Environment 155–56
    brand mascots 161–62, 162, 163
    defining 154, 156
    measuring 157
    value of 157–58
brand positioning 144–52, 266
    and the Brand Experience
        Environment 144–45
    competitors, identifying 149–50
    'jobs to be done' 149
    defining 146–47
        points of difference 146
        points of parity 146
    positioning statements 151, 151–52
brand promise 137–43
    and the Brand Experience
        Environment 138–39
    features vs benefits 139–42
        allocating to stakeholders 140
        benefit types 140–42
brand purpose 265–66
brand stories 208–12
    communal stories 212
    'neural coupling' 209
    stakeholders, your 209
    template for 211
brand values 115–27, 265
    and behaviour 117
    and Brand Experience Enablers 120–21
    and the Brand Experience
        Environment 116
    defining 115
    opinions, expressing 122–23
    qualities of
        active framing 124–25
        balance 126–27, 126–27
        deliberateness 125, 126

brand values (*continued*)
    specificity 124
    uniqueness 123
  in recruitment 178–80
  and stakeholder values 117–19, *118*
brand vision 266
BrandZ *60*
  Top 100 Most Valuable Global Brands
    5, *5*
Branson, Richard 118, 253
Briggs, Andy 54
British Airways 132, 204
British Council 147, 148–49
British Gas 61
Britten, Tony 224
Brock, Betty 8
Brooke Bond Red Label tea 122–23
Bryant, Kobe 159–60
Brynley-Jones, Luke 203
BUPA 218
Burberry
  'Art of the Trench' 45
  artificial intelligence (AI) 8
  brand control 65
  Burberry Acoustic 224
  Burberry Bespoke 77
  retail experience 82
Burton 120, 131

Cadbury 266
Cadillac 225
Calpol 141
Calvert, Gemma 101
Capitol Records 161
Captain Birdseye 162
Caribbean Airlines 176, 177
Carling 197, 198
Caterpillar 72
Cats Protection 204
CBS 150
Champions League 224
Charles Schwab Corporation 179
Chesky, Brian 235
Chick-fil-A 52
Christensen, Clayton 37
Churchill Insurance 161
CIBC 198
CIMB 58–59
  brand promise 142–43
  training 185
Cisco 181
Clooney, George 158
Coach 77
Coca-Cola
  bottle design 220
  brand positioning 146

  in China 219
  growth rate 61
  happiness 71
  'Labels are for cans' 122
  'Share a Coke' 1
co-creation 75–80
  empowering customers 77
  and profitability 77
  tools for 76
Coleman, David and Coleman, Mark 210
colour, use of 218
communications 192–214
  and the Brand Experience Essentials *193*
  brand language 204–05, *205*
  brand stories 208–12
    communal stories 212
    'neural coupling' 209
    stakeholders, your 209
    template for *211*
  communities 199–204
    benefits of 201
    building 203–04
    'need for belonging' 200
  content, use of 196–99
    conversations, starting 197
    transparency 198
  gamification 212–13
  internal 193–94
  mobile, using 205–08
    apps 207
    'jobs to be done' 205–06
    location 206
    payment 208
    personalization 207
    privacy 206
    timeliness 207
    visual nature 208
  social media, risks of 194–95
competitors, identifying 149–50
  'jobs to be done' 149
Confucius 71
control, loss of 65–67
  influencer marketing 65–67
  social media monitoring 65
Cook, Tim 178
Costco 219
Crayola 223
Credit Suisse 141
customer empathy maps 227–28
customer journey maps 228–33, *230*, *232*

Damasio, Antonio 71
Daniels, Ron 121
data, using 87–102
  biometrics 101
  holistic measurement 101–02

mixed methods, using 87
neuroscience 101
qualitative insight 98–101
    qualitative methods 99–*100*
    subjectivity, overcoming 98
quantitative insight 88–97
    Big Data 96–97
    'inferential statistics' 88
    quantitative methods 89–92
delivering brand experiences 70–84
    co-creation 75–80
        empowering customers 77
        and profitability 77
        tools for 76
    emotions, role of 3, 70–75
        B2B markets 72–74
        brain physiology 74, 74–75
        prefrontal cortex 74
        value of emotional connection 71,
            71–72
    omnichannel experiences 80–84
        airline example 80–82, *81*
        augmented reality (AR) 84
        beauty market 83
        'ecosystems' 83–84
        Internet of Things (IoT) 84
        luxury market 83
        virtual reality (VR) 84
Dell 31–32
Deloitte 186
design 216–38
    and the Brand Experience Essentials *216*
    business case for *217*, 217–18
    multisensory design 217, 218–26
        smell 222–23
        sound 223–25
        taste 225
        touch 225–26
        visual 218, 219–20, 222
    service design 226–
        case scenarios 233–34
        customer empathy maps 227–28
        customer journey maps 228–33, *230*,
            232
        mood boards 235
        personas 227
        service/experience prototyping
            234–35
        stages of 226–27
        storyboards 235–37, *236*, *237*
DHL 48
Di Somma, Mark 67
Diesel 220
differentiation, and brand experience 7
Dillman, D A, Smyth, J D and Christian, L
    M 88

Direct Line Insurance 156
Disney 6
    brand essence 131, 132, 134
    Disney, Walt 175, 228
    employee training 185
Dobrea, Alin 197
Dollar Shave Club 201, 220
dopamine 6
DoubleTree Hotels 225
Dove 123, 141, 254
Dubai Model for Government Services
    (DMGS) 43–44
Duracell 161

Edelman 122, 199
Edgbaston Priory Club 231–33, *232*
electroencephalogram (EEG) 101
Emirates Airline 159
Emirates NBD 195–96, 198
emotional benefits 141
emotions, role of 3, 70–75
    B2B markets 72–74
    brain physiology 74, 74–75
    happiness, and brand experience 6–7
    prefrontal cortex 74
    value of emotional connection 71, 71–72
employee behaviour 8–9, 175–90
    appraisal 186–88
        annual reviews 186–87
        artificial intelligence (AI) 8
        B2B markets 9
        bonuses and reward 188–89
        and the Brand Experience Essentials *175*
        exit interview 189–90
        financial value of 176, *176*
        induction 183–84
        recruitment 178–83
            attracting candidates 182–83
            and brand values 178–80
            diversity 180
        training 184–86
            empowering employees 184–85
            interactive tools 186
employee metrics 245, 252–53, *253*
enablement benefits 141
enrichment benefits 142
enticement benefits 141–42
ESPN 150
Estee Lauder 66
Etihad 159
Expert Insights 10
    brand personality 159–60, *160*
    brand positioning 147–48, 148–49
    brand promise 142–43
    brand stories 210–11
    brand value and health 5, 5–6

Expert Insights (*continued*)
  brand values 119–20, 121–22
  China, branding in 219
  co-creation 78–80, *79*
  communities 201–03, *202*
  content 197–98
  control, loss of 67
  data, using 93–95, *94, 95–96*
  digital communications 195–96
  emotions, role of 73–74
  employee behaviour 177
  holistic mindset 55–56, 57–58, *58*
  'jobs to be done' 38
  recruitment 181–82
  retail experience design *221,* 221–22
  service design 226–27, 229
  social media communities 203–04
  stakeholder engagement 41–42, 43–44
  transparency 52–53

Facebook 36, 41
  Facebook Live 199
  growth rate 61
  Messenger 66, 199
  recruitment 182
  Watch 150
'fake news' 52
Fedrigoni 225
Fernandes, Tony 46
Ferrari 126
Ferrero, Michele 228
FIFA 52, 198
Fifth Avenue 207
financial metrics 245, 250–52
Financial Times 141
FKA Twigs 66
Food Aid Foundation 42
Ford 206, 224
  Ford, Henry 36
Fortnum and Mason 220
Four Seasons Hotels 193
Foxtel 226
Franklin, Benjamin 75
French, Ed 56
Fuji Film 149
functional benefits 140–41

Gallart, Álvaro 93
Game of Thrones 84
gamification 212–13
Garageio 84
Gatorade 225
Gaultier, Anne-Marie 212
General Electric (GE)
  design 218
  emotions, role of 72

employee appraisals 186, 187
Industrial Internet events 181
recruitment 180, 181–82
Ghazali, Rafiza 41
Glassdoor 182
Glenfiddich 185
Godin, Seth 137, 208
Goldman Sachs 182
Google 1, 181
  brand wellness 6
  Daydream 84
  growth rate 61
  research 36, 72
Goosebumps 199
GoPro 200
Greenpeace 52
Gucci 126
Guinness 1, 209–10

Hallmark 75
Handbook of Brand Management Scales, The 260
Handbook of Marketing Scales, The 260
Handel, George F 224
Harley Davidson 141
Harrison, Joel 73
Harrods 219
Harvard Business School 37
Harvey Nichols 185
Hasbro 220
Hasson, Uri 209
HCL Technologies 199
Hellmann's 53, 123, 207
Hendrick's 185
Herbie 157
Hermes 183
Hewlett Packard 213
Hobson, Michael 56
Holiday Inn 158
Hon, Linda 56, 57
HSBC 146
Huawei 66
Hudson, Kate 82
Hunt, Jeremy 43
Hyundai 127

IBM 198
  artificial intelligence (AI) 8
  benefits 141
  brand personality 154
  design 218
  emotions, role of 72, 141
  employee appraisals 186
  growth rate 61
  Institute for Business Value 176, *176*

recruitment 182
research 47
Iceland 66
IKEA 76, 207
InBev 176
influencer marketing 65–67, 209
    audience for 65–66
    brand advocates 66
    micro-influencers 66
ING 199
Instagram 32, 66, 77
InterContinental Hotels Group (IHG) 88, 93
Internet of Things (IoT) 77, 84

J W Marriott 158, 209
Jackson, Samuel L 160
Jaguar Land Rover 147–48
    Range Rover 77
Janata, P 224
Jean Paul Gaultier 225
Jenner, Kendall 66
Jia, Junman 147, 148
Jobs, Steve 36, 147, 195
John Lewis 220
Johnson & Johnson 66, 266
Jubelirer, Michelle 161
Just for Men 141

Kahneman, Daniel 71
Kantar Millward Brown 60
Keitel, Harvey 156
Kelleher, Herb 253
Kenco 122
Keohane, Kevin 178
Kidman, Nicole 159
Knorr 123
Kodak 1, 149
KPMG 265
Krishna, Vikram 195
Kumar, A, Killingsworth, M A and
        Gilovich, G 6
Kuzmina, Ksenija 226

L'Oreal
    Age Perfect 159
    Chinese market 83
    influencer marketing 66
    recruitment 208
LaCroix 32
Lane Keller, Kevin 130
Lean Six Sigma 58, 142
Lee Yohn, Denise 178
Lego 77, 98, 220
Leica 225
Lidl 61
Ligoure, Dionne 176, 177

limbic system 74, 74–75
Line 66, 150
Lineker, Gary 159
LinkedIn 182
Liu, Lucy 159
Lloyds Banking Group 146, 220, 221–22
'Locate a Mate' 39–40
Loeb, Ben 93, 95
logo, your 218
Lucent 149
Lululemon 47, 156
Lynx 123

magnetic resonance imaging (MRI) 101
Mandarin Oriental 159
Mantua-Kommonen, Kirsi 218, 219
Marketing Leadership Research
        Council 260
Marks and Spencer 197–98, 207
Maybank 56, 57–58, 58, 185
McDonald's 61, 162
McKechnie, Sally 147
McKellen, Ian 148
McKinsey 159
    brand positioning 146
measurement, of brand experience 16,
        244–61, 263
    Big Picture metrics 245–46, 247
        brand metrics 245, 252, 253
        employee metrics 245, 252–53, 253
        financial metrics 245, 250–52
        social media sentiment metrics 245–46
    causal relationships 258
    constructs 256, 257
    dimensions 256, 257
    holistic approach, taking a 250–54
    indices 256–57
    measures 256, 257
    scales, choosing 260–61
    touchpoint metrics 246, 248, 249
measurement, of brand experience 10, 16
Media Rating Council 53
Mellor, John 70
Mencius 71
Mercedes Benz 141, 212
Messi, Lionel 159–60
Metro Bank 146, 185
Michelin 161
Microsoft
    data-driven approach 93, 95–96
    ecosystem 83, 84
    employee appraisals 186
    retail spaces 176
    Surface 84
    Windows 84
    Xbox 84

Milner, Gary 200
Milo 213
Mini 37, 38
Mirren, Helen 159
Mitsubishi 52, 210
Mode 161
Mondelez 45, 182
Movenpick 158
Mullen, Kathleen 180, 181
Mumsnet 38

Naccari, Claudio *162, 162, 235, 236*
Nair, Hari 41
Narellan Pools 97
Nestlé 52, 65
Netflix 150, 186
Neuhaus 185
Neuromarketing 101
neuroscience 101
New Markets Advisors 37
Nielsen 32, 71
Nike 47, 198
    brand essence 131, 132, 134
    brand positioning 146
    hashtags 45
    iD 76, 77
    influencer marketing 66
    'Just Do It' 135
    NikeConnect 45
    Sina Weibo 206
Nooyi, Indra 251

Olay 161
Olcay, Harun 55
OMO 199
Ooredoo Oman 78–80, 79
Orange 206
Oreo 45, 77
Owen, Bryn 59
Oxo 161

Pacha 142
packaging 220
Pan 97
Pandora 225
Patagonia 53, 265
patience 61–64
    introducing 64
    quick wins 64
    world's most valuable brands 62–63
PayPal 150
PepsiCo 218
Periscope 220
Pernod Richard 77
personalization 1

and co-creation 76, 77
on mobile 207
perspective, your 51–68
    control, loss of 65–67
        influencer marketing 65–67
        social media monitoring 65
    holistic mindset 54–59
        CIMB example 58–59
        practicalities of 55, 59
        siloes 59
    patience 61–64
        introducing 64
        quick wins 64
        world's most valuable brands 62–63
    transparency 51–54
        B2B markets 53
        Blockchain 53–54
        'fake news' 52
    value vs price 59–61, 60
        commodities markets 60
        supermarkets 61
Pfizer 36–37
Pine, Andrew 54
Pitt, Brad 161
Porcin, Mauro 209
Porsche 1
    Porsche Exclusive 77
    'Sound of Porsche' 224
    Vehicle Delivery app 228
Prada 220
pre-frontal cortex 74
Premier Inn 256
Pret A Manger 185, 189
Princess 146
Pritchard, Marc 53
Prius 38, 117, 120
Procter & Gamble 53, 126
PwC 186

QQ 84
Quaker Oats 162

Ralph Lauren 220
Red Arrows 148
Red Bull 1
    brand essence 132
    brand personality 154
REI 195
Reuters 141
Revenant, The 101
Ritz-Carlton 67
    emotions, role of 75
    scent, use of 223
    training 184

Rolls-Royce 222
    Rolls Royce Aerospace 77
Rothschild 141
Rowntree, Joseph 266
Ryanair 60

Saatchi & Saatchi 38
Saks 207
Salesforce 122
Samsung 45, 146
SAP 218
Saunders, Gemma 119
Sears 1
self-expressive benefits 141
Sephora 83
Sharp, Bryon 61
Shinola 77
Siilasmaa, Risto 251
Sime Darby 27, *28*
    Young Innovators Challenge 41–42
Singapore Airlines
    flight attendant 161
    scent, use of 223
SK-II 83
Skype 149
Smirnoff 1
Snapchat 182, 207
    Spectacles 209
social benefits 141
    building communities on 203–04
    'fake news' 52
    influencer marketing 65–67, 209
        audience for 65–66
        brand advocates 66
        micro-influencers 66
    monitoring and control 65
    in recruitment 182
    risks of 194–95
    sentiment metrics 245–46
    and your stakeholders 32
SoftBank 8
Sony 199, 203
Sour Patch Kids 182
Southwest Airlines 179, 189
Spotify 225
StaaG 133
stakeholder, defining 4
stakeholders, your 25–49
    brand personality 157–58
    'jobs to be done' 36–41, 76
        competitors, identifying 149–50
        examples 37
        'Locate a Mate' service 39–40
        template for 40–41
    managing expectations 48

profiling 25–36
    B2B markets 35–36
    biases, challenging 32–33
    brand stories 209
    personas, developing *33*, 33–34,
        34–35
    profiling template *29*, *29–31*
    Sime Darby 27, *28*
    stakeholder-based experiences 26–27
    values 32, 117–18
stakeholder engagement 41–48
    Government of Dubai 43–44
    role of customers 45–46
    role of employees 46–48
    UK Sepsis Trust 42–43, *43*
Standard Chartered 197, 198
Starbucks
    brand wellness 6
    Card Mobile App 208
    in China 219
    'My Starbucks Barista' 224
    Red Cup Art 45
Stolichnaya 225
Sun-Pat 203
Sunseeker 146
Supermalt 203
Swiss Airlines 225

Taco Bell 66
taglines 135
TD Bank 7
Tencent 84
Tenpay 84
Tesco 42
Thompson, Caron 201
Tiffany 82
T-Mobile 45
Toms Shoes 46, 53, 265
tone of voice 204–05, *205*
touchpoints, managing 3, 7–8
Towers Perrins 253
Toyota 161
transparency 51–54
    B2B markets 53
    Blockchain 53–54
    'fake news' 52
Triodos 265
TripAdvisor 80, 82
Trust Accountability Group 53
Turkish Airlines 159–60
Twitter 198, 199
typography 220

Uber 117
UK Sepsis Trust 42, *118*, 118–19, 121–22

Under Armour 47, 117
uniforms, using 222
Unilever 123
    'Grow with Us' campaign 53
    recruitment 182
Universal Music Group 224

Van Boven L and Gilovich, T 6
Vans 131
    'House of Vans London' 200
    'Living off the Wall' 200
vehicle livery 222
Verizon 97
Versace 117, 218
video, use of 220
Virgin
    brand essence 132
    brand positioning 211
    logo 218
    Virgin Active 47
    Virgin Atlantic 204, *205*
    Virgin Holidays 228
virtual reality (VR) 84
Visa 61
Voice over Internet Protocol (VoIP) 149
Volcom 131
Volkswagen 52, 157
Volvo 75, 141

W Hotels 180
Waiting Room, The 201–03, *202*

Walkers Crisps 159
Walshe, Peter 4, 5–6
Warby Parker 154, 182, 204
WeChat 84, 150, 212
Wee Abdullah, Mohamed Adam 58, 142
Wendy's 225
WhatsApp 66, 150, 207
Whole Foods 67
William Grant & Sons 185
Witherspoon, Reese 82
Wizarding World of Harry Potter, The 6
Wong, Matthew 228, 229
Woolworths Group 1
WPP 5
Wrangler 224
Wunker, Stephen 37, 38

Xeljanz 36–37
Xerox 149

Yazıcı, Ayşegül 159
Yeti 32
YouGov 48
Young, Molly 154
YouTube 150
    YouTube Labs 66

Zalando 187
Zappos 180, 182
Zara 47
Zurawicki, L 101